*J*ames H. Gray is one of western Canada's leading popular historians. Born in Manitoba in 1906, he worked for the *Winnipeg Free Press* for many years and was editor of several other publications. He is the author of many bestselling and award-winning books on the social history of western Canada, including *Booze, Red Lights on the Prairies, The Winter Years,* and *The Boy from Winnipeg.* Gray has received numerous honours, including the Alberta Order of Excellence in 1987, the Order of Canada in 1988, and the 1995 Pierre Berton Award for "distinguished achievement in popularizing Canadian history." He lives in Calgary.

Courtesy Provincial Archives of Manitoba/N18331

Men Against the Desert

JAMES H. GRAY

FIFTH
HOUSE
PUBLISHERS

SASKATOON & CALGARY

Front cover photograph courtesy Glenbow Archives/ND-3-6343
Hand colouring by Laurel Wolanski
Frontispiece courtesy Provincial Archives of Manitoba/N18331
Cover and series logo designed by Sandra Hastie
and John Luckhurst/GDL

The publisher gratefully acknowledges the support received from
The Canada Council and Heritage Canada. The publisher also
wishes to thank the PFRA, Glenbow Institute, Saskatchewan Archives
Board, and the Provincial Archives of Manitoba for their assistance
with photo research.

Printed and bound in Canada by Friesens, Altona, MB
98 99 00 / 5 4 3 2

Canadian Cataloguing in Publication Data
Gray, James H., 1906–

Men against the desert
2nd. ed. -

(Western Canadian classics)
Includes index.
ISBN 1-895618-70-3

1. Reclamation of land - Prairie Provinces.
2. Droughts - Prairie Provinces. I. Title.
II. Series

HD1790.P7 1995   630'.9712   C95-920082-7

FIFTH HOUSE LTD.
#9 - 6125 - 11th Street S.E.
Calgary, AB Canada
T2H 2L6

CONTENTS

ℱOREWORD

*M*ore lies have probably been told about the weather of the Dirty Thirties than about any other subject except sex; yet most of the lies could have been true." That's how James Gray, in characteristic fashion, opens one of the chapters in *Men Against the Desert*. The remark aptly captures the horrendous conditions farmers faced in the short grass prairie district of Western Canada, otherwise known as Palliser's Triangle, during the 1930s. Every conceivable calamity—from unrelenting drouth and scorching temperatures to insect plagues and crop diseases—descended upon the region and its people. The rescue of this area from possible extinction as a farming district, and the reclaiming of the desert, however, remained largely an unknown victory, until Gray published *Men Against the Desert* over a quarter-century later.

The impact of the depression on western agriculture and the response to the ecological problems were something that James Gray came to appreciate during the latter part of his journalism career. Although born in rural Manitoba, in 1906, Gray grew up in Winnipeg and was essentially a product of the urban prairie west; in fact, most of what he knew about farm life had been gleaned from his days on the Winnipeg Grain Exchange and later as a reporter for the *Winnipeg Free Press*. In 1946, while working as a member of the Ottawa Press Gallery, the 40-year-old Gray prepared a personal account of the dismal 1930s, drawing upon his own experiences and observations as a relief recipient. "The Winter Years" was initially turned down by Macmillan because of internal editorial bickering and languished for over 15 years until the publisher agreed to take another look at the manuscript. Gray, in the meantime, had relocated to Calgary, where he had served as the editor of the *Farm and Ranch Review* and then the *Western Oil Examiner* before joining the Home Oil Company as public relations officer.

This second opportunity to have "The Winter Years" published thrilled Gray. But equally important, it gave him a chance to rework the manuscript to include some of the fascinating material on the agricultural depression that he had absorbed from Prairie Farm Rehabilitation Administration (PFRA) officials, experimental farm scientists, and everyday farmers during his six-year tenure with the *Farm and Ranch Review*. He consequently quit his position with Home Oil and hurriedly added some 80,000 words on the rural west to the original manuscript. The reception to the revised version was mixed. Macmillan agreed to publish "The Winter Years" on the condition that the new agricultural chapters were dropped; the publisher was not only concerned about the length of the book, but believed that Gray's personal memoirs would have greater public appeal.

When *The Winter Years* finally appeared in 1966, James Gray found himself the author of an instant bestseller. One Calgary bookstore, for example, reportedly sold 1,000 copies during the fall season. Carlyle King, an English professor at the University of Saskatchewan and Cooperative Commonwealth Federation activist, however, believed that the critical acclaim for the book was unwarranted. In a review for *Saskatchewan History*, he dismissed *The Winter Years* as "a city man's account of the Depression" and argued that Gray was "less successful when he tries to convey the impact of the Dirty Thirties on the rural population." These comments caught the attention of Tom Melville-Ness, the editor of the Saskatoon-based *Western Producer*, who sent Gray a copy of the review, along with a note that King was right and that the story of the great dust bowl had yet to be told; he also promised to publish whatever Gray might write on the subject as part of the Prairie Books imprint.

When Gray received Melville-Ness's challenge—to do for rural history what he had done for city life—he immediately called his old newspaper friend to tell him that the book had already been written. He then took the chapters Macmillan had dropped from *The Winter Years* and after some minor tinkering, including the addition of some vignettes, sent the manuscript, titled "Men Against the Desert," to Saskatoon in the spring of 1967. There it sat untouched for several months, until a call from Gray later that fall spurred Melville-Ness to send the typescript to the composing room—unedited! Gray first learned about the book's appearance from a Calgary radio reporter, who had received a review copy in late November and wondered what had happened to the author's trademark moustache. The author soon discovered to his horror that the dust jacket carried a photograph of the late L.B. Thomson of the PFRA masquerading as James Gray. What was perhaps even worse was that the text was riddled with errors.

These initial problems aside, *Men Against the Desert* quickly emerged as the PFRA bible and was adopted and distributed by the federal agency as "our story." And it is easy to understand why. While preparing articles for the *Farm and Ranch Review*, Gray constantly heard how the depression had forced a major rethinking of Western Canadian agricultural practices and how PFRA personnel and experimental farm employees, in cooperation with determined farmers, had tackled the ecological problems of the decade with a missionary zeal and a healthy dose of prairie innovation. This story was now told for the first time in *Men Against the Desert* in a comprehensive and evocative fashion. It was nothing less than a war of conquest, complete with helpless victims, unlikely remedies, and production miracles: families madly spooning out a concoction of sawdust, "paris green" poison, and water along the edges of grasshopper-infected fields before dawn; farmers ploughing their land with listing blades into high wave-like furrows to stop the soil from blowing away so that it could be brought under control; or fencing crews turning several

thousand acres that had first been broken by eager homesteaders in the late nineteenth century into community pastures. And although many have since questioned the wisdom
of opening the southern grasslands to farming, the story of
how "the wounds of the Palliser Triangle were bound up and
healed [and] its productivity . . . marvellously restored" re-
mains an unrivalled classic in prairie agricultural literature.

BILL WAISER
UNIVERSITY OF SASKATCHEWAN

Men Against the Desert

Jack Hamilton said:

You remember the crazy things. Like the caterpillars. We had no grasshoppers around Killam that I can recall. But one year we were ankle deep in caterpillars. They covered everything. Unless you wanted to walk on them you had to sweep a path across the porch floor from the door to the steps. They ate everything–the garden, the caragana, the flowers and then they were gone.

Then there was the fence building. We built barbed wire fences on top of fences. The fences would catch the weeds, the weeds would catch and hold the soil. In a single year there would be enough soil blown along a fence line so that the barbed wire was covered. So we'd get another load of posts and some wire and string another fence. We did that twice and I've heard of them doing it three times in southern Saskatchewan.

And there was horse hair. The best you could get for a prime steer was 2 cents a pound, but horse hair brought 25 cents. We had about 40 horses on the 2 farms, my uncle's and ours. So we thinned down all the horses' tails one fall and raised enough money for new skates. We were too greedy with one horse and took off too much of his tail hair. His tail froze and the tip fell off.

This is a book with a point of view and a conviction. The conviction is that the conquest of the desert in the Palliser Triangle in the 1930s is the greatest Canadian success story since the completion of the Canadian Pacific Railway. The point of view is that Canada could not have existed without the settling and farming of the Palliser Triangle; and that Canada could not have survived, economically or politically, if this vast area had been permitted to go back to weed-covered wasteland and short grass cattle range. Would it have gone back to a wind-blown wasteland of sand dunes, buckbrush and pasture sage without the massive campaign that was mounted to save it? That is at least arguable.

What is not arguable is the contribution which this campaign made not only to Canada but to world agriculture and to a humanity caught in the population explosion. The things that Canadians did in those years, the discoveries they made and the methods they devised will pay dividends in increased food production in the semi-arid areas of the world for generations to come. Who were the people who did all this, and what did they do? "They" were the 50,000 bankrupt farmers who lived on relief throughout the "Dirty Thirties" inside the famous Triangle that Captain John Palliser said should never be settled; who fought the scorching wind, the blowing dust, the drouth, hail, frost, grasshoppers and rust from one crop failure to another, and never gave up. "They" were the dedicated legion from the Dominion Experimental Farms who provided not only the leadership but the muscle and equipment that was required to mount the campaign against the desert. "They" were the agricultural engineers,

1

and the university researchers, the soils scientists, entomologists, plant breeders and animal husbandmen who often worked around the clock with the farmers in the fields. "They" were the people who brought the Prairie Farm Rehabilitation Administration into existence—more, the people who *fought* it into existence.

This, I say, is one of the great Canadian success stories of all time. Yet it is completely unknown to 99 out of 100 Canadians, and known only vaguely at best to 99 out of 100 people who inhabit the Palliser Triangle today. The 99 out of 100 who know it only vaguely included myself who, of all people, should have been intimately familiar with it. I was engaged in journalism on the Prairies for 25 years, including a period of six years as editor of the *Farm and Ranch Review*. I got to know my way around the Federal Department of Agriculture in Ottawa during the time I spent in the National Press Gallery. I travelled back and forth around the Prairies during my tenure with the *Farm and Ranch Review*. I knew the Dominion Experimental Farms well, many of their key employees and the heads of all the Prairie Wheat Pools. As a reporter I had travelled through the dust bowl in the Dirty Thirties; I had covered Royal Commissions on grain marketing and on co-operatives. So I knew there had been widespread privation during the depression. I knew that it arose as much from the collapse of farm prices as from drouth in many areas. I had seen farm life at its lowest level, and I had heard it described in detail by a parade of witnesses under oath. Yet withal, my knowledge of the agricultural depression was rather vague. I knew the PFRA had been established in 1935, that it had built thousands of dugouts on prairie farms and had later established the Community Pastures system and built great dams to store irrigation water. But I assumed, if I assumed anything, that the dust bowl had disappeared of its own accord when the rains came back in 1938.

I could not have been more wrong, which was something I discovered during the researching for my book *The Winter Years*. In my reading and conversations I kept stumbling over facts of tremendous significance—the development of Fairway crested wheat grass by Dr. L.E. Kirk; Sidney Barnes's truly monumental work on the effect of wind on soil; the development of strip farming by Leonard and Arle Koole; the invention of the blade cultivator by C.S. Noble and the discer by R.A. Johnson and, above all, the extent of both the desert that developed and the counterattack launched against it by the Experimental Farms personnel from Swift Current, Lethbridge, Scott, Indian Head and Brandon.

Perhaps "discovered" is the wrong word. I knew many of these things already and perhaps it was only during my research that I began to put them together and relate them to each other. In any event I began to see that no history of the Dirty Thirties would be complete without more and more chapters on the conquest of the drouth. The manuscript got completely out of hand, until it became clear that I had not one book but two. The first could be limited to a personal history of the depression, the second confined to the development and the ultimate overcoming of the desert within the Palliser Triangle. It could be a short history of the Prairie Farm Rehabilitation Administration, except for one fact: the emergency was largely over before they got the PFRA off the ground as an effective organization. The real work was done by the Experimental Farms people with the money provided by PFRA. Even after the PFRA was in business, it was the personnel of the Experimental Farms who carried out the job of regrassing and reclaiming the hundreds of thousands of acres of abandoned land that were taken into the Community Pastures.

Why has this great Canadian achievement gone unnoticed by Canadian writers? Largely, I suspect, because there was nothing very dramatic about it. The drouth years came slowly, the desert developed slowly and it spread slowly. Nothing much was done about it until after 1935 when it became recognized as a truly national emergency. What was done was never dramatic or exciting, unless 50,000 farmers planting crested wheat grass seed on five-acre plots is dramatic, or unless never counted numbers of farmers ridging their fields against the wind is dramatic and exciting. The threat of the desert to the West did not end suddenly, by some massive stroke of genius or good fortune. It was only nibbled away over a period of five years during which time it rained enough to give the desert-fighters a chance to catch their breath and redouble their efforts.

On the other hand, there was surely drama enough in the 10,000 farm families who walked away from their farms in the Palliser Triangle and trekked to the north. Much has been written of the farmers of Oklahoma and Arkansas who loaded their families in their trucks and flivvered to California. But the Okies and Arkies were bound for the "promised land", while the Canadians were headed into a land that God forgot, to the Big River country, the Torch River country, the outer fringe of the Peace River country, and the Carrot River country, for which they were worse fitted and worse equipped than for the dust bowl they had left.

The difficulties that derive from writing a history without a climax will be apparent to the readers of this book. One example will suffice. Some sort of thundering if fraudulent climax might have been created by laboriously compiling the year-by-year reseeding of the Community Pastures until 80,000 cattle were grazing on 2,000,000 acres of new grassland that had once been wind-blown wasteland. But the climax was not in the end of the story but in the beginning. In the construction of the first barbed wire fences around half a dozen wastelands in 1937. It was not the seeding down of 1,000,000 or 2,000,000 acres that counted. It was the reclaiming and restoring of the first few thousand acres out of the 500,000 acres that were blowing out of control. Once the first steps were taken, the rest followed naturally, given the dedication, energy and intelligence of the people involved. It is for this reason that the emphasis of this work is on beginnings, on getting things started rather than the glossing over of the start in pursuit of a dramatic climax.

The PFRA is, of course, a great success story in its own right, but getting it into existence at all was fraught with endless difficulty and frustration. Its architects in Ottawa and the men trying to contain the desert in the field shared the same problems: "Where do we start?" The massive emergency that was caused by the violent dust storms that blew across the Palliser Triangle cannot be exaggerated. But how did the Federal Government, in 1934 and 1935, go about coping with it? What kind of an organization was needed? It should be recalled that this was before there was much machinery for federal-provincial collaboration of the kind that developed after the Rowell-Sirois Commission. The Prairie Provinces were only lately possessed of their natural resources and were most reluctant to have the Federal Government take them back. And doing something about the number one natural resource, the topsoil, was the categorical imperative, and only the Federal Government could finance the kind of an effort that was needed. None of the provinces had either the money or the people who could do the work, but it was *their* land, *their* municipalities and *their* people who were at the bottom of the problem.

The complexity of the problem of organization cannot be passed over lightly. What was involved was the putting together of an organization that would teach 100,000 farmers how to farm. How do governments, living in gold-fish bowls anyway, go about doing that without even admitting to themselves that is what they must do? The physical task of organizing the teaching cadres was difficult enough without inventing a dominion-provincial-municipal superbody to master-plan the project. Fortunately, the organizational problems were not allowed to detract from the job at hand. Parliament voted the needed millions to finance countermeasures to control the dust-blowing. The people who had all the answers were conscripted to do the job, and three years later a formula was found to get the PFRA into operation.

Most of the difficulties were sorted out by the mounting pressure of the crisis, but that took a great deal of time. This complicated history, for it makes it impossible to tell the story chronologically. It was not simply that the PFRA was organized, investigated what had to be done, and then went out and did the job. Rather it was that previous investigations had long since discovered what had to be done. Money which was appropriated to PFRA enabled others to do the job, and then the PFRA was organized. By then the authorities had come to the unanimous conclusion that stopping the dust storms and containing the desert were not enough. The whole face of Western Canada had to be radically altered and in the process the agricultural industry had to be revolutionized.

All that has come to pass and the revolution still goes on. The fabulous crops that have been reaped in Palliser's Triangle in the post-war years have not been grown by accident. They are the demonstrable results of the discoveries that were made by Canadians in their struggles to contain the desert. They are discoveries which, if put to use, can work productive miracles for the peoples of all the world. In those testing years Canadian agriculture assumed a new role in the world. It ceased being only an important agricultural producer and became a leader of world agriculture in the fullest meaning of the word.

This, then, is the story of the era in which Canadian agriculture grew out of parochialism into international stature. It is not a complete history for there are unavoidable gaps in it although it was researched as carefully and thoroughly as time would allow. That research included long interviews with all the key figures of the time. Most of the interviews were tape recorded and the tapes have been deposited with the Saskatchewan archives in Regina for the use of future historians. Included with the tapes so deposited are interviews with Dr. E.S. Archibald, Dr. J.G. Taggart, Dr. L.E. Kirk, Grant Denike, Gideon Matte, George Spence, Asael E. Palmer, Peter Janzen, Baden Campbell, R.H. Painter, Jack Byers, G.D. Matthews, Raymond Youngman, Allan McKinnon, Gerald and Shirley Noble.

In addition to the taped recordings there were many other interviews with Don Allen, who was executive assistant to the Rt. Hon. J.G. Gardiner for more than 20 years; Harry Hargrave, deputy director of PFRA, who was in charge of the Manyberries Range Experimental Station during the worst drouth years; H.A. Purdy, who helped organize Agricultural Improvement Associations in western Saskatchewan; J. Roe Foster, who had a similar responsibility in eastern Saskatchewan; and several dozen farmers and ranchers who lived through the worst of it. The files of the Dominion Experimental Farms were made available as were all the early records of the PFRA together with subsequent reports and other data. The pinpointing of a good deal of the unfolding history was made possible through access to the microfilm of newspaper files in Edmonton, Calgary, Lethbridge, Regina, Saskatoon and Winnipeg.

JAMES H. GRAY

A Farmer's Wife
(In the drouth area)

The crop has failed again, the wind and sun
Dried out the stubble first, then one by one
The strips of summerfallow, seered with heat,
Crunched, like old fallen leaves, our lovely wheat.
The garden is a dreary, blighted waste,
The very air is gritty to my taste.

And now I ask, O Lord, a mother's prayer!
Help me to know these fields so brown and bare;
Art not of Thee, that all this stricken land
Is not because of Thine avenging hand,
But ours the fault; we did not farm it right
And now it answers us with wind and blight.

I don't know how we'll face another year–
Help us someway to know that you are near.
The children need so many things, and I–
I don't mind much, but oh, I'd love to buy
A nice new dress, a soft blue silk that clings.
O God, forgive me for such trivial things!

I know we'll manage somehow, but today
It is all dark, I cannot see the way;
The months loom up with all their snow and cold.
Oh, give us something, Lord, some faith to hold.
Something that we can count on, look ahead
Above these stricken fields so brown and dead.

And even as I wait before Thy throne
New strength flows in, and I am not alone;
This hour with Thee has brought me strength and grace.
I shall go on with courage now to face
Whatever comes, the children will be fed:
Give us each day, O God, our daily bread!

EDNA JAQUES

George Blundun said:

I taught school in Alameda in 1933 and 1934 for $50 a month plus the teacherage. Phyllis and I might have managed on that, except for one thing. We had to save enough out of it to tide us over the summer while I was getting my degree at the University of Saskatchewan summer school. However, we were lucky to be musicians of sorts–Phyl played the piano and I played the saxophone–and we were able to augment our income by playing for Saturday night dances. There was one somewhere in the district every week. Nobody had much money in south east Saskatchewan but that never stopped us from having fun, and the Saturday night dance was always crowded.

Being musicians created a real problem. We needed clothes. Phyl had to have a couple of good dresses that she could alternate and fix over so that she didn't turn up at every dance every week in the same outfit. Nobody ever took better care of their clothes than we did those years in Alameda.

Then one frightfully hot Saturday night we came home from a dance and probably didn't lock the screen door. In any event, it blew open during the night and we were awakened along toward morning by the damndest clatter and uproar in the living room. I leaped out of bed expecting God knows what. I got into the living room just as a gaunt and starving steer disappeared out the front door with one of Phyl's best dresses in its mouth and the other torn and trampled in the manure it had left all over the living room floor and furniture.

CHAPTER ONE

The Land of Beginning Again and Again

hen the Rt. Hon. J.G. Gardiner arose in the House of Commons on February 11, 1937, to present his bill to amend the Prairie Farm Rehabilitation Act, the atmosphere of the House was in sharp contrast to what it had been two years before. The partisan politicking that marked the debate in 1935, when the Hon. Robert Weir launched the PFRA was notably absent. The Rt. Hon. R.B. Bennett, whose dislike for Mr. Gardiner was all embracing, was restrained in his comments and helpful in his questions. At the end of Mr. Gardiner's two-hour speech, Mr. T.C. Douglas congratulated the Minister of Agriculture on having presented the best case he had ever heard on behalf of the farmers in the drouth areas of Western Canada. Partisanship would return later in the debate, but on that day all members in the House of Commons seemed united in the recognition that the worst calamity in Canadian history was in the making on the western plains.

The people of the West had just survived the worst year, climatically, within living memory. Not only had 1936 been the coldest, bitterest winter ever recorded but the torrid summer had seen high temperature records shattered between Winnipeg and the Rockies. And even as Mr. Gardiner spoke the winter of 1937 had started in where the winter of 1936 had left off, presaging worse disasters to come. Life on the dust bowl farms might have been tolerable for the 200,000 farmers and their families on dried-out relief if they had been well housed and well clothed. For the most part they shivered or sweltered in shack-houses with paper thin walls, without modern conveniences, comatosely holding to a fading hope that next year had to be better; and for seven years each next year had been worse than the one before.

The desert, which had begun in 1929 with the swirling up-drafts on the parched summerfallow from Hanna to Monarch to Cadillac to Melita, now threatened the entire Palliser Triangle. Blowing topsoil drifted like snow across the railway tracks in Alberta. It blew from the poor land onto the good land in Saskatchewan and kept Regina, Moose Jaw and Swift Current coated with dust inside and out. It bathed Winnipeg in a perpetual yellow overcast. Roads made impassable by snowdrifts in the winter were drifted into impassability again with blowing topsoil in the summer. The drifts built up till they covered the fences, choked out the shelterbelts and gardens, reached the roofs of the chicken houses, blew in through the cracks around farmhouse windows and under farmhouse doors to drive the inhabitants out of their houses and out of the country.

Each year the disaster area had expanded until it now embraced 250 municipalities and 18,000,000* acres—a quarter of all the arable land in Canada. As Mr. Gardiner pointed out, it threatened the social and economic survival of 900,000

---

* Throughout the text which follows various figures will be used to estimate acreage affected by soil drifting, insect infestation, crop failure and drouth in various degrees. It should be understood that all figures are fairly rough estimates made at the time by Government agencies. No accurate count was ever made of the actual number of acres ruined by wind erosion, severely damaged by wind erosion or severely affected by wind erosion. An omnibus definition—blowing out of control—was frequently used to encompass both land from which the topsoil had been blown and where the denuding was still in process. At the peak of the windstorm periods some 250,000 to 300,000 acres were within this category. The land which was affected in varying degrees of severity by wind erosion has been estimated from 3,000,000 to 6,000,000 acres. Not all the 2,000,000-odd acres taken into the Community Pastures were wind eroded, and severe damage by wind erosion was by no means confined to land eventually made into pastures.

people. If prairie agriculture could not be saved, if the desert could not be contained and then reclaimed, the cities that lived off agriculture could not survive. And without productive and prosperous and populated Prairie Provinces, could Canada itself survive? This was the unasked question on everyone's mind.

There was more to it, however, than even the physical disaster with which Mr. Gardiner dealt. There was a financial disaster of equal magnitude. The calamitous collapse of farm prices between 1930 and 1933 had reduced farm purchasing power to near zero and there had been little real recovery by the winter of 1936-37. Livestock shipped to the Winnipeg stockyards returned barely enough to pay the freight charges to get them there. One of the measures the Government had taken in 1937 was to pay the freight charges so that the farmers would have two or three cents a pound net for their animals. Prices on the Winnipeg Grain Exchange had fluctuated wildly at times, after the Liberals fired the McFarland Wheat Board in 1935 and took the wraps off the futures market. The result was temporarily high prices when the farmers had little grain to sell, depressed prices when they had. But as the farmers within the Palliser Triangle were enduring successive crop failures anyway, the fluctuating prices had little relevancy for them. In 250 municipalities there was almost total destitution and the distribution of relief to the destitute had become Saskatchewan's biggest industry. The province itself functioned mainly as a distribution agency for federal assistance, which was provided both as loans and grants. Most of the municipalities within the Palliser Triangle were in default on their debentures, the school teachers went unpaid and even the councillors who dispensed the relief were themselves on relief.

There was no cause and effect relationship between the natural disaster and the economic disaster, except this: the economic collapse made everything worse. The collapse of prices added to the drouth to double the impetus which drove thousands of settlers off the land and out of the Palliser

Triangle. Had they received reasonable returns for their labors, some of these refugees might have been encouraged to stay on and wait for one more "next year." Indeed, had there been a shadow of validity to the theories of the liberal economists, the crop failures would have produced sky-rocketing prices for the lucky ones who had a crop to sell. Instead the prices of everything the farmers produced went down and stayed down. As a result those who stayed on the land wore out their machinery, their horses and themselves and were in no condition, physically or financially, to undertake the steps that became necessary to combat erosion. Their problems were complicated further by the abandoned land from which the topsoil blew. When crops were occasionally raised as a result of spring showers and thunderstorms at the right time, the meagre returns were as damaging to morale, almost, as a crop failure would have been. Nothing, however, was quite as shattering to morale as grasshoppers and rust. Until the grasshoppers descended in their clouds in 1933, a good crop was in the making in parts of the Palliser Triangle. When the grasshoppers passed, there was nothing of crops and less of gardens. A good crop was in prospect too in 1935 until the rust attacked it. Then it was not even good enough for horse feed.

The challenge of the dust bowl demanded heroic measures and Mr. Gardiner urged Parliament to think in heroic terms, in terms of the expenditure of $10,000,000 a year and an overall cost of $50,000,000. In the context of 1937, when there were still 1,250,000 Canadians on relief out of a population of 13,000,000, these were truly heroic figures to be bruiting about. Yet only those who had travelled through the Prairies in those years could appreciate the magnitude of the task that faced the country. And only those whose judgment of the possible was distorted by frenzied desperation could have had much confidence that the country could yet be saved. Mr. Gardiner perhaps expressed it best when he said there was no alternative, that it would be physically and financially impossible to evacuate 900,000 people from the stricken area. Somehow, the West had to be saved.

Given time and money, grasshoppers could be controlled. Experiments in Manitoba had provided the scientists with a nearly foolproof method of doing that. Rust could be overcome by the use of resistant varieties of wheat. The soil scientists were confident that wind erosion could be unfanged with time, money and machinery. It was all these that Mr. Gardiner hoped to achieve once he had changed the form and substance of the PFRA. But, for the economic problems that afflicted the farmers, his Liberals had nothing to offer but a hope that world markets and world prices would somehow find their way back to normal. On balance, however, Mr. Gardiner was putting first things first. Unless the marching desert of the Palliser Triangle was contained, arguments over farm prices and economic policies would soon become wholly academic.

And how had all this come to pass, in a land that had been broken to the plow for less than two generations? Essentially, the disaster in Saskatchewan was part of a much larger whole which extended backwards to the dawn of time, and geographically from the Battle River to the Gulf of Mexico. It began, possibly, when the first cave men domesticated the first goats which over-grazed and trampled out the grass on the hillsides to open the soil for wind and water erosion. Archaeologists in Mesopotamia have uncovered the village of Khorosabad which was buried in 15 feet of soil blown over it 2600 years ago. At the time of Cleopatra, Tarsus in Turkey was a thriving port which her fleet visited regularly. Today it is 10 miles inland, separated from the sea by the millions of tons of rich topsoil that have been eroded away by wind and water. The Romans destroyed Carthage, and then took only 200 years to turn the rich soils of North Africa into a desert wasteland. Whether they were Chinese, Syrians or Spaniards, living 1000 years before or 1000 years after Christ, people everywhere have tended to follow the same pattern—cut, burn, plant, destroy, move on. It has been a pattern that has prevailed throughout the new world as well, from the tobacco farms of the Confederate south to the Valley of the Gananarska in Ontario. At first glance, what was happening in Canada seemed to be a carbon copy of all that had happened before, and a mere extension of the disaster that was gripping the American Midwest. Pictures of Okies and Arkies in Model T caravans heading for California made their periodic appearance in Canadian newspapers along with a great deal of publicity about the black blizzards of the United States.

As the rest of Canada became gradually aware of the seriousness of the drouth in the West, a bumper crop of freelance wiseacres sprouted with a brash eagerness to diagnose the trouble. Their diagnosis began usually with a quotation from Palliser, touched caustically on the harm caused by the "wheat miners" and concluded with a Jeremiad on a population motivated only by a desire to "get in, get rich and get out!"

It was true of course that Captain John Palliser had explored the south country in 1857 and had decided it would never be able to support a viable agriculture. But Palliser had made the same mistake the latter day critics were to make. He had seen only part of the country in a dry year and in the main he had treated the whole vast area as having a single homogenous soil type. The truth, of course, was that an infinite variety of soils were scattered over a wide area, and even within rather small areas there was rich land and poor land. Thus while the Palliser Triangle included millions of acres of land which should never have been broken to the plow, it included more millions of near-perfect grain-growing soil. Palliser's judgment of the quality of the land in his famous Triangle was, unhappily, based at best on a superficial acquaintanceship and at worst, no knowledge of it at all. His journeys were mainly around its periphery. In any event, those who leaned on Palliser ignored the much more important and more thorough examination made by Professor John Macoun in the 1870s, during a string of wet years.

It was Macoun who demonstrated the fallibility of annual rainfall statistics and the importance of summer rainfall to the Great Plains. It was Macoun's report which helped guide the CPR through the southern prairies and led to the settlement of Saskatchewan. A second event which further vitiated the validity of Palliser's opinion was the happy accident at Indian Head. There, in the early spring of 1885, the farm horses were all conscripted to haul supplies for the army that was suppressing the Rebellion of 1885. By the time they were released it was too late to put in a crop. However, the land was worked during the summer, and the following year it produced a splendid crop of wheat despite an almost complete crop failure everywhere else. Angus McKay, the first superintendent of the Dominion Experiment Station at Indian Head, was so intrigued by this development that he launched a series of experiments with summerfallow as soon as his station was established. Out of these experiments came the invention of the system of summerfallowing that turned Palliser's Triangle into the sometimes bread basket of the world. It is true, of course, that summerfallowing was a prime factor in creating the dust bowl. But summerfallowing made the growing of bumper crops possible where none was possible without it. That fact was decisive in the settlement of the West. That, and the discovery of early ripening Red Fife wheat, and the development of Marquis wheat.

It was becoming apparent, however, that regardless of the opinion of Palliser or anyone else, an "on paper" settlement of the prairies would not be enough to allay fear of the area being absorbed by the United States. A new cloud no larger than the proverbial man's hand had already appeared on the horizon, in the form of a man on horseback driving a herd of cattle northward across the Saskatchewan River. He had driven them all the way from Texas, and behind him were legions of other cowboys looking for ranches, driving cattle looking for grazing land.

Between Winnipeg and the mountains in 1885 there were barely 100,000 people in the settlements concentrated along the CPR main line and from Brandon to Saskatoon to Edmonton to Calgary. Outside the cities there were less than 20,000 people in the whole Palliser Triangle in 1901 between Manitoba and the mountains. The RCMP had put the run on the American whiskey traders and quieted the Indians; but could a corporal's guard of red coats hold the whole Triangle against the peaceful invasion of the American cattlemen? As the westward rush of American homesteaders closed the old buffalo pastures to the cattlemen, the ranchers were forced ever westward and northward into Wyoming and Montana. The wide open and unsettled spaces of the Palliser Triangle looked inviting indeed to the displaced beef producers. The American ranching industry drifted quickly north of the border on the spill-over from Montana of the Texas-bred herds. As Wallace Stegner has pointed out, the great pioneer Canadian cattle spreads like the 76 Ranch, the Turkey Track, the T-Down-Bar and the Matador were simply extensions of American cattle empires.

The orientation of the cattlemen was naturally southward whence they drew supplies and to where they shipped their cattle. Whether they were Canadian, American or British, they had a friendly familiarity with the Montana cattle towns of Shelby, Havre, Malta and Glasgow. Moreover all the folk customs of the American cowboy were soon adopted in Canada, with the possible exception of gun-toting.

How far the encroachment might have extended geographically without the aggressive settlement policies of Sir Clifford Sifton is, of course, purely conjectural. Perhaps history by then had moved past the point where a repetition of the Oregon grab could have been possible. In any event, if the railways and the nation had followed the course Palliser recommended, 100,000 square miles of superb range land would have been held open for the cattlemen. This would have confined settlement to the Winnipeg-Saskatoon-Edmonton axis, and the Prairie Provinces could never have functioned on such a population base. The bridge that would make Canada a country by connecting Ontario with British

Columbia had to be a bridge of people. No mere cattle economy could have nurtured the hundreds of thousands of people who were needed to get the country going.

The die was cast for settlement, even before the cattle barons crossed the Whitemud River and headed for the South Saskatchewan. With the decision, the forces were set in motion which led, inexorably, to the creation of the dust bowl, even though settlement itself fluctuated between flood and trickle. In response to the blandishment of the recruiting agents, the settlers came from the United States, from Ontario, the British Isles and continental Europe. Some of the most experienced farmers settled in the cities, some of the poorest equipped went homesteading. Many of those who went on the land were birds of passage rather than settlers. Their main objective was to prove up their homesteads, sell out for a profit and move on. Free land was the attraction, not the idea of turning a prairie homestead into a family farm. Between 1896 and 1914, the Dominion Government gave away millions of acres of homestead lands while the railways and land companies sold millions of acres more. William Pearce believed only a third of the homesteaders ever intended to become farmers. At one time the CPR had a list of 50,000 names of absentee landlords who had acquired land in the West and left the country.

Nevertheless there was a high percentage of experienced farmers among those who settled the Palliser Triangle. They and their forebears had learned how to cultivate the soil over 1,000 years in the Ukraine. They were experienced farmers and farmers' sons from the Midwest of the United States, from the British Isles and from Ontario. It is one of the ironies of Canadian history that the worst damage to the soils of the Palliser Triangle was done by the best farmers. The land recovered quickly from the wounds inflicted by the touch-and-go homesteaders who flitted in, stayed awhile and drifted away. It was those who followed the best scientific methods, those who plowed and manicured their summerfallow with infinite care and patience, who were the primary fashioners of the disaster.

The experienced settlers of the Palliser Triangle had one thing in common regardless of their origin—they came mainly from high rainfall areas. They had learned how to farm where a cow could be kept on an acre or two of land, where all the horses needed to farm 100 acres could be kept on the forage and pasture from a 10-acre field. They had learned their trade with moldboard plows, discs and harrows, in an environment where the need never existed to rush the planting of their seed to catch the spring rains, where work could proceed at a horse's walking pace.

The skills they brought to the Palliser Triangle were as wrong for that area as they could possibly have been, as totally wrong as the tools they brought, or bought. But they had to find these things out for themselves. Once they reached their homesteads they were on their own—dumped in the middle of nowhere to root-hog-or-die. Attached to the glittering bauble of "FREE LAND!" that had brought them to the Triangle was a price tag which was never deciphered for them in advance. The price tag was 10 years out of their lives—the time it would take them to become established farmers—with good luck on good soil. There were no soil surveys to guide them. No one told them to look first for a source of water before they picked their homesteads, or to test the topsoil, or anything else. Agricultural extension services had not yet been invented and the authorities were too busy recruiting settlers to bother with those who had come in. The settlers turned to their neighbors for advice, and learned by doing, even copying the mistakes of their neighbors.

Those who had any financial resources when they arrived got somebody with a steam engine and a breaking plow to turn the first sod for them. Then they went off to work for wages while the sod was rotting and to get money for more breaking, for horses and lumber and plows and harrows and binders. Those who came without resources followed almost the same path and it took a lot longer. One factor which helped them in two ways was the boom in railway construction that added 1,000 miles of trackage in southern Saskatchewan just prior to World War I. The work gangs who built the roads were recruited from among the settlers who got first call on jobs. The new lines cut the distance they had to haul their supplies and take their grain from 30 or 40 miles to 8 or 10. It made the whole process of getting settled on their own land less onerous. To most of them, when they first looked over the 160 acres they had filed on, across to the quarter section they would pre-empt, it had to seem that they owned all the land in the world. They compared it happily with the land they had left, convinced that a man had to get rich someday farming so vast a spread.

It took time, but they learned one fact at a time. The horses they required to work their new farms needed an astounding 10 acres each to sustain them. So did their cows. They learned about summerfallowing and those who survived learned about the categorical imperative of dry-land farming—timing. As Grant Denike has pointed out with such forceful conviction, the twin scourges of the dry-land were untimely and inadequate tillage, both of which could be traced to the necessity of the settlers relying on horse power. Unless the crop was seeded at the right time, it would miss the rains and yields might be cut in half. Unless the land was properly cultivated the soil would be robbed of its moisture, humus and fertility and the way left open for wind erosion. Cultivation too early would miss the weeds, too late would mean a loss of moisture.

All this was knowledge that would be acquired later, though some would never learn. The settlers before World War I were far too busy trying to get established to have much time for observing and learning. So they profited least in the good years and suffered most in the poor years. The conditions which would produce bumper crops 50 years later often spelled near crop failure for the settlers before World War I. By that time, however, the blandishments of the railways and Government had proven so effective that the south country had become overpopulated. There were too many people trying to make a living on too little land. Farms of 320 acres could produce a living in a bumper crop year, but that happened only once in five. The process of desettlement was already underway. As economic circumstances squeezed the least efficient or least lucky off their holdings, the more successful farmers sought to expand their holdings in search of the optimum farm size. There were two developments, however, which retarded this process. The first was the outbreak of the war, and the second was the crop of 1915.

Immediately upon the declaration of war on August 4, 1914, a great drive was launched by the Federal Government to bring more land under cultivation. Every piece of equipment that could be made to work was engaged breaking sod that fall. The result was that 4,800,000 more acres were being cultivated in 1915 than the year before. The pressure for more and more grain production was kept on for the next four years and 12,000,000 acres in all were added to cultivation, of which more than 5,500,000 acres were broken in the Palliser Triangle alone.

It was the crop of 1915 that changed the complexion of Western Canada and ended all doubts about its future as one of the greatest wheat growing areas on earth. Yields of 30 to 40 bushels per acre were common in the Palliser Triangle. The Prairie Provinces produced 360,000,000 bushels of wheat from just under 14,000,000 acres that year, almost twice the crop they had ever produced before. The average yield of 26 bushels to the acre was destined to be a record for 40 years. The most interesting thing about that crop was that it was produced with little more moisture than had fallen the year before, when "crop failure" was written across most of the face of Western Canada. The rains of 1915 fell everywhere and always at the right time. The big crop of 1915 accentuated the drive to put more acres under cultivation. However, it did nothing for the soil of the Palliser Triangle because it encouraged the breaking of thousands of acres of submarginal land. The farmers, forced to struggle on without adequate help, were less and less thorough in their attention to their soil, and crop failure followed crop failure in 1917, 1918, 1919 and 1920. The high gloss the country acquired in 1915 started to tarnish in 1917 and the succession of crop failures also dimmed the lustre on "provincial status" for which everybody in the North-West Territories was agitating at the turn of the century.

Neither Alberta nor Saskatchewan had the tax sources needed to sustain their services in bad times. Neither did the municipalities. But as the population doubled and redoubled there was need for doubling and redoubling of services, including the construction of roads, schools and public buildings of all kinds. Much of the needed expansion was financed with borrowed money and interest charges began soaking up ever-increasing portions of provincial revenues while the recurring depressions created greater demands for relief. In 1911, the Province of Saskatchewan budget provided $192,812 for debt charges. Ten years later the figure had shot up to $2,259,000. Public welfare costs rose from $192,000 to $1,281,000 in the same period.

As Ottawa still held title to the natural resources of both provinces, and was responsible for bringing in the settlers, the provinces turned to Ottawa for assistance. It was always forthcoming, often in large sums. But as the cost of relief mounted with settlement, grave doubts were raised about the basic wisdom of settling the country at all. Could the country stand such a steady drain? What was wrong with the settlers or the country that they could not become self-supporting? When blowing soil began to make its appearance, both Alberta and Saskatchewan decided it was time for a dispassionate re-examination of the Palliser Triangle. Alberta set up a survey commission in 1920 and Saskatchewan established a Royal Commission to study the problems of dry-land farming.

Neither report found much to recommend. Alberta, which was having some success in the Lethbridge area with irrigation, thought that more irrigation might be helpful. Saskatchewan and Alberta agreed that some of the strain would be eased for farm families if they paid more attention to keeping a few dairy cows and poultry. It was Saskatchewan, however, that provided the suggestion which history will probably judge one of the most important ever to come out of a Royal Commission. It urged that a special experimental farm be established at Swift Current to make scientific investigations of problems of dry-land farming and find the solutions to them. It also urged that an agricultural extension service be established which would be staffed by trained agrologists who would spread the latest information from the scientists to the farmers on the land. The Dominion Government was impressed and moved immediately to establish the Experimental Farm at Swift Current. It was 30 years later, however, before the Saskatchewan Government got around to the second, and in many ways just as important, recommendation.

As the Royal Commission on the South Saskatchewan River pointed out in 1952, the reports of both inquiries underlined the dilemma of dry-land farming. Summerfallowing was the great moisture-conserving device and was hence indispensable. But in the succession of extremely dry years, summerfallow could not conserve enough moisture to produce a crop. It was basic to the summerfallow theory that the surface of the soil had to be kept free of weeds and covered with a dust mulch which protected the sub-surface moisture from yielding to the suction of the sun and winds. But the finely tilled summerfallow with its dust mulch became increasingly subject to wind erosion. By 1920, wind erosion had become a serious problem in the border country and was threatening to engulf other areas as well. The situation was summarized by the Royal Commission into Farming Conditions in Saskatchewan as follows:

The report said in part:

> The summerfallow method of using the precipitation of three years to grow two crops, or of two years to grow one crop, has made possible the growing of grain

in areas in which it is doubtful whether any other system of tillage and cropping would have produced equally good results. To summerfallow has meant to plow the land late in May or early in June and keep it free from vegetation during the remainder of the year so that what rain falls on it is absorbed by it and a considerable portion retained as a surplus for the next year's crop . . . The early efforts of the homesteader have to do with breaking up the prairie and destroying native vegetation so as to have a place in which to grow crops. Soon, however, he has to consider what is the most profitable method of treating stubble land, and this introduces the summerfallow and with it come some of the problems of the summerfallow.

For over thirty years, the summerfallow once in three years has been the practice upon which successful grain growing has been carried on in Eastern and Central Saskatchewan. Until this plan of storing moisture was devised, crop failure was as frequent and just as serious in the eastern part of the province as it is now in the southwest. But while it stabilized grain growing it was learned that when the root fibres of the native prairie plants had been worked out or destroyed by frequent plowing and cultivating, the land developed a tendency to blow and drift, and this has been the history of most open plains districts where grain growing has been carried on for a dozen years or so, while some have reached this stage much sooner. The southwest being more recently settled than any other part of Saskatchewan should not yet experience soil drifting, but this has developed in some districts, and it may therefore be assumed that the soils which have already proved very troublesome in this respect are naturally deficient in fibre, and that provision will have to be made to restore organic matter if these soils are to continue in use for grain production according to prevailing methods. Soil drifting is one of the most serious conditions in connection with grain growing on the lighter soils in Saskatchewan and calls for immediate action.

What the cure will be is not fully apparent . . .

While the experts were palavering in search of a cure, farmers by the thousands found their own solution in the manner farmers have solved this problem since history has been recorded. They pulled up stakes and moved off to greener fields. In Alberta the movement out of the border country became almost a stampede between 1921 and 1926. Over the whole of the Triangle the previously heavy immigration became heavy emigration. When the census was taken in 1926 more than 10,000 abandoned farms were counted in Alberta. Half of them were in census divisions three and five, which hug the border north of Medicine Hat. In the division immediately north of Medicine Hat population dropped by 30 percent within five years. The count of abandoned farms in Saskatchewan reached only 4,900, and these were fairly well scattered. Nevertheless, the count in the area north of Swift Current adjoining the Alberta border exceeded 900.

The exodus out of the eastern area of Alberta became further stimulated by the Provincial Government itself. It undertook a resettlement project and moved between 600 and 700 families to new land in the Red Deer-Rimbey area. The municipalities were abolished and the whole area was placed under a special board which was given wide powers to regulate land use in the area.

Alberta reversed its previous order of importance from grain and livestock to livestock and grain. With two or three sections of pasture land, plus a section of wheat land, Alberta officials thought a farmer might prosper even in the dry belt. In the area east of Tilley, where there had been 2,400 families in 1911, population was down to around 1,500 when the Government began to de-populate it still further in 1926. By the end of the decade there were scarcely 500 people left.

Gradually a large part of eastern Alberta was taken out of grain growing and restored to grass.

Though the Saskatchewan exodus was much lighter it did help in part to allay the wind erosion problem for the time being. Some of the poorest land went back to weeds and ultimately to grass. Then, just as the exodus was in full swing, the rains came back. Good crop followed good crop from 1922 until 1928 and with top prices farm income soared to previously unparalleled heights. Economic statistics for Western Canada tend to distort the picture in the Palliser Triangle because the figures are averaged over very wide areas. Nevertheless, the overall statistics for farm income indicate that even if the farmers in the Triangle earned less than their more fortunate compatriots in the sure-crop parklands, they did very well indeed. The cash farm income of the farmers of Saskatchewan was very close to $300,000,000 a year on the average over most of the 1920s. It was small wonder as the decade drew to a close that no one was worrying publicly about the problem of wind erosion. But the scientists at Swift Current, Lethbridge and Scott knew that the problem was far from solved. There were areas in both Saskatchewan and Alberta where wind erosion was worse than ever. But the goose hung high and the decade closed with farmers everywhere poised at their implement dealers for the great leap forward into the golden age of farm mechanization that the tractor and combine would usher in. Instead, the Dirty Thirties arrived with great black blizzards and the near disappearance of cash farm income from the entire Palliser Triangle.

Olaf Field said:

When I went to the barber in Swift Current in the summer of 1937 to get a haircut and a shave he said the haircut was okay but he had quit shaving people. I asked how come and he said: he couldn't keep an edge on his razor any more. With the terrible dust and shortage of water, he said sharp particles of sand got imbedded in the skin, or stuck to the surface somehow. Despite the extra honing he gave his razors, a couple of strokes down the side of a customer's face took off the edge completely. Either he had to keep honing after each stroke or two, or the customers got mad. So I settled for a haircut.

CHAPTER TWO

The Bench-Mark Years of Decision

ates are important even to informal histories and the immediate background of the conquest of the desert that threatened to destroy Western Canada can be assembled around five: June 2, 1886; August 1, 1931; May 12, 1934; September 14, 1934; and April 11, 1935.

The first date marked the establishment of the Dominion Experimental Farms system, without which nothing would have been possible. The Experimental Farms did most of the thinking, provided all the solutions, supplied most of the organization, drive, legs and muscle which were to save the country. It was able to do all this because it had been set up like no other Experimental Farm service anywhere. Its uniqueness lay in the fact that it was one interconnected and centrally controlled and directed system. The prairie farms, first at Brandon and Indian Head and then at Lethbridge, Morden, Lacombe, Scott and Swift Current, were established to serve the farmers on the land. Their objective was to find answers to all the problems that beset the farmers of their localities, the choice of strains of seed, what cultural practices were best suited, which livestock types were best for the particular environment. As the farm problems differed from area to area, so naturally did the activities of the stations. Ottawa co-ordinated the activities of each station with the others, provided both overall control and direction, but did so with a very light rein.

Without the Experimental Farms, there could have been

no Prairie Farm Rehabilitation Administration, and it was in the performance of the PFRA that the Experimental Farms had their finest hour. For the dedicated people in the service, this was doing what they had been trained to do—serve the farmers on the land, work with them in solving their problems and make their very lives a part of the community around them. Soon degree-festooned careerists would take over and the publication of scientific theses in technical journals would be the highest activity to which a government employee could aspire. Ultimately the Experimental Farms would be derogated clear out of the *Canada Year Book* index. But that was not to come until a later date.

The agricultural community of the United States was also well served with Experimental Farms, but there each state operated its own research station with the help of federal grants. Thus the American experimenters lacked the co-ordination and direction the Canadians enjoyed. There was however the closest collaboration between the Canadian and the American agricultural scientists, and in this co-operation Canadians gave as much as they received.

The second date, August 1, 1931, marked the day on which the rest of Canada discovered that there had been a series of crop failures in the Palliser Triangle. The Canadian Red Cross launched an appeal for food and clothing for 125,000 destitute farm families who had now suffered three consecutive crop failures. Without help on a massive scale there would be severe privation and suffering in the winter to follow. The Red Cross appeal was important for two reasons. It underlined a truism of the Dirty Thirties, that nobody outside the Palliser Triangle ever was told much, or knew much about what was going on inside. The grain trade in Winnipeg knew that the average wheat yield in crop districts two through seventeen would average less than six or five or three bushels to the acre. Owners of debentures for 150 municipalities would discover that no interest was being paid on their investment. Employees of mail-order houses in Regina and Winnipeg would wonder what had happened to the flow of orders they once got from southern Saskatchewan, western Manitoba and eastern Alberta. In Toronto and Montreal the banks and mortgage companies would lay in a new supply of red ink for their debt collection records.

There was no conspiracy of silence in Canada comparable to the condition which prevailed in Kansas. There the secretary of the Board of Agriculture was so concerned with the State's image that he would permit nothing derogatory to be printed about the drouth in any government publication. The story of the developing drouth in the Palliser Triangle went unreported because it simply was not the sort of phenomenon which could be reported. It was not a spectacular natural disaster, like a volcanic eruption, a tornado, a hurricane, or an earthquake. It was a "nothing" story for nothing changed from day to day. The rains never came, the seed did not germinate, the grain did not grow, there was no grain to harvest. When something unusual happened in the farm communities a report would likely be carried in the *Leader Post, Lethbridge Herald, Winnipeg Free Press* or *Tribune*. But only when the drouth was prolonged enough to affect the prices on the Winnipeg and Chicago Grain Exchanges would it be carried with any prominence. At other times the stories of wind storms that blew the roof off the poolroom at Forget, of the army of worms blackening the sidewalks in Killam, of wind driving the dust to a depth of three feet into the straw stack at Shaunavon—these were the trivia of journalism that found publication space deep inside the newspapers. Or they made two-sentence items to fill out the tail end of national news broadcasts on the radio.

Nor was the slowly developing disaster something that lent itself to pictures. None of the newspapers in Saskatchewan or Alberta boasted of staff photographers. Most pictures Canadian newspapers published were supplied in mat form by feature syndicates which went in heavily for Hollywood movie stars and foreign crises in Europe and Asia. Even had there been a lively interest, what was happening seldom lent itself to photography. Nothing would have been more difficult to capture on film than a dust storm, grasshopper infestation or rusted wheat field.

This unawareness was by no means confined only to the far away places. Few Manitobans or Albertans knew much about conditions in central Saskatchewan. The severe drouth was concentrated within a triangle that had Saskatoon as its apex, the international boundary as its base and the Manitoba and Alberta boundaries as the corners. In 1927, this area had produced $90,000,000 worth of wheat. In 1936 it produced $3,000,000. Not only had the wheat crop failed in 1929 and 1930, the fodder crops had also failed so that thousands of tons of feed for livestock had to be shipped in. In addition to the farm distress there were more than 100 villages within this 100,000 square miles that were unable to care for their people.

Within the impoverished area the farmers in the late 1920s had made all the mistakes the people in the cities had made. They had paid off the debts they had accumulated prior to 1922. Then they had added to their holdings, and with easy credit being forced on them they had begun the big switch from horses to tractors, trucks and combines. During that decade most of the 25,000 tractors, 6,000 combines, 10,000 trucks and 50,000 cars that were sold went into this area. When the crops failed and grain prices collapsed they were faced with the prospect of paying debts they had assumed when wheat was $1.25 a bushel with income from 50-cent wheat, and they had no wheat to sell. The Canadian Pacific Railway Company, seemingly the only group aware of what was happening, cancelled all interest on farm loans for 1931.

The unawareness of Canadians generally was understandable too because everybody else had their own problems to worry about. In every city the relief rolls mounted steadily, massive layoffs in industrial plants were followed by wholesale wage cuts. Crisis piled on crisis and by the summer of 1931 even bank presidents had stopped issuing re-assuring statements about the return of prosperity.

If the world in which they lived gnawed away on men's faith in human nature, the response of Canadians everywhere to the Red Cross appeal was enough to restore it. Throughout the rest of the country, and particularly in Ontario, the people made the cause of the impoverished in Saskatchewan their own. Churches became the collection centres. Hundreds upon hundreds of tons of clothing were rounded up, washed, pressed and packed. In all 247 carloads of food and clothing were donated, of which the United Church alone supplied 135 cars.

The response to the Red Cross appeal had one important side effect—it did more to remove West-East antagonism than anything that happened before or since. More than 30 years later, when disaster struck the farmers of the Ottawa valley, western farmers reminded themselves publicly of their gratitude for the 1931 donations and tried to repay their debts. Nor was the campaign of 1931 to be a one-shot affair. More fortunate farmers in Ontario began to trace long-forgotten relatives and send relief parcels to them. They continued sending them periodically for the rest of the decade. Interest in relief projects to help the West never quite subsided among the fruit growers and fishermen on the east and the west coast. Whenever a surplus developed in any crop, the first thought was to donate it to the Red Cross and send it to Saskatchewan. Sometimes these generous gestures caused widespread embarrassment to the recipients, as when a carload of salted cod was distributed. Few there were in the whole Palliser Triangle who had ever tasted salted cod, or knew how to cook it. The last idea to occur to any cook was to de-salt the fish, so most of it was wasted. When conversation lagged at dances or church socials one question would start it up again. The question was "What on earth did you ever do with that fish?"

The events that took place on May 12, 1934, occurred far from the Canadian trouble centre. On that day the Associated Press reported huge clouds from the American midwestern dust bowl being sighted at a height of 10,000 feet over the Atlantic Ocean. Statisticians began calculating the volume of topsoil that had been removed in this storm alone. When they reached 300,000,000 tons, the exercise became pointless. It was probably the worst black blizzard in recorded history. It swept from the Rocky Mountain states to New York and Washington, seeped in and around the windows of both cities and permeated the minds of the members of the United States Congress. When, to the dust they could see and feel and choke on, were added stories of grasshopper plagues destroying millions of acres of growing crop in a matter of hours, panic gripped the country. And some of it rubbed off on Ottawa. The Canadian Press reported to Eastern Canada that the dust storms were blowing across Western Canada from the Rockies to the Great Lakes and the West was faced with the greatest grasshopper invasion in history. The next day Ottawa announced that $500,000 was being appropriated to set up 1,000 mixing stations in 200 municipalities to mix 10,000 tons of poison bait to combat the insects.

The Americans, long before the week of the black blizzards that May, had become far better aware of wind erosion than Canadians. In addition to grasshoppers, great heat waves periodically swept the country to compound the problem of soil drifting. The exodus of the people from Oklahoma, Kansas and Nebraska to California, created great social upheavals and nationwide publicity. Some aspect or other of the agricultural crisis was seldom off the American front pages or out of their radio newscasts. But the black blizzard was something else again.

It recalled to Americans that the area beyond the Mississippi had been known to travellers for 200 years as the Great American Desert. Palliser so referred to it in his diaries, and so had many other writers. The storm reminded them too of the flight from the western prairies that followed the severe and prolonged drouth after 1886. Before that the western limit of settlement had been pushed through the Dakotas and Nebraska to Colorado and the Rockies. By the turn of the century, the western border for dry-land farmers was thrown back 350 miles to a line down the centre of the Dakotas, Nebraska and Kansas. When the normal rainfall returned, resettlement was resumed but it proceeded much more slowly. The summerfallow practice spread south from Canada and made dry-land farming more practical in the arid areas of the Great Plains states. But, as in Canada, summer-fallow also burnt the fibre out of the soil and made the top soil vulnerable to the wind.

During the summer of 1934, Americans stopped talking about the "return of more normal rainfall" and became genuinely alarmed at the threat to the fertile soil of Iowa, Illinois, Ohio and Kentucky which was posed by the blowing soil from the west. Their concern was not so much with saving and restoring the West but to contain the spreading desert and save the rest of the country.

The great blizzard of the week of May 12 brought the agricultural emergency to the top of Congress's agenda. The year before, Congress had appropriated $5,000,000 to set up the United States Soil Erosion Service. It rushed through an act establishing the U.S. Conservation Service and quickly appropriated $150,000,000 for buying and moving cattle out of the dust bowl. It passed the Taylor Grazing Act to turn 80,000,000 acres of Government land into grazing districts. It announced that it was mobilizing the Civilian Conservation Corps to launch a massive tree-planting project.

Tree planting as a means of combatting wind erosion has been a recurrent idea for many hundreds of years. The Russians, in 1696, tried to establish an oak forest clear around the Sea of Azov by planting millions of acorns. The Mennonites on the Volga, in 1792, built shelterbelts around their farms. In 1890, when Russian scientists stumbled onto the tough and hardy caragana growing where no other shrub would grow, they adapted it to shelterbelts. The first U.S. Arbor Day was held in Nebraska in 1873 and in Canada in 1886. Tree planting on a large scale was started in Canada in 1901. The project announced in Washington dwarfed anything previously imagined, let alone anything previously attempted.

The United States Government proposed to plant a wind-break 100 miles wide and 1,000 miles long between the

Canadian border and the hills of Oklahoma. Trees would be planted in rows 100 feet apart, billions of them over millions of acres. Not only was the project imagined, it was started and carried on for eight years, during the course of which 200,000,000 trees were planted over 228,000 acres. To the windward of the area selected for tree planting, armies of employees from the Reclamation Bureau, the Federal Emergency Relief Administration, and the Department of Agriculture, among others, were sent out in 1934 to work with the states and the farmers in taking emergency measures to stop soil blowing.

Thus the great May blizzard had this important result—in the United States it evoked national recognition of the soil erosion as a national emergency about which something could be done and about which something must be done. This recognition, however, spread slowly in Canada. The western Members of Parliament from the farm belt tended to regard the siege of drouth as the sort of act of God to which prairie farmers were accustomed. There had been drouth before. It had been followed by good years. The drouth would end and the good years would return.

"From my own experience going back 53 years—I doubt if there is anything we can do—until the good rainfall comes back—" et cetera, ad infinitum.

But there was much that could be done. The files of the Experimental Farms at Lethbridge and Swift Current were full of the results of studies of the arid prairies over 15 years. Dr. L.E. Kirk had long ago developed a superb new strain of drouth-tolerant crested wheat grass. Gordon Taggart, Asael Palmer and L.B. Thomson knew what could be done and what had to be done and were impatiently waiting orders to mount the attack. In Ottawa, developments in Washington stirred the head of the Experimental Farms System, Dr. E.S. Archibald, and his staff to ponder the nature and the form of an organization which could do for Canada what half a dozen separate agencies were trying to do for the United States.

But the time for action was not yet. It was, however,

brought closer by the publication on September 14, 1934, of the first of a series of reports on the drouth conditions in Saskatchewan. The reports were written by D.B. McRae, the editor of the *Regina Leader-Post* and R.M. Scott, assistant agricultural editor of the *Winnipeg Free Press.* Both newspapers, with the *Star-Phoenix* of Saskatoon, were owned by the Sifton family. Victor Sifton, who was in charge of the publications, was then living in Regina and had first-hand knowledge of the dust bowl. The McRae-Scott articles were published in the three Sifton newspapers and were widely extracted in Eastern Canada in the weeks and months that followed.

McRae and Scott zig-zagged back and forth across the whole of southern Saskatchewan, covering over 2,000 miles in two weeks, talking to farmers and townspeople, and writing as they went. It was the first, and probably the last, on-the-spot survey of conditions on the farms reported in detail over so wide an area.

That year there were fair crops only along the main line of the CPR between Winnipeg and Calgary. But even the good crops were interspersed with areas of complete failure. McRae and Scott stopped for their first survey in the Mortlach-Chaplin area where there had been no crops since 1928 and the farmers had harvested every scrap of Russian thistle they could find for winter feed for their horses and cattle. In one of the municipalities, 95 percent of the farmers were on relief, in another the secretary-treasurer put the figure at 98 percent, in another 890 out of 895 people.

The next day, in the Shaunavon area, they found things somewhat better. A single good rain in June had given the district a crop of sorts. Some fields would go as much as 15 bushels to the acre on summerfallow, though stubble and feed crops had failed. But with low prices, and heavy arrears of debts and taxes, the farmers would have little left for themselves. South of Shaunavon at Loomis, Frontier and Climax there were miles and miles of complete crop failure. Even the gardens had failed.

The next day they criss-crossed three municipalities along

the western side of the dust bowl around Kincaid, Cadillac and Gravelbourg. They collected the opinions of the settlers that two whole townships out of the 30 that made up the three municipalities would have to be permanently abandoned. They were shattered by the experience of one of the best farmers in the area whose land was well above average. He had managed to thresh 400 bushels of wheat from 150 acres. After paying for harvesting and putting aside enough seed for the following year, he would have about $50 on which to keep his family. In the whole section, which had sent 1,500,000 bushels of wheat to market in 1928, there would be less than 60,000 bushels for sale.

In the Gravelbourg, Mossbank, Assiniboia, LaFleche enclave they found many places where soil drifting and grasshoppers were rated ahead of the drouth for crop destruction. The schools were open but few of the teachers were being paid. The highest level of teachers' salaries was at Mazenod, where they were getting $30 a month. The municipalities had voted to guarantee payment of the bills of the local doctors to encourage them to stay. But as the municipalities were collecting little in the way of taxes and were themselves in default on their debentures the inducement had a hollow sound.

In farm houses, lard pails had replaced kettles that had worn out; clothing had patches on patches; little girls went to school in faded and threadbare overalls that their brothers had outgrown; cardboard replaced glass in the windows. Farm machinery was badly worn and had been patched and wired together because there had been no money for parts or repairs for five years. Harness, too, was wearing out and the horses had gone without grain for so long they were no longer capable of doing a hard day's work.

Despite five years of privation and a sadly declining standard of living, McRae and Scott nevertheless discovered there was faith in the country everywhere. From one side of the province to the other they found the people going about the business of being farmers almost as if no disaster had overtaken them. They had worked their summerfallow for "next year," put up their feed for the winter, hauled in their relief fuel and kept one eye always on the sky for the appearance of the return of the good fall rains. The good crops of 1928 were still remembered and even in the worst of the drouth districts there was a fierce confidence that prosperity would return when the rains came back.

This conviction was one of the things that troubled McRae and Scott. If the governments ever got to a point where they decided to move the people out instead of keeping them on relief, it would be a tough job for anyone to say who should go and who should stay.

At the end of their journey neither McRae nor Scott could offer much in the way of a solution. Their investigation cast serious doubt on many of the suggestions that were being offered from the sidelines. Damming creeks and coulees to provide irrigation water for cereal crops appealed to nobody they had met, though they thought small stock-watering dams, and dams which could flood natural hay meadows, might be worthwhile. Both rejected the charge, as did the farmers themselves, that soil mining was the root cause of the trouble. The land would still produce good crops with adequate moisture. That was demonstrated every year where timely summer showers had fallen. Diversified farming was all right where it was proven practical and economical. But in the drouth area livestock were often a liability, and a serious liability, for feed had to be imported for them. Strip farming, which was being tried around Shaunavon, might be further experimented with, but it would need substantial government support. Tree growing was discarded as impractical over the large areas that had been suggested. Certainly something would have to be done about farm debt, which would have been intolerably burdensome, if anyone had been worrying about it. McRae and Scott put it this way:

> It was near the U.S. border that we heard statements of the morale of the people breaking. Some have adopted the 'what's the use?' attitude. Some young people

have grown tired of waiting until times are better and have married. A depression generation of babies is appearing.

Nowhere, however, did persons talked with, attack anybody in particular. They say they do not see how debts can ever be paid at present levels, but it is obvious that many have quit worrying about the future of debt. The necessity of the present has its foot too firmly planted on their necks for them to worry much about what will happen if they can get that foot even partially removed.

McRae and Scott saw much land that should have been permanently taken out of cultivation. A succession of farmers failing on the same farm over a period of 10 years should dictate that such land be returned to the Crown. What to do about it and with it was the concern of scores of municipalities. Poor land was the biggest problem the Government would ultimately have to solve, they believed. But they had no solution.

The McRae-Scott articles were collected into pamphlet form and 10,000 copies were distributed. They had taken the reporting of the agricultural depression out of the episodic stage in which it had languished for five years. They fixed public attention on the magnitude of the problem just as the black blizzard had attracted public attention in the United States. They, moreover, brought attention to focus sharply on a previously unnoticed dark patch—the drouth in Manitoba. Five municipalities were already within the total crop failure area, seven or eight others were marginal and concern was felt elsewhere as well. In western Manitoba much of the land was covered with thin stands of weeds. The farmers said the land was too dry to cultivate for if the weeds were cut the soil would blow.

It was in Manitoba where the exodus of farmers from the drouth area was most noticeable because Manitoba had been longest settled. The windows of fine brick homes on farm after farm were boarded up and the farmyards were empty. Where had all the people gone? No one seemed to know. Some had left the country, some had gone north. Some had driven into Brandon and Winnipeg to go on relief. Every municipality by this time was encouraging its relief recipients to move out, and taking drastic action to prevent relief recipients from outside municipalities from moving in. The authorities in Winnipeg suspected, by the trek of destitute farmers into the city, that rural municipalities were subsidizing some of the migration. They agitated for the extension to two years the period of self-sustaining residence required for relief eligibility. These facts, however, are from other sources.

Concurrently with the McRae-Scott articles, many other discussions were taking place. Premier Bracken of Manitoba came out a month later with a four-point program with which to lay the foundation for a campaign to solve the crisis. Prior to his entry into politics, Mr. Bracken was head of the Manitoba Agricultural College and was an authority on dry-land farming. He proposed:

> —That the provinces provide without charge all the technical people required for a major emergency program;
> —The Dominion establish a co-ordinating body to correlate all the efforts being made by individual farmers, government departments, universities, etc., over many thousands of square miles;
> —The Dominion provide the funds needed to finance a large scale but well balanced program over the 10 year period;
> —The support and co-operation of the railways, banks, municipalities and individuals be sought in connection with the working out of the program.

J.G. Taggart, who had been in charge of the Swift Current Experimental Farm from its inception in 1921 until he quit the service to enter politics in Saskatchewan, became Minister of

Agriculture after the 1934 election. He proposed that a special economic and soil survey be undertaken at once by technical experts from the universities. Each person would be assigned eight municipalities. After he had gathered all available crop and weather data he would talk to the municipal officials, farmers and ranchers and make recommendations for remedial action. Taggart's purpose was to do no less than reorganize the whole of the agricultural economy within the Palliser Triangle on a scientific basis.

Taggart, however, had no need for any further scientific investigations to provide him with the answers to the problems of dry-land farming. Most of the answers were in the files of the Swift Current Experimental Farm or, for their own special aspects of the problem, in the files at Lethbridge, Scott and Brandon. At the time Taggart was leaving Swift Current for politics, Asael Palmer at Lethbridge was gathering all the relevant data together for the Barnes-Palmer-Chepil manual, "Soil Drifting Control in the Prairie Provinces." In it was the best judgment of the Experimental Farms system, based largely on the imaginative and painstaking research at Swift Current and Lethbridge. There were 5,000 copies of this 40-page pamphlet in print when Hon. Robert Weir on April 11, 1935, moved final reading of his bill to establish the Prairie Farm Rehabilitation Authority.

The problem was no longer how to control soil drifting on the prairies. It was how to find a way through a jungle of legal complexities so that the task could be undertaken. As in the United States, only the Federal Government had the financial resources necessary to mount a large-scale, long-range program. Agriculture, however, was both a provincial and federal responsibility and the division between the two was not clear. The titles to the lands which were blowing were in an unholy mess. Some were Crown lands, some were owned by the Canadian Pacific Railway, the Hudson's Bay Company and a number of large mortgage companies. Most of the farmers were so far in arrears in their municipal taxes that they had no real equity left in their farms. The municipalities which could have taken the farms for taxes were as stricken with "next-year fever" as the farmers. They held off in the hope that a good crop could be harvested so that tax arrears might be collected. The mortgage companies by this time no longer pressed their rights to foreclose, rights that had been severely restricted by debt-adjustment legislation anyway. Besides, as there was no market for farm land at any price, they too encouraged the farmers to stay on in hope for the return of the good years. Yet in spite of the leniency of their creditors, farmers by the uncounted thousands picked up their belongings and moved away. The details of this mass migration will be filled in later. Here it is sufficient to say it was the desertions of the settlers which caused the biggest headache of all.

Very often it was those on the worst land, the rough light soil most subject to wind erosion, who were driven off the land. They went. The erosion problem remained, but it was nobody's responsibility. The soil just blew and blew and destroyed the crops growing on the better land. In Alberta, the Government thought it could solve everything by passing a law. It made it an offense punishable by a heavy fine for a farmer to allow soil from his farm to blow onto his neighbor's farm. No charges were ever laid.

The complexity of the problem can be illustrated by the case of Canada Land and Irrigation Company at Vauxhall, Alberta. This company had acquired some 400,000 acres of land in the Alberta Palliser segment at the turn of the century. It had installed huge irrigation works and placed between 300 and 400 settlers on irrigated farms. It also supplied water to scores of ranchers in the district. The operation was never a success for the company. With the collapse of grain prices the farmers who stayed on the land could no longer meet their mortgage payments, interest or water charges. After the company had sunk $15,000,000 in the project it went into receivership.

It was broke. Of that there was no doubt. But could it be permitted to cease to operate and leave 300 farmers stranded without water? The company had no money left and no credit. The Province of Alberta was just as badly off. If the irrigation ditches and other works were not maintained the system would fall apart. Then what would become of the people? They would have to abandon their homes and be settled elsewhere. So the Federal Government, which had sold the land to the company in the beginning, came into the picture and advanced the $100,000 a year required to keep the irrigation system operating.

The practical problems which had to be worked out undoubtedly delayed the start of any wide-front offensive against the drouth and blowing soil. There was a psychological problem as well. In the eyes of eastern politicians Saskatchewan was becoming an albatross around the necks of the Canadian economy and the Federal Government. Or, to switch metaphors, it was the dog with the bad name. It seemed to be forever camped at the national treasury begging for help to meet some new crisis. When taxpayers and bank presidents thought of the burden of relief expenditures they thought of Saskatchewan. (The fact was, as Mr. Taggart was able later to demonstrate, that more federal money was spent in the city of Montreal for relief than in Saskatchewan.) So the province had no reservoir of goodwill to draw on in the search for a solution to its problems.

Finally, widespread opposition was certain to arise to any proposal that would involve the Federal Government directly in anything. The business community throughout the depression had one fixed idea which was sounded with almost psychopathic ferocity—cut government expenditures and ease the intolerable tax burden! Premier Bracken of Manitoba sought to achieve this end by suggesting that the three prairie governments be amalgamated. Nothing happened to that proposal, but the Bracken and Taggart suggestions were incorporated in the setting up of the PFRA.

In face of the magnitude of the task that confronted it, the objectives of the PFRA seemed modest enough to appease the opposition but large enough to satisfy the clamor from the

West that something be done. A five-year plan was outlined under which Ottawa would provide $1,000,000 a year for some large erosion-control demonstration projects, the subsidized construction of small water-storage reservoirs on individual farms, and investigation of feasibility of larger dams and engineering projects. The entire program would be under the direction of a committee composed of Federal Government experts, representatives of the three Prairie Provinces, the railways, the banks and the mortgage companies, and farmers and ranchers selected for their special knowledge in their particular fields.

Despite the high hopes of 1935, it would take three more years, and two more disasters, before the PFRA itself would become an effective instrument to contain the desert in Western Canada.

L.B. Thomson said:

The engineers all tell me there is absolutely no scientific basis for water witching, or as some say–water divining. They'll tell you that you'll get as many wells by throwing a stone over your shoulder and drilling where it lands as by having some witcher select a spot with a willow stick or a bent wire or a crow bar. Well, they know more about water reservoirs and the behavior of water than anybody, so a man would be a fool not to pay attention to them, everything else being equal. But out here everything else is seldom equal, and reliable water supplies are awfully hard to find. If you were a dry-land farmer and you only had money enough to drill one well to 100 feet, would you have the courage to drill it where a witcher said there was no water, or not to drill it where he said you'd get water? I doubt that I would, when all my own chips were down.

CHAPTER THREE

Grasshoppers, Rust and Sawflies

A nature worshipper, contemplating the natural history of the Palliser Triangle in the 1930s, would have been able to advance compelling arguments on behalf of this proposition: Nature had anticipated the campaign which the PFRA would launch to beat back the desert and had committed its reserves and secret weapons long before the PFRA counterattack was even thought about.

Certainly the task of arresting the blowing soil and the expanding desert was difficult enough without complications. The complications were endless. Native insects were reinforced by clouds of invaders that blew in from the United States. Minor blights suddenly became totally destructive to crops over vast areas. The trash cover and stubble strips left to protect the surface of the soil from the winds became incubation beds for new insect threats to whatever could be made to grow. Russian thistle growing on abandoned farms became the host plant for the Say's grain bug that attacked the nearby stands of wheat and barley. A bacterial wilt blew into southern Alberta and destroyed the potato crop. Types of sawflies, caterpillars and cutworms never before seen in Canada were borne by the wind into Alberta and Saskatchewan and multiplied prodigiously. The ubiquitous gophers moved into the abandoned fields by the thousands, and out of the abandoned fields into whatever crops were growing by the tens of thousands. About the only pests that did not seem to thrive in the drouth years were the field mice and the pocket gophers or moles.

By far the worst pests were the grasshoppers that came on the winds from Montana and North Dakota in numbers beyond all calculation, even beyond the exaggerative genius of the yarn spinners of the prairies. Single flights would descend out of nowhere, devour everything in sight and move on. They ate the handles off pitchforks, armpits out of shirts on farmers' backs, clothes off the lines. A single flight was once trapped by a cold wind over Lake Winnipeg, fell into the water and when blown toward land covered the shoreline for 20 miles to a depth of several feet.

The plague of grasshoppers began with the depression and did not end until well into the war years. An Alberta statistician once estimated that over the decade of the 1930s, the total area cumulatively infested with grasshoppers would have exceeded 290,000 square miles—16 times the total crop area of the province. In the first year of the outbreak in Alberta, the infestation covered 1,600 square miles. By 1939 the infested area exceeded 60,000 square miles. In Saskatchewan the area grew from a mildly infested 1,600 square miles in 1931 to over 100,000 square miles.

The great drouth made the grasshopper plagues far worse than they otherwise would have been and the grasshopper plagues helped to hasten the spread of the drouth-made desert. The abandoned land became the incubation areas for the insects which were carried by the winds onto the farms on which crops were still being grown. As the extent of abandonment increased, so did the size of the incubation beds. The irony of the grasshopper plague was surely this: Had it not been for the wind-blown influx from North Dakota and Montana, and the spreading incubation areas of the dust bowl, Canadian entomologists would have been able to bring the outbreak under control before it could do serious damage. The fact was they were able to contain it very well in Manitoba, with an assist, it is true, of the wet year of 1935.

The grasshoppers' nemesis, and the man who worked out

the method of controlling infestation, was Norman Criddle, one of the few authentic geniuses the West produced. Mr. Criddle had emigrated to Canada from England as a small boy with his family in the early days of Manitoba. The elder Criddle settled on a ranch 25 miles southeast of Brandon and Norman Criddle grew up there. Whether it was from the famous grasshopper plague of 1885, or a natural bent, young Criddle developed an insatiable curiosity about all growing things and particularly about insects. Grasshoppers held a special interest for him and it was from observation on his father's ranch that he developed the first poison bait with which to combat them.

Criddle noticed, when he cleaned out the stables in the early morning, that the grasshoppers swarmed onto the fresh horse manure. They would stay for a while and fly off for the rest of the day. When the hoppers began an assault on the Criddle family garden, Norman Criddle began his poison bait experiments. He mixed Paris Green with the manure and had a puzzle immediately on his hands. When the mixture was made with the fresh manure in the early morning, it killed the grasshoppers instantly. But later in the day the insects refused to be attracted at all. Criddle tried adding things to it. Salt was one ingredient that was used, on the principle no doubt that most animals can be attracted to food with salt. In the end he found the answer: It was a moisture need of some sort that brought the insects to the manure. When it dried and cooled it was no longer an effective lure. These and scores of other experiments were later to enshrine Criddle's name permanently on the world's honor roll of entomological discoverers. The Paris Green and manure mixture became known the world over as the Criddle mixture and for many years it was the standard poison wherever grasshoppers were a problem.

The Criddle mixture had one drawback. It worked perfectly to protect relatively small areas from grasshoppers. But the farmers, even in the days of horse power, seldom had sufficient manure to bait the large areas required in a heavy infestation. Once Criddle had made his discovery, however, others took up the search for the substitute moisture carriers and, like Criddle himself, tried both bran and sawdust with success.

In addition to his interest in insects, Criddle developed a professional competence as an artist with water colors. His naturalist bent gained him employment with the Dominion Department of Agriculture and in 1913 he contributed 27 paintings of grasses for the standard reference book—*Fodder and Pasture Plants.* Eventually he was appointed Dominion Entomologist for Manitoba and for 30 years was engaged in field work in Manitoba in the summer and in research in Ottawa in the winter. In 1919 he published one of the world's first papers on grasshopper control which was still being quoted by the *Encyclopedia Americana* 40 years later. The Russian Government once paid him the ultimate in compliments by sending a delegation to Brandon to obtain his advice about their own grasshopper problems.

In the words of R.H. Painter, who shared an office with Criddle in Ottawa and was his assistant in Manitoba, Criddle knew everything there was to be learned about the three species of grasshoppers that were common on the prairies. He was not content only to study them in their Manitoba habitat. He took quantities of eggs back with him every fall to Ottawa so he could hatch them and study them during the winter. So expert was he in spotting the nests where the hoppers had laid their eggs that he could almost do an egg-count from behind the wheel of his car. It was Norman Criddle who developed and perfected the widely used techniques for counting eggs and predicting infestations. In the autumn of 1931 his field work indicated that Manitoba in 1932 was threatened with the worst hopper infestation in 15 years.

In the spring of 1932, he laid plans for a province-wide organized campaign to combat the menace and took Dick Painter back to Brandon with him from Ottawa to help him run the campaign. He talked the Manitoba Government into establishing poison bait mixing stations at 50 towns in southern Manitoba. Painter was given the job of instructing the mixing station employees on how to mix the poison, and advising the farmers how to spread it. Using the Criddle system, entomologists in Saskatchewan and Alberta also swung into action and that summer the three provinces spread between 25,000,000 and 30,000,000 pounds of poison along the edges of 2,000,000 acres of hopper-infested land. It was the first of what would be annual anti-grasshopper mobilizations. The Provincial Governments, working through the municipalities, got the farmers organized as they had never been before.

"We had three very bad areas in Manitoba," Dick Painter said, "at Arnaud in the east, south around Cartwright and around Melita in the west. The farmers co-operated to the hilt, though you could see they were pretty dubious about whether the bait would work or not. Mind you, it was pretty hard to convince them that they had to be out spreading poison at dawn if they wanted to get an effective kill."

P. J. Janzen, who was in charge of a large area in southwest Saskatchewan, also found the farmers co-operative but doubtful.

"But we accidentally poisoned a few head of livestock here and there, and when the word of that spread it sure convinced the farmers that poison bait which would kill cattle would certainly kill grasshoppers," he said. By then, of course, the effective poison had been changed from Paris Green to powdered white arsenic and then to liquid sodium arsenite. The latter was such a threat to livestock and human life, however, that a search was begun for a milder poison and eventually the standard sodium siloco fluoride was chosen as the safest and most effective.

In Manitoba the control programs set up by Criddle kept the grasshoppers pretty well concentrated in the three badly infested areas. In Saskatchewan the first severe outbreak was along the south bank of the South Saskatchewan and in the area south of Regina. Gradually the grasshopper belt widened until it took in the entire centre section of the province between Saskatoon and the border. This was the most seriously infested section most of the time. Periodically the insects broke out of this general area to seriously infest the rest of the Palliser Triangle. In Alberta the most severe impact of the insects was along the Lethbridge-Drumheller axis spreading out gradually to the eastern border until the whole of the province south of Red Deer was more or less seriously affected.

Norman Criddle was an entomologist, not an engineer, so he never got around to inventing an easy way of spreading his poison bait. The farmers, perforce, had to do it the hard way until they developed techniques of their own. At first they carried it in pails and scattered it with a spoon. This tended to land it in gobs rather than in small grains. Manitoba farmers devised chunk-breaking dispensers by driving shingle nails around the edge of wooden spoons. This increased both the speed and efficiency with which the job could be done. But the pails of bait still weighted them down and the mixture burned their hands wherever they were cut or nicked. The epidemic was almost over before the Alberta farmers perfected a method of spreading the bait mechanically. Alberta also invented a system of central dry mixing of the bait, which got away from the laborious work at scores of local mixing stations. The poison was mixed dry with the sawdust and bran and shipped to the farmers in bags. All they had to do was add water and serve.

The big campaign of 1932 developed many problems. The unskilled laborers in the mixing stations tended to skimp on the poison. When the non-potent mixture was spread it in turn tended to jolt confidence in the efficacy of the treatment. There was a belief abroad that the mixture needed additives to attract the hoppers, so farmers laced it with molasses, orange peel, lemon peel and salt, all of which they were continually running out of. The mere transportation of the bran from the flour mills to the mixing stations was no small problem. In a program the size of the one undertaken in 1932, the available supply of bran was quickly exhausted. The substitution of sawdust for bran was undertaken with more hope than confidence but when results showed sawdust was equally effective the entomologists turned to its use wherever it was available.

The egg census taken in the fall of 1932 covered the entire Palliser Triangle and from it the authorities were forewarned that the infestation in 1933 would require a substantial expansion of the network of mixing stations. When the hatching season started the preventive forces were well organized and had the local pests fairly well in hand when the invasion from the U.S. exploded. Nothing could have withstood that onslaught, and nothing did. Millions of acres of crop were ruined in Saskatchewan and Alberta. There was scarcely a farm garden between Brandon and Calgary that was not seriously damaged. Only in Manitoba was there any kind of dividend from the pests. There the insects searched out and devoured all the sow thistle in sight and completely eradicated one of that province's most troublesome weeds. Not only did they feast upon the plant itself, they ate the roots as far down as they could reach. Unhappily, they did the same to carrots, beets and turnips.

When the damage done by the grasshoppers in 1933 was totalled it was revealed that more than $30,000,000 worth of crop had been destroyed and the blow to morale was even greater than to the pocket books of an already near-destitute farm population. Through the spring of 1933, over a wide area of the dust bowl, it appeared as if the long drouth was broken at last, and that there would be a crop to harvest again in the Palliser Triangle. But the grasshopper invasions of late June and July ruined the dream, and in the process spread the alarm that 1934 would inevitably produce much more of the same.

The campaign that was mounted in Saskatchewan and Alberta to combat the grasshoppers in 1934 was easily the greatest thing of its kind ever seen in Canada. It began in the late autumn of 1933 and went on until the harvest was completed in 1934. Alberta, with less area than Saskatchewan to cover, set up 89 mixing stations to serve 4,500,000 acres and organized 15,000 farmers into bait-spreading teams and provided them with 31,637,000 pounds of bait to spread.

In Saskatchewan the entomologists, university specialists and key people from the Dominion Experimental Farms were drafted by the Provincial Government to help make up the Grasshopper Control Committee. The working members of that committee were J.G. Taggart, S.H. Vigor, K.M. King, F.M. MacIsaac, F.H. Auld and Prof. M. Champlin. Their first assignment was to divide up into two-man teams to interview the councils of 223 municipalities, an onerous task in itself. Out of this came no less than 1,097 emergency committees to organize 47,000 farmers who would spread the bait around 22,000,000 acres which would be infested the following year. Of that total, between 6,000,000 and 8,000,000 acres were identified as severely infested. The affected area in Saskatchewan was divided into 24 districts. The Dominion Department of Agriculture turned its Experimental Farms staffs into overnight experts and extension workers on grasshopper control. Field crops men, livestock men, dairymen and soils scientists all dropped what they were doing to become supervisors of the grasshopper campaign. In Alberta, the same things happened at Lethbridge and Lacombe and the province's own technical experts also went out to supervise.

The Saskatchewan committee laid in 90,000,000 pounds of sawdust, 35,000,000 pounds of bran and 180,000 gallons of sodium arsenite. In addition to spreading these materials, the farmers in both provinces plowed protective strips around their crops to channel the hoppers into the baited areas. The directors of the campaign in the fall of 1934 called it a definite success, though a tenth of the crop was destroyed and $20,000,000 in damage done. The test that year was not the destruction but what was saved and a conservative estimate was that within the Palliser Triangle 40 percent of the entire grain crop was saved from destruction by the exertions of the farmers and their expert advisers. Unfortunately, in the heart of the Triangle what they were able to save did not amount to much for the wheat that was harvested that year barely exceeded four bushels to the acre. In the following year the damage was much lighter—from grasshoppers. There was more moisture, the crop got away to a fair start in 1935 and conditions, particularly in Manitoba, were right to spawn the fungus that was the natural enemy of the grasshoppers. However, these conditions were also ideal for wheat stem rust and in the southeast corner of the Triangle the rust epidemic wiped out the entire crop, over 3,000,000 acres, and materially cut the yield and quality over most of Manitoba and Saskatchewan. Marquis wheat, which had done so much to make grain growing possible on the prairies, reached a dead end to its usefulness in the south country that year.

The rains that brought on the rust also provided the environment which brought back mosquitoes with a vengeance to southern Manitoba and parts of Saskatchewan. With the mosquitoes came the first big outbreak of equine encephalomyelitis—sleeping sickness. Like all the other wind-blown epidemics, this was brought in by the mosquitoes from North Dakota. Once established, horse sleeping sickness became an ever-increasing problem for the next few years. Thousands of horses died of it—how many thousands will never be known. The disease also spread to the human population and though there were few fatalities the occurrence spread a lot of panic abroad for there was a widespread belief that infantile paralysis and sleeping sickness were related diseases.

The grasshoppers were a diminishing problem in 1936 and over most of the area in 1937. They had been brought under control to so great an extent in Manitoba that in 1938 Dick Painter was transferred to Lethbridge to take charge of the hopper campaign in eastern Alberta. By 1937 the organizations for combatting grasshoppers had been shaken down into more or less routine operations. The mapping was done automatically and the areas were identified in which the more severe problems were expected. But nothing in the experience of 1937 prepared anybody for the disaster of 1938.

Once again it was the influx from the United States which did the damage, and it came at a time when the farmers of the Palliser Triangle were ill-prepared for any more buffeting from nature. The Saskatchewan crop of 1938 was planted almost entirely from $20,000,000 worth of relief seed which the governments had to provide after the total failure in 1937. As had happened in 1933 and 1935, the crop got away to a good start. But it was 1933 and 1935 all over again, and the worst of both rolled into one. Again the grasshoppers blew in from the south in clouds that obscured the sun. This time the attack was concentrated in Saskatchewan and western Manitoba with control measures working fairly well in Alberta. At the height of the grasshopper invasion in July, rust struck again in epidemic proportions. Then hail storms of unprecedented severity swept across the prairies. On top of everything else, the depredation of wireworms, which had been growing steadily, reached its peak and wiped out more than $8,000,000 worth of grain crops. Grasshoppers, wireworms, sawflies, hail and rust cost the farmers of Saskatchewan alone $50,000,000 worth of wheat production that year. In the Palliser Triangle, the crops were cut in half in less than a month.

It was not only the physical aspects of the struggle against the desert which the insect invasions complicated, though that was complication enough. The grasshoppers were just as deadly in the rows of rye the PFRA was nursing along in an effort to stop the blowing soil as they were in the wheat fields of the farmers whose land was still safe. The infestation of sawflies along the edges of the strip-farmed fields discouraged farmers from adopting stripping to wind-proof their fields. Infestation of stubble fields by wireworms gave the farmers an excuse to burn off their stubble and take a chance on the wind. Each of these constituted a setback to the struggle to contain the desert, and serious setbacks they were. Yet it was to the morale of the farmers of the Palliser Triangle that the multiplying pests did the worst damage. No one kept track of the suicide statistics. No one tried to correlate the rising toll of farm abandonment with grasshopper plagues.

But even in the sterile prose of the government reports there are references to the defeatism of farmers who were doing nothing about grasshoppers because their crops were not worth saving.

The cloud of discouragement hung heaviest over Saskatchewan, for the very simple reason that in season and out, Saskatchewan had it worst on all counts—worst drouth, worst grasshoppers, worst rust, worst cutworms, worst hail. It was in an effort to give the farm population some reason for hope that Saskatchewan organized a massive scheme of agricultural short courses for the winter of 1938. In a dozen centres scattered around the province it arranged to bring as many young farm people as would come to a 10-day course in farm subjects. The province billetted and fed the young farmers, the universities and Experimental Farms supplied the speakers who each spent a day at each centre then moved on to the next. In the process they used every measure of transportation yet devised. They rode in freight train cabooses, in cutters and straw-filled sleighs, in rudimentary snowmobiles with airplane propellers, on railway scooters and once in a while in automobiles. The schools were held wherever a room could be obtained and churches, garages, poolrooms and hotel basements were all pressed into service.

"The astounding thing about these courses was the interest the people took in them," Dick Painter recalled. He was on the circuit for six weeks talking about insects and grasshoppers in particular. "This was the absolute bottom of everything. You couldn't have raised $5 if you'd emptied all their pockets. But they were as interested and alert as any audience a man could have."

The Government of Saskatchewan and the PFRA were both committed to the proposition that the land was worth saving, that it could be saved and it would be saved. The influx of the insects into the Palliser Triangle shifted some of the responsibility for trying to save it off the shoulders of the soils specialists onto the entomologists. It was up to them to find out how to eradicate the new insect menaces which had suddenly found the climate of Western Canada so much to their liking.

"I have never ceased to marvel at the great work the entomologists did for us in those days," Asael Palmer said. "You couldn't find men of more complete dedication and they have never received the credit they deserve." Palmer had better reason than most to know. The Dominion Entomological Laboratory was at the Lethbridge Experimental Farm and Palmer worked in the closest collaboration with H.L. Seamans, the entomologist in charge. It was Seamans, working with Ron Peake of the forage crops division, who devised the method by which the wheat stem sawfly could be controlled at a time when it was threatening to force dry-land farmers to give up strip farming after they had adopted it to prevent soil blowing. What started out to be simply an exercise in low cunning became an experiment in beautification that transformed the face of Western Canada.

Unlike the grasshoppers, which voraciously launched a mass offensive over the whole of a wheat field, the sawfly was both lazy and a nibbler. It never flew any farther than it had to to find a hollow-stemmed plant in which it could lay its eggs. Thus it could always be found around the edges of wheat fields. In strip farming, alternative patches of wheat and summerfallow gave the sawflies many more edges to work along than a solid field would have. The flies deposit their eggs inside the hollow stems of grain and grasses. The larvae hatched from the eggs feed up and down the inside of the stems until the grain is approaching ripeness. Then they move to the bottom of the stems, girdle them from the inside and retire down into the root for the winter. After being girdled the stem falls over, hence the name sawfly.

The adult flies emerge from the ground in late June and go looking for hollow-stemmed plants in which to lay their eggs. If they happen to choose either the stems of brome grass or oats it is the end of the cycle for them, because both those plants are poison to sawflies. So Seamans and Peake perfected a system of planting poisonous trap crops around the edges of the susceptible grain crops. Down the road allowance next to a wheat field they planted brome grass to attract the flies. Brome grass, which needs more moisture than was usually available within the Palliser Triangle, flourished in the roadside ditches where the run-off from the roads collected.

Around the stripped patches the ground for 10 or 15 feet was seeded to oats before the wheat was sewn. Thus the oats were much further advanced in June, when the flies hatched, and they would choose the lethal oat crop in which to lay their eggs. By seeding brome grass along the outside of the field in the roadside ditches and oats on the inside, the menace of the sawflies to strip farming was eventually overcome. Part of the solution had to be the seeding of roadsides to brome grass. Before it could be seeded the roads had to be cleaned up, tidied up and cultivated. Thus the campaign against the sawflies had the secondary effect of providing Alberta with the tidiest and best kept of roadsides.

When L.B. Thomson at Swift Current became privy to what was being done with brome grass in Alberta he took time out from dust fighting to launch a roadside seeding program of his own. This was the first casualty of the economy wave that hit the Experimental Farms after war was declared. Eventually, however, thousands of miles of roadways in Alberta, Saskatchewan and Manitoba were seeded to brome grass and later to alfalfa. From these ditches thousands of tons of hay were being harvested annually long after the sawfly had ceased to give any cause for concern.

How many tons of gophers were harvested within the Triangle during the decade would not be too difficult to estimate, given the weight of one gopher. Both Saskatchewan and Alberta paid bounties of a penny apiece for gopher tails and municipalities in badly infested districts added a penny or two to the bounty. Snaring gophers was a source of candy money for the town children and a popular amusement for the farm children. In each province, bounties were paid on around 700,000 gophers a year, of which two-thirds went to school children. In 1934, for example, the children of the

Indian Head district collected $765.14 for killing 76,514 go-phers. In Instow, Saskatchewan, the local storekeeper, act-ing as municipal agent for the gopher bounty, accepted gopher tails as cash and filed them in a tin can behind the cash register. Other storekeepers kept them in cans under the counter, out of sight of mischievous small boys who might be tempted to snitch a handful and sell them over again to the unwary merchant. Yet despite the ceaseless assault of small boys with traps and snares the gopher population continued to multiply and take a toll of what-ever grain was grown.

In the United States, squirrels are hunted as the basic ingredient of Brunswick stew. The Canadian gopher is a species of squirrel and was used not infrequently for food in Saskatchewan and Alberta. It was this use that no doubt gave rise to the canard that the people of the Palliser Triangle were reduced to eating gophers in order to survive. The gophers were eaten as delicacies, and for no other reason, though those who fancied gophers as a delicacy were in a very decided minority. The people of the prairies are almost pathologically squeamish when it comes to exotic food. The mere mention of food that is eaten with pleasure elsewhere in the world will turn prairie dwellers blue. Oysters, for example. Hundreds of thousands of Western Canadians would blanch before a dozen Malpeques on the half shell. And such titillating items as lamb fries, frog legs, snails, fish heads and chicken livers would send them reeling for the rails. But those who fancy off-pattern foods are not likely to be put off by such squeamishness.

"Why shouldn't gophers be good to eat?" they demanded. "They exist almost exclusively on a diet of grass and grain, and there is no reason why the meat of a grain-fed gopher should not be as good as the meat of a grain-fed steer."

As food, the gophers shared one drawback with the squirrel. It took a lot of them to make a meal, and in the dust bowl the gophers were likely to become scrawnier than the people. Nevertheless a family of small boys with snares might well harvest a pailful of gophers in an afternoon and that would be enough to make a stew or two.

After being skinned, cleaned and dressed, gophers were cooked in just about every way a rabbit could be cooked. When simply popped into a pot and boiled, they excited few appetites. This undoubtedly led to experiments with gopher stew. If gopher quarters were mixed in with vegetables and chicken, there were those who insisted that no one could tell chicken and gopher apart. Around Swanson, Saskatchewan, there were farm wives who turned gopher cookery into a fine art. In addition to stewing, the gophers were canned in the same way they canned chicken. One farm family called on memories of eating squirrel pie in the United States and came up with gopher pie. The meat was simply placed in a pan, covered with a crust and baked in the oven. Another favorite dish was smoked gopher which was regarded by some as the ultimate delicacy of the Dirty Thirties. The meat was hung on sticks in the bright sun with a fire going constantly to smoke the gophers and keep off the flies.

Pickling gophers was common throughout southern Saskatchewan. A school teacher, visiting a farm home east of Canuck, arrived just as the farm wife was completing the pickling of a 10-gallon crock of gophers. Preserved in brine, they helped to stretch the winter's food supplies. There are not too many reports of fried gophers, though a farm housekeeper in the Stettler area said that the children developed a strong liking for gophers that were breaded and fried like chicken. Others did the cooking in two steps. The meat was first parboiled and then breaded and fried.

As a food, however, the gophers never repaid the farmers for the damage they did to their crops. That damage was estimated at almost $4,000,000 for the province of Saskatchewan alone in 1938. No estimates were ever made of the toll that the minor menaces took of the grain crops. Through the decade there were reports of army caterpillars in eastern Alberta, and damage from crickets in Manitoba. Colorado potato beetles were a universal nuisance and there were outbreaks of aphids, psyllids, leafrollers and spider mites from time to time. Throughout the decade the entomologists seldom had time to stop to catch their breath before some new insect was chewing on their plants.

One of the most important programs undertaken by the entomologists developed as a sort of carom off Dick Painter's field work in Alberta in the grasshopper campaign. Before going to Alberta, Painter's interest in livestock was less than casual. In Alberta, however, his grasshopper territory took in most of the ranching country. He soon discovered that the ranchers had a serious insect problem about which nobody was doing anything. The insect was the warble fly. It jabbed its needle-sharp ovipositor through the hide of the cattle to deposit its eggs into the flesh of the animal. The eggs hatched into large grubs in a gelatinous mass under the hide along the back of the animal and often became a suppurating mass when the grubs emerged to become flies and complete the cycle. The insects were seldom if ever fatal to livestock, but they ruined the hide, caused lack of thriftiness and downgraded the carcasses when they went to market.

By the time Painter moved to Alberta in 1938 the infestation had become endemic over most of the Palliser Triangle wherever cattle were kept in any quantity. In his circulation among the farmers at short courses and AIA meetings, Painter became quickly aware, from the questions frequently asked, of the warble problem. He boned up on the subject and provided the standard answer—scrub the backs of the animals with derris dust or other insecticide. The advice was useful enough to a farmer with a half-dozen dairy cows but was totally impractical for the ranchers with herds numbering in the hundreds. During the tail end of the dust bowl era—the date is lost to history—Doug Matthews at Scott conducted a far-out experiment. His men were spraying some shelterbelts for insects and a farmer wondered whether the high-powered orchard sprays would direct enough of the insecticide onto his cattle to kill the warble flies. The spray was turned onto the cattle to see what would happen. It did not produce a complete kill, although the effects were quite noticeable. Painter too had been wondering about spraying and borrowed an orchard sprayer from the Lethbridge farm and took it out to Gene Burton's ranch at Claresholm. The cattle were penned, given three separate sprayings and the experiment was completely successful in eradicating the warbles. The orchard sprayer was by no means a perfect instrument and, while the search for a better nozzle went on, Painter was put in charge of a nation-wide warble fly control program which Gordon Taggart sponsored to safeguard the short supply of meat that developed during the middle war years.

All this was in the future, after the menacing desert had been contained, but the campaigns against the insects indicated the closeness of the co-operation and teamwork that existed between the entomologists and the Experimental Farms scientists with the farmers on the land. It was a relationship, moreover, in which the hardship was not all on one side. During the height of the crisis, there was not an entomologist, plant scientist, irrigationist, forage specialist or Experimental Farm director or administrator who had a normal homelife. They were on the road constantly, missing meals or eating wherever food could be found; sleeping in stifling and dusty hotel rooms, in their cars or curled up in the corner of a country elevator toolshed. Where something more than advice was called for, they pitched in with muscle to help convert farm machinery, to adjust a listing machine or seeder, help work a cat tractor through a sand dune or demonstrate how to mix and scatter grasshopper bait. Nor was the advice of any of the scientists sought after more frequently than that of the entomologists. Not being able to supply answers for the new problems being created by cutworms, wireworms and Say's grain bug was not too embarrassing to the scientists. They knew that in time the answers would all be found. What was most trying was the spread of the grasshoppers, year after year, when they had the means to control them. But until they could also control the wind, and get the millions of acres of abandoned land back into grass and out of the business of incubating grasshoppers, the insect was something that had to be endured. And it had to be endured by the farmers, ranchers and city gardeners as well as by the frustrated bugmen.

J.A. Sutter said:

Feed was so scarce in southwestern Saskatchewan in 1936 that many farmers had to turn their horses loose to fend for themselves. I had 18 horses and I kept a chore team at home and sent 16 over into the Loomis district. The horses got away from the herder, became mixed in with the big herds and when I went to collect my horses in 1937, only four of them could be located.

In those years we learned to waste nothing. In 1937 not a blade of grass sprouted but the Russian thistle grew so we cut the thistle green, mixed it in with relief hay and kept two cows milking all winter. Butter then sold for five cents a pound but we had to pay 16 cents a pound for axle grease. So we mixed two-thirds unsalted butter and one-third beef tallow and made some very satisfactory axle grease for ourselves. When things were at their toughest, we gathered buffalo chips in the pastures for stove fuel and in the winter collected the screenings from under the separators and mixed the stinkweed seeds with coal. We got more heat from the stinkweed seeds than from the coal.

The best thing that could be said for those years was that they were great years for baseball. With no work to be done, and nothing to do it with, we played ball twice a week and everybody for miles around turned out.

CHAPTER FOUR

The Dirtiest of the Dirty Thirties

M ore lies have probably been told about the weather of the Dirty Thirties than about any other subject except sex; yet most of the lies could have been true. There was the legend of the children reaching well into school age before they had ever seen rain; of children rushing terror stricken to their mothers when they first felt rain on their heads. Each of these events might have happened somewhere in Palliser's Triangle for the incomparable dirtiness of the weather was the outstanding characteristic in the 1930s. But there were very few areas in which the extreme drouth extended much beyond five years. This is not to suggest that a five-year drouth was not an unmitigated disaster. It was, and there were areas in which a general drouth extended up to seven and eight years, but within even the driest areas there were farmers who almost seemed to attract the summer showers that produced crops of some kind. South of Swift Current, for example, farmers on a small hill frequently got rain when none fell anywhere else in the district.

Perhaps the main factor which created an atmosphere conducive to remembering things that did not happen was the weight of the economic depression. Good times were always associated with good crops. But a good crop during the depression was almost as disastrous as a crop failure. The news of a big crop could arouse farmers' creditors from their lethargy and intensify their efforts to collect long-overdue accounts. That happened, for example, in 1932. The crops were excellent that year over the whole of the western half of the Palliser Triangle, though the drouth intensified in the east. But the returns where there was a good crop were barely enough to pay for the cost of harvesting it.

The crop of 1932 was the one for which the price dropped to 40 cents a bushel. To the creditor, the arithmetic was simple. A farmer with 400 acres of wheat that went 20 bushels to the acre would have 8,000 bushels which, at even 40 cents a bushel, would give him $3,200, a small fortune in 1932. Unhappily for both the farmers and their creditors, there was a sad flaw in this simple arithmetic. The non-farmers never seemed to learn that 40 cents a bushel was for No. 1 Northern, and it was for wheat delivered to Fort William. To most farmers No. 1 Northern was a mythical grade which neither they nor their neighbors ever grew. The bulk of the crop was likely to grade No. 3 Northern or No. 4 Northern which sold for discounts of 5 to 10 cents under No. 1 Northern. In normal times, when these discounts might have meant the difference between $1.30 a bushel and $1.20, the flawed arithmetic would not have been as important. But during the depression grade discounts could cut a farmer's gross income by 25 percent of the quoted price. And this was only the start. The farmers had to pay the freight to Fort William out of the selling price of their wheat. Again in normal times, this might reduce the income from $1.20 a bushel to $1.00. During the depth of the depression it cut the farmer's cash return from 30 cents to 10 or 15 cents per bushel on the farm. Instead of the $3,200 cash income he would have had, the way his creditors did the arithmetic, his cash return would be closer to $320. In those years, moreover, the farmers had to take what they could get for their wheat as quickly as they could get it hauled to the elevators. They were in no condition financially to be able to hold back in hope of getting a higher price later on. Prices did come back in the weather markets of July 1933. By then the wheat grown in 1932 was long gone from the farmers' hands. Having survived three successive crop failures, the returns from the 1932 crop were so shattering to morale that dust bowl farmers tended to remember 1932 as one of the great disaster years. The point is that 1932 was much more financially disastrous than climatically disastrous. As Gordon Taggart has emphasized, at least half the privation of the depression was of financial origin. Had it not been for the collapse of prices for all farm products, many of the farmers in the Palliser Triangle might have been able to take measures of their own to control the black blizzards. There were, indeed, several years when fair crops were grown in the dust bowl. In 1935, for example, when between 50,000,000 and 60,000,000 bushels of wheat were destroyed by rust in the southeast, the whole of the north country reaped a crop that averaged 20 bushels to the acre. West of Outlook, and around Swift Current, there were fields that went 25 bushels to the acre. In the central area from the border to Saskatoon the overall average was between 10 and 15 bushels; not bumper crops but not failures either. Here are some production statistics for Saskatchewan for the depression years:

Year	Acres	Yield	Production	Value of Wheat Sold off Farms
1928	13,791,000	23.3	321,215,000	$218,000,000
1929	14,445,000	11.1	160,565,000	134,932,000
1930	14,714,000	14.0	206,700,000	72,293,000
1931	15,026,000	8.8	132,466,000	44,407,000
1932	15,543,000	13.6	211,551,000	56,889,000
1933	14,743,000	8.7	128,004,000	52,301,000
1934	13,262,000	8.6	114,200,000	57,950,000
1935	13,206,000	10.8	142,198,000	68,400,000
1936	14,596,000	8.0	110,000,000	81,000,000
1937	13,893,000	2.7	37,000,000	16,000,000

Because crop production statistics are gathered from and averaged over a wide area, it is easy to draw distorted conclusions from them. Except for 1937, there is no indication of the dust bowl disaster in such tabulations. The explanation, of course, is that, year after year, good crops were harvested generally in the north above the Yorkton-Saskatoon-Battleford line. A better picture of what the combination of crop failure or short crop and low prices meant to the people in the dust bowl can be drawn from the following table:

Cash Returns per Acre of Wheat in Crop Reporting
Districts of Saskatchewan 1930–37

District	1930	1931	1932	1933	1934	1935	1936	1937
South Eastern	$5.83	$1.29	$3.63	$3.29	$2.01	$1.40	$3.96	$2.31
Regina-Weyburn	4.56	.11	3.32	5.13	2.01	2.95	7.39	nil
South Central	3.25	.61	2.37	1.18	1.28	5.98	2.82	nil
South Western	5.74	1.60	4.96	1.32	1.60	4.20	nil	nil
Central	4.28	2.66	3.53	1.93	3.98	7.38	7.93	nil
West Central	8.65	4.52	5.39	1.23	4.33	5.00	3.34	nil

The Government of Saskatchewan estimated that the minimum return per acre of wheat required to permit a farmer to survive without relief, provided he paid no taxes, was $5.30 per acre. A mere doubling of wheat prices would have made survival possible in some areas in some years. This question, it might be emphasized, is of more than academic importance. The growing opposition in Eastern Canada to the mounting costs of farm relief for the West arose largely from the conviction that western agriculture could not be saved, and that it was not worth saving. Few understood that the fiscal policies of Canada were just as important a cause of distress as the climate. Nevertheless, even written down by 50 percent, the weather in the Palliser Triangle in the Dirty Thirties was frightful.

Conditions somewhat similar to those that prevailed in 1932 developed again in 1933 over much of Saskatchewan. Spring moisture conditions were excellent and the crop got away to a fine start. But in June myriads of grasshoppers blew in on the high-level winds from the United States and destroyed millions of acres of growing grain. Not only did they devour the heads of the grain, they fouled the stems and grass so that it was no good even for pasture. And not only grain. The grasshoppers ate everything in sight. They chewed pitchfork handles into unusability, ate clothing off the lines, chewed through the shirts on the backs of motorists in cars and farmers in the field. The grasshoppers seemed addicted to the residue of human perspiration for they concentrated their chewing where sweaty hands and necks had rested. Or it might have been that it was only moisture which attracted them for they ate everything moist and particularly if it was green. They stripped caragana hedges of leaves in a matter of minutes, devoured gardens at one swoop and left the country completely devoid of vegetation.

Whether a farmer's crop was destroyed by grasshoppers, rust or drouth was, of course, incidental to the fact that it was destroyed. And there were large areas where the rainfall statistics distorted the production picture. On the Regina plains, for example, the farmers grew large crops in 1928 and again in 1929. In order to get rid of the straw and get their land in shape for seeding they burned off the stubble. The years 1930 and 1931 were not particularly dry years but years when hot winds blew strongly across the plains. These winds picked up the sand from the soil and blew it with such force that it cut the growing grain off at the ground. In later years, moreover, soil erosion reached a stage where rain increased wind erosion rather than retarded it. The topsoil acquired the textile of talcum powder which shed the heavy rain and then eroded worse than ever when the sun came out and the winds came back.

Nevertheless, though the weather may not have been as bonedry for as long as survivors remember it was, there is no question about the general climatic conditions of the 1930s. The Dirty Thirties were well named. The drouth conditions that developed on the Great Plains of Canada were directly connected to similar conditions in the United States. The big drouth was almost like a great flood sweeping northward from the Gulf of Mexico. Each year it extended farther north and got worse as the years passed. In Nebraska, for example, it caused a great crop failure in 1931 and then grew until all temperature records were broken in 1934. In the spring of 1934 there was an abundant water supply in the top two feet of soil in Nebraska. By July it was completely depleted down to a depth of six feet. Temperature rose to 111 degrees, humidity dropped in places to as low as 3 percent; and this was the story from the tip of the Palliser Triangle to the Texas border. In the weather statistics of the Great Plains, the years 1931 and 1934 appear consistently among the 5 or 10 driest years on record.

In Canada there were no temperature records established in 1931 or 1934. Within the Triangle it simply got hot and stayed hot. The winds blew strongly and steadily and the crops that germinated at all quickly exhausted the moisture left over from the melting snows. By Dominion Day, 1931, the south country wrote the wheat crops off as complete failures. But if the temperatures of 1931 and 1934 were not spectacular, the winds and storms they blew up certainly were. In 1931 a huge thunderstorm dropped three inches of rain on Outlook in a matter of hours, then swept southward and flooded the basements of Moose Jaw. That July a near-tornado blew the windows out of stores and the roofs off homes in North Battleford. Two days later an even more violent storm struck Regina at midnight, set buildings afire, blew out power stations and tore up the paving blocks across the intersection of Hamilton and Twelfth Streets. Wild hail storms were reported from a dozen places in Alberta and a tornado swept out of North Dakota and destroyed farm buildings and homes along a 25-mile front in southwestern Manitoba.

In 1934, the story was generally the same, with long sieges of hot though not extreme temperatures punctuated by hail and wind storms. The 12th of July was marked in Alberta by one of the worst hail storms ever experienced. It buried the crops under an 8-inch blanket on a 90-mile front between Stettler and Carstairs. Some of the Alberta storms carried deep into Saskatchewan to Biggar and Elrose. Others swept down from the north on winds up to 100 miles an hour, scattering poultry, barn roofs and hail over the countryside from Davidson to Lumsden, or blew up into black blizzards that turned day into night from Acme to Medicine Hat to Swift Current. It was in 1934 that the first serious damage to community life became more apparent. Soil blowing off abandoned land drifted onto good land administered the coup de grace to both gardens and crops. For the first time anyone could remember, the local summer fairs were cancelled all across the south country. People had nothing to exhibit, and there was nothing to spend any money on even if they had any money. It was the year in which the blowing dust came to resemble a refinement in the Chinese water torture. There was no escape from it, least of all inside the farm houses. The farm families ate dust with their food, walked on it, dressed in it and slept in it.

It was not, however, until 1936 that the records for high temperatures were established which still stood 30 years later. Eighteen American states recorded temperatures above 110 degrees in July. It was 121 in North Dakota, 120 in South Dakota, 121 in Kansas and 118 in Nebraska. For the Canadian Prairies, the suffocating heat of the summer of 1936 followed hard on the worst winter ever experienced. Nothing like that winter had ever been known even to the oldest settlers, for it covered the whole of Western Canada. Thermometers dropped to 30 and 40 below zero soon after Christmas and below-zero temperatures were still being recorded in April. The mean temperature of -17 at Edmonton for February was 25 degrees below normal, and an all-time record. Calgary had a record-low mean of -12 for the same month. Winnipeg had the coldest January in 50 years and the coldest February in 60. Not since 1875 had January and February put together such mean temperatures as -13.2 and -14 and never before had such extreme temperatures been recorded as in the first four months of 1936. Coldest of all, and by far, was Saskatchewan. Regina's mean temperature was -19.8 in February and its long siege of desperately cold weather was featured by blizzard after blizzard that choked the country roads and piled drifted snow to window height in the cities. The bitterness of the winter was particularly trying to the people of the south country. Their clothes had worn thin, their stoves and heaters were wearing out, they were short of bedding, and as half the people lived in flimsy, submarginal housing anyway, the mere business of keeping warm occupied most of their waking hours.

But there was one ray of hope that winter, the hope that the abundance of snow would get the crop off to a good start in the spring. The improved moisture conditions in 1935-36 gave farmers reason to believe that the extreme drouth was over. That prospect was dashed by the extreme heat in May and June and July. From Lethbridge to Winnipeg, temperatures rose to the 100 degree mark and stayed there for days on end. Each day seemed hotter than the one before. The hot winds grew stronger and the dust clouds that hung over the whole of the mid-continent plains grew thicker and thicker. By the second week in July the crop was gone. The thermometer touched 110 at Brandon and Morden, 108 at Winnipeg and during the third week of July it went over 100 every day somewhere within the Palliser Triangle. The city newspapers kept a box score on deaths from heat prostration but there was nobody to gather the statistics for the dust bowl.

There was a noticeable change in the drouth pattern of 1936. In the previous years the crop failure areas were concentrated mainly in the southern part of the provinces. There was a slight improvement in the southeast, in 1936, while the west side of the Palliser Triangle from Lethbridge east to the Saskatoon-Regina line and north to Lloydminster and Turtleford became the zone of total disaster. The wind started to blow the soil off the land in May. It blew intermittently in June and then built into huge dust storms in July. It blew the topsoil off the cattle ranges west of Kindersley, upended barns and granaries from McRorie to Zelma and beyond. There were cyclonic winds in Regina and the midway was blown down at the Saskatoon Summer Fair. In Alberta the crop failure area extended as far west as Calgary which had the hottest 30-day heat wave since the turn of the century.

Between the big wind storms the dust blew continually so that the whole of the Palliser Triangle lived in a perpetual haze. But dust was only part of the weather record of 1936.

That was also the year of the insects, the year when the grasshoppers suddenly blew back into southern Manitoba east of Morden to devour all the sow thistle over an area of more than 5,000 acres. It was in 1936 in which the first epidemic of equine sleeping sickness hit the horse population of the West. The grasshoppers never reached epidemic proportions that year though there were many pockets of rather severe damage. Of much greater consequence was the outbreak of army worms which destroyed the farm gardens on a line from Valley Centre to Quill Lake, a distance of 150 miles in Saskatchewan, and into Alberta as far west as Killam. Along the Saskatchewan-Alberta border the army worms had to compete with the pale western cutworms which destroyed the crops that had survived the winds and 100 degree temperature.

The effect of the weather of 1936 was to give governments at all levels a new sense of urgency to attack the problem of the spreading desert. In 1934, the Saskatchewan Wheat Pool recorded 157 reports of serious crop damage from soil drifting in the south country. In 1936 it would not have been difficult to tabulate statistics from three or four times that many localities.

The rains that disappeared in the summer of 1936 failed to return in the fall so that the autumn of 1936 was the driest in almost two decades within the Palliser Triangle. It was followed by another extremely cold winter, a dry spring and the long hot summer to end all long hot summers. Outside the Triangle in Manitoba and Alberta, fair crops were to be made. Even in the arid southwest of Manitoba the best crop in almost a decade was grown in 1937. But inside the Triangle the heat settled in early and stayed late. A violent wind storm that swept clear across Saskatchewan started the dust blowing on May 24th. On June 8th the worst dust storm in 30 years swept through the Shaunavon area and reduced visibility to three feet. The small towns were being emptied as the people began to desert them. Saskatoon reported it had 600 families from outside on its relief rolls and asked the Provincial

Government to accept responsibility for them. By mid-June the PFRA estimated that disaster had engulfed 60,000,000 acres of land, three-quarters of it good land on which people were living. It was also estimated that 500,000 head of cattle faced starvation in the drouth area and the stockmen sent an urgent appeal to the Government for relief feed as the cattle were eating the leaves off the trees. The temperatures then moved high into the 90s and a dust blizzard that swept across western Saskatchewan forced the cancellation of horse races at the Moose Jaw Fair.

June was the hottest ever recorded in Saskatoon and the city gardeners kept their hoses going 24 hours a day to save the vegetation of the city. In Regina there was no water to spare and the grass died in Victoria Park. Lake Johnston south of Moose Jaw went dry and the high winds coated the plains with alkali dust which gave the heavy clouds between Moose Jaw and Regina a ghostly whitish cast. In Regina itself dust covered everything, the sidewalks, the streets, the lawns and gardens, the interiors of the hotels, even the foam on the beer. There were many times that summer when it was impossible to see across the street—any street. Nor was Johnston Lake the only body of water to disappear. Fife Lake, near Rockglen, which once covered a township, went dry. The Lake of the Rivers dried up to reveal hundreds of tons of buffalo bones which the farmers gathered and shipped to fertilizer plants. It was their first good cash crop in seven years.

There was no such dividend for the farmers of the Outlook area from the natural disaster there. A rainless thunderstorm set the prairie ablaze and destroyed more than 10 sections of pasture land before it burned itself out. And there was no comfort for anybody in the week of July 4th. It included the hottest day ever experienced in Canada. On the 5th of July the thermometer touched 113 above in Yellow Grass and Midale, 110 above in Regina and Moose Jaw and in nine other smaller places in the south country. By then the Government had made a frantic appeal to all farmers to cut any wheat that was still alive for winter feed and to turn their cattle into the fields. In Saskatoon, the University of Saskatchewan put every available man to cut Russian thistle for feed for the institution's valuable experimental cattle herd.

Then, abruptly on the 16th of July, the drouth ended in Saskatchewan. The rains came pelting down all over western Saskatchewan, flooding roads, filling ditches and germinating a trillion Russian thistle seeds that had lain dormant in the soil. Within a matter of days, the country was blanketed in the most beautiful shade of green anyone could remember. The cattle were turned into the Russian thistle and the farmers went out to cut it for winter feed.

Winter came early that year, but it came with snow instead of dry frigidity and it snowed all winter, more than it had done for several years, and it melted slowly in the spring of 1938 and went deep into the parched soil of the Palliser Triangle. When the time came to sew another wheat crop the soil was ready for it and the growing season was marked by the arrival of good showers when the crop needed it the most. But the forces of destruction still seemed to have something left for a dying kick or two. At the end of March, the worst storm ever known struck the Alberta side of the Palliser Triangle just after the southern ranchers had turned their yearlings out on the range. Winds reached hurricane speeds of upwards of 80 miles an hour. The temperature dropped to zero and at Manyberries the wind blew at the rate of 60 miles an hour for a solid 24-hour stretch. Though the snow that had accompanied the wind was comparatively light, it was drifted to a depth of 50 feet in the coulees and trapped and smothered hundreds and hundreds of yearling calves in the fence corners and drifts. It was the storm that made simple truth totally unbelievable.

Two other blows were to befall. The first was the infestation of rust that decimated one of the best wheat crops the south country ever grew. At the beginning of July, the Saskatchewan Wheat Pool estimated the Saskatchewan crop at 200,000,000 bushels. First the rust hit it and then great clouds of grasshoppers descended on the Regina plains from the north. Within a matter of days rust, drouth and insects cut the crop from 200,000,000 bushels to 132,000,000 bushels. These were the dying kicks of the disaster years, but to the people who received them they were nature's unkindest cuts of all.

Alvin Geddes said:

I went to work for Westinghouse after graduation and in 1929 was calling on the power companies of Alberta, selling generators, turbines and transformers. The heavy end of the electrical business died in 1930 but Westinghouse kept me on by switching me to appliances. It got to the point where all I ever sold were fuses, light bulbs and radio tubes. But I kept trying, and when I found a store that was still in business I sure gave him service.

I had a good customer at Hanna which in 1933 was the only town in the whole of eastern Alberta that had any survival potential. One day I decided to take a short cut back to Calgary from Hanna and I got down into the country around East Coulee and I got lost. What a day! It was at least 100 above and the dust was blowing. Eventually, a thousand miles from nowhere, I came to an inhabited farm. The house was scarcely more than shack-size and the stable was more a lean-to than a building. There was a water wagon in the yard and a few discouraged chickens were scratching around outside the back door. A couple of small children peeked around the corner of the house. Then the farmer sort of materialized out of nowhere.

"Howdy," he said. "Could you tell me who won the Stanley Cup last spring? My radio went on the blink half way through the fourth game and nobody has come by since who's interested in hockey."

He drew another blank. Who ever knows, five months later, who won the Stanley Cup?

CHAPTER FIVE

From Strip Farming
to Trash Farming

As the dust storms blew higher and wider and thicker across the Palliser Triangle it was most ironic that a coterie of dedicated agricultural scientists who knew how to solve the problem of wind erosion waited impatiently for the opportunity to do so. The question was not what had to be done. That question was answered. The question was how to go about the task, how to marry know-how to muscle and equipment in a massive campaign never before imagined, let alone undertaken. It was this that took the time, time for negotiation, for letter writing and for conversation between representatives of all the governments and private interests which were legally involved in the country that was being destroyed. The time for study and research and questioning had all been spent and the spending had provided more knowledge about dry-land farming in less than 20 years than mankind had previously acquired in 20 centuries.

The investigation of dry-land farming was put on a scientific basis for the first time with the establishment in 1922 of the Dominion Experimental Farm at Swift Current. When Gordon Taggart arrived from the School of Agriculture at Vermilion to establish the farm, his terms of reference were clear enough. He was to investigate all matters concerning the production of grain and livestock on the dry lands of the Palliser Triangle. Taggart, though he was a well-trained scientist, conceived his job as being broader and deeper than the mere investigation of the technology of wheat production. Rather it was to include the whole scope of the agricultural industry—to find out how to sustain a consistently profitable agriculture in an area which had been notoriously unprofitable in the years between the booms.

Before doing anything he consulted Dr. W.H. Fairfield, the dean of the prairie agricultural scientists at the Lethbridge Experimental Farm. Out of these conversations came the decision to make a fresh start at Swift Current and get answers to the questions that have troubled every farm boy. Why does the wind blow? What makes the wheat grow? Why do farmers plow and disc and harrow? It would be possible, perhaps, to find the right way by doing things the wrong way. But why was one way right and another wrong? Necessity seemed to dictate that the land of the Palliser Triangle had to be summerfallowed to conserve moisture or crops would fail. But in dry years the summerfallow blew off down to the plow sole and destroyed the fertility of both the fallow land and the adjacent land to the lee of it.

How much moisture did wheat need to germinate, grow thriftily, set seed and ripen? Laboratory experiments could supply answers, but laboratory results could seldom be repeated in open fields. What effect did the wind have on temperature, and temperature on wind, and black soil on temperature, and wind? How much land did a farmer need to sustain his family at a reasonable standard of living? It was on this last question that everything else revolved. Unless it was answered, the answers to all the other questions would have little meaning for any save the coroners who would conduct the inquest on the great settlement experiment. But could the question ever be answered satisfactorily? Perhaps not, but the mere pursuit of it turned up evidence that much larger farms and radically different ways of doing things were essential. As the years passed from 1922 toward the 1930s Taggart and his fellow workers began to think they could see the outlines of an answer. Particularly when the tractor and the newly developed reaper and thresher—the combine—opened fascinating new areas of investigation.

Swift Current played a vital role in the development and improvement of both pieces of equipment. The idea of replacing the lugged steel wheels on tractors, for example, came to Grant Denike as he and a fruit-growing scientist from Florida watched a Ford Tri-motor "Flying Boxcar" make a landing in Chicago. The Florida scientist had been explaining that they had seen their hopes shattered of using tractor power to cultivate orange groves. The lugs on the wheels cut the surface roots of the citrus trees. Denike remarked that in Canada the tractor tended to both pack the earth and pulverize the topsoil too much. They wondered about putting some of the huge airplane tires from the Ford planes on tractors. When Denike came home he contacted the Goodyear Rubber Company and got some airplane tires to tinker with. His research showed considerable promise, until Ottawa suggested, with a mild rebuke, that he halt such foolishness.

Similarly the Swift Current station became the first anywhere to become excited about the self-propelled combine. Most of the early attempts at combine designing tended to be simple modifications of the old stationary grain separators, pulled around by 20-horse teams. However in heavy crops it took too many horses to haul the machines because the threshing mechanism was driven by power from the moving wheels. Massey-Harris came up with the idea of mounting a Waukesha engine on the machine to run the thresher and hence make it easier to pull. After trying one out, the Experimental Farm at Swift Current bought a machine and it became the vehicle for a prolonged researching spree that yielded many modifications and improvements.

It would be wrong to give the credit for any one development to any one individual at Swift Current because it was the sort of place where everybody had a finger in everything, because everybody was interested in everything. For example, the conclusion which Sidney Barnes came to from his long studies of plant moisture needs became the foundation for a crop forecasting system worked out by P.J. Janzen. Janzen applied Barnes's laboratory results to field conditions and succeeded in giving very accurate guidance to the farmers. Barnes pointed the way and Janzen had the vision to carry the information much further afield. Nor did Swift Current function in a special vacuum of its own, despite the special tasks set for it. Everything that was done at Swift Current was quickly reported and checked by the Experimental Farms at Lethbridge, Scott and Indian Head. Similarly, the other stations kept each other advised of results and directed questions germane to their specialties to the other stations. All this was natural enough because during the 1920s they all lived with the same problems.

Perhaps a better appreciation of the role of the Experimental Farms scientists can be obtained if the establishment of the Swift Current station in 1922 is placed within the context of its times. It came into being scarcely 20 years after Abbé Mendel's science-shaking theory had been re-discovered and brought to light in Vienna. The word "agronomy" had only been in general circulation for 25 years and the science itself was in its infancy. The mechanization of agriculture had barely been foreshadowed and both the methods and the equipment still in use had come down through the ages. What science there was, was often indistinguishable from folklore.

It was true that Angus McKay's discovery of summerfallowing to preserve moisture had been widely adopted throughout the Great Plains. American farmers and scientists not only demonstrated that summerfallowing worked, they worked out a scientific theory to explain why it worked: By capillary action, moisture was drawn to the surface and when the surface of the soil was cultivated it broke up this capillary movement. It followed, therefore, that scientific summerfallowing required that a fine, dry dust mulch be maintained on the surface and that the land be plowed after every rain to prevent surface caking and clods from developing. All this was spelled out in detail in H.W. Campbell's *Soil Culture Primer,* which was a required text in the agricultural colleges of the United States and Canada. It was only with the questioning of the scientific basis of summerfallowing, by Sidney Barnes at Swift Current and Dr. John A. Widtsoe in Utah, that the first scientific steps could be taken toward the solution of the problem of wind erosion. It was not only the absence of fundamental information which handicapped our Experimental Farms researchers. They had to clear away a lot of unscientific debris before they could even get started.

The hiring of Sidney Barnes for the Swift Current Station was a 10-strike. In Gordon Taggart's words: "Sid Barnes was our scientific everything. He was our meteorologist, botanist, engineer, soils specialist. He was dedicated, imaginative and inventive with a monumental curiosity about everything."

It was Barnes who devised the method of filling galvanized iron tanks with soil and growing plants in them to determine the moisture requirements of all the varieties of crops it was possible to raise within the Palliser Triangle. He segregated the tanks into those which had only normal rainfall, those which were given carefully measured quantities of water artificially, those in which the moisture supplies were restricted, and those given unlimited moisture. Over a 10-year period he was able to discover the upper and lower moisture limits of all the plants in the area. Barnes also worked out and adopted a completely new and comprehensive system of measuring and recording the sunshine, wind velocities, total flow of wind and most important of all, evaporation under varying conditions.

In addition to his other qualities, Barnes was a man of infinite patience and it was well that he was. The lines of inquiry he had undertaken took years to complete. Unhappily, he died in 1935, with his work only half done. But he had lived long enough to put Canadian agriculture forever in his debt and to explode the theory of capillary action. He proved that it was weed growth and not capillary action that took the moisture from the soil. It was Barnes's experiments which led to the accurate measurement of moisture loss by weeds and as a result of his experiments the whole basis of summerfallowing had to be reversed. Instead of chewing the earth into a fine powder after every rain, the farmers were advised to stay off their summerfallow except to control weed growth.

While one team studied the way the wind blew, another under H.J. Kemp and Grant Denike endlessly worked with machinery. It was determined that the best protection against soil drifting on summerfallow was a cloddy surface of the soil. The next problem to be solved was how to produce cloddy surfaces. The first rule that was universally agreed upon was that the less done to the soil the better. Instead of plowing, discing and harrowing the soil intensely, it should be left as much alone as possible, and cultivated only enough to keep down weed growth. Just as different soil reacted differently to the wind, so did the results from using different tillage equipment and methods differ from soil to soil. This helped explain why it took years of experimenting to come to definite conclusions, but one of the surest they came to was that the moldboard plow had to go. In its place the one-way disc was recommended, at least for the first pass over the stubble; instead of the harrows, the duckfoot cultivator and rod weeder provided better results. Plowing of dry soil at any time was rejected and so was fall plowing in the high wind country.

All this ran counter to everything the best farmers of the Palliser Triangle had regarded as the hallmark of good farming. It was axiomatic that the summerfallow had to be kept black and the soil could not be allowed to dry into rough chunks. A poorly cultivated summerfallow was a sure indication of a sloppy farmer. Once on a Field Day inspection tour in the Maple Creek area a party with whom Gordon Taggart was riding stopped to admire the excellent job of plowing a corn patch a local farmer was doing.

"He would be better off sitting in the shade having a sleep with his horses in the barn," was Taggart's brash comment, and the argument was on. There was still a good deal of distrust of the college graduate among western farmers, yet this was one proposition which the Swift Current scientists found easy to sell. Walking behind a set of harrows on a hot day, eating dust and pursued by flies, was not the kind of work any farmer relished. It was only a deep and abiding instinct of craftsmen that kept them at it. Convincing them they should stay off their fields unless weeds were becoming rampant was not as difficult as might have been expected.

The abandonment of the dust mulch theory was symptomatic of the whole process that began with Swift Current—the process of unlearning and forgetting most of the practices which the farmers had been taught to follow over the generations. A great many common-sense notions, things which "stood to reason," had to be abandoned. One of the hardest of all to overcome was the belief that there was some sort of magic in tree planting as a cure for wind erosion. Observation wherever trees grew indicated that soil did not blow on the lee side of the trees. Trees seemed to attract rain, just as rivers seemed to attract rain. Trees caused snow to drift on the lee side, so it "stood to reason" that planting trees could be a partial answer to the drouth problem. It had seemed to rain more on the Prairies when there were sloughs in the centre of the fields and along the roads. But the farmers had drained the sloughs, and ditched the roads, the sloughs had dried up and the summer showers fell some place else. It "stood to reason" that drainage had caused the trouble, that something should be done to restore the sloughs.

It once took Dean A.M. Shaw of the University of Saskatchewan a full hour to catalogue, and to demolish, the folk notions that accumulated in the wake of the dust storms. Yet it is doubtful if the advocates of tree planting at that Regina Board of Trade luncheon were ever wholly convinced, although a year later they could have seen shelterbelts wilting from the onslaught of the winds.

It was not as if Swift Current was an agricultural Menlo Park out of which poured a steady stream of startling new inventions for the farmers on the land. It more closely resembled an evaluation centre to which the farmers could come with their ideas and find people with the resources, intelligence, experience and interest to test them out. While Swift

Current was carrying out its prolonged soil moisture and wind velocity tests and measuring the results against crop production, farmers themselves were endlessly engaged in experiments of their own.

Wind erosion was identified as a menace to Alberta agriculture as early as 1910 when a section of fine land owned by the Knight Sugar Company blew out down to the plow sole near Raymond. In 1917, Leonard and Arle Koole, who farmed north of Lethbridge, invented the system of strip farming that was, literally, to revolutionize grain growing in Alberta. A farmer from Montana, 17 years later, brought the idea back to Canada to launch a strip-farming campaign in the Shaunavon area of Saskatchewan. The farmer was W.H. Read and he farmed 2,000 acres south of the Saskatchewan border. Just after the First World War, Read made a trip through southern Alberta to Banff, at a time when the soil was blowing badly. There were huge drifts along the railway line and down the fence lines between Calgary and Lethbridge. Ten years later, Read repeated the journey and the landscape had changed beyond all recognition. Strip farming was everywhere in evidence. With a wind erosion problem of his own at home, Read interrupted his journey at Lethbridge to investigate the idea, which he subsequently put into operation on his own farm. In 1934 the Shaunavon Board of Trade started to agitate for the adoption of strip farming methods in southwest Saskatchewan. Mr. Read came to town, invited everybody down to Montana to see how effectively the Alberta system was containing soil erosion, and making wheat production possible even in dry years. A cavalcade of 100 farmers from the area made the trip and came back sold on the idea. A strip farming association was organized and it became the first successful step taken in Saskatchewan to overcome the dust bowl.

Strip farming itself had grown out of a period of wind erosion and black blizzards in Alberta in 1917-18-19 that was as bad or worse than anything that happened in Saskatchewan in the 1930s. One of the worst blowing areas was the Chinook belt around Lethbridge where winter and summer winds up to 60 miles an hour were common.

The farmers themselves knew they had to summerfallow to raise any sort of crop. But if they tried to summerfallow, their fields blew away. The situation became so critical that several pioneer Lethbridge-district farmers went down to Idaho and Utah in search of new farms. The black blizzards convinced them they could not summerfallow their farms, and if they could not summerfallow they could raise no crops. So they were going to get out of the country. It was J.H. Bohanon of Sibbald who came up with the first constructive idea. Instead of plowing his stubble and turning the straw under to start his summerfallow, he left the stubble unplowed and on the surface. Then he worked it with a duckfoot cultivator before seeding. This innovation produced a big crop, and the plowless fallow idea was launched when it was written up in the *Farmer's Advocate* and a number of farmers in the Lethbridge area adopted it. What happened next illustrates how closely the Experimental Farms and the farmers in the Lethbridge area adopted it. What happened next illustrates how closely the Experimental Farms and the farmers worked together in the development of new ideas. The episode revolves around and involves Asael E. "Ace" Palmer.

Asael Palmer's interest in the control of wind erosion was aroused by a Lethbridge Chamber of Commerce meeting on soil blowing in 1918. Until then his special concern had been irrigation and its problems. He set out to inform himself on wind erosion, only to discover the literature on the subject was sparse to the point of non-existence. And wherever his journeys took him he took special notice of the action of the topsoil in the ever-present winds from the west. He was on the move a great deal. He had a farm of his own, taught school at Raymond and was a consultant to the CPR irrigation systems on their salinity problems. As the only farmer-teacher-consultant with a college degree for miles around, his advice was frequently sought by his neighbors. One day in the spring of 1920, one of the most prominent farmers in southern Alberta came to see him. The visitor was Thomas O. King and he wanted Palmer to take a look at his soil-drifting problem.

Up until that moment Palmer had been convinced that Bohanon's plowless fallowing was an excellent way of preventing soil drifting. But King had adopted plowless fallowing, and his land was blowing so badly it was almost blown out. It looked as if the new system caused the soil to blow worse than ever, rather than preventing soil blowing. As they talked, Palmer noticed that there was one part of the field that was not blowing. He wondered why.

King explained that he had burned off the stubble before summerfallowing on most of the field but had missed that part where it was not blowing. The solution to King's problem was staring them in the face—if they were going to use plowless fallow they would have to leave the stubble on the surface—unburned. That spring Palmer examined many other plowless cultivations. Wherever they burned off the stubble to kill weeds and to make cultivation easier, there was soil blowing. Where the stubble was left unburned, there was not.

The Lethbridge Experimental Farm was also testing plowless fallow but on a small-plot basis where the blowing problem did not arise. When Palmer went to the station in 1921 as assistant superintendent, the station expanded its staff of illustration supervisors. They were called in for a conference regarding the pros and cons of plowless fallowing. The meeting, curiously enough, broke into two opposite schools of thought. One held that plowless fallowing prevented soil blowing. The other claimed it increased it. It developed that the first group all came from west of Lethbridge while the second came from east of the city. In other words, they divided on the Russian thistle belt. The "tumbleweed" did not grow west of Lethbridge, so the farmers there were not burning their stubble to control Russian thistle. It grew profusely in the east and they burned the stubble to get rid of it.

Plowless fallowing was clearly the answer to soil blowing

in the Chinook belt, and if it could stop it there it would stop soil erosion anywhere. But there remained the problem of weed control. Some means had to be found of cultivating the soil to kill the weeds and still leave the stubble on top. On light soil with a light crop of stubble, a duckfoot cultivator could be used. But it would not work otherwise. The search for effective machinery to get the job done was on.

In the Lethbridge-Monarch-Nobleford area, the farmers went searching for long-abandoned steam gang plows. They took out every other beam, removed the moldboards from the beams they left in, and converted them into 32-inch duckfoots. Unhappily the old equipment was quickly used up so there was far from enough to supply the need. In any event the arms on the gang plows were too short and clogged with weeds. The search lost much of its steam during the series of wet years in the 1920s. The strip farming practice became more widely adopted. New cultivating equipment was gradually coming in—the one-way discs, the rod weeder and much heavier duck-foot cultivators. But the idea of maintaining a black summerfallow died hard.

When the badly blowing years returned in 1929 there was a resurgence of interest in plowless fallow. Soil drifting became so serious in the Chinook belt that a group of farmers headed by C.S. Noble organized a meeting at Nobleford and invited Dr. Fairfield and Palmer to come up and lead a discussion on plowless fallowing. To the meeting came farmers to whom plowing the soil was a religion, who looked with contempt on those who would ever be satisfied with less than a black summerfallow. They had gone in heavily for strip farming and it seemed to be the answer to the soil drifting problem, though with some important exceptions. Every year, more soil from summerfallow was sifting onto the growing grain. The strips of growing grain also tended to attract grasshoppers and sawflies and the wind carried weed seeds.

Some of the farmers who had tried strip farming had given it up in favor of plowless fallowing. A long argument developed between the two camps. Those who had lost faith in strip farming pointed out that the strip farmers emphasized that the soil from their summerfallow was sifting onto the crop area, that ridging around the edges of the strips was a problem and that insect and weed infestations increased with strip farming. Out of the discussion, the most dedicated plowman at the meeting agreed, as an experiment, to convert one half of one of his strips to plowless fallow and test the results. Within two years he abandoned strip farming for plowless fallowing.

At this meeting, as at most of the other gatherings of farmers, discussion inevitably turned to farm machinery. Some of the newer implements worked reasonably well on some soils in some circumstances. But none worked with complete satisfaction. The one-way buried too much straw, rod weeders did not work on rocky land, duckfoots did poorly in very hard soil. The search for new implements that would cut down the weeds and leave the stubble on the surface went on and on. It ended on a fruit ranch in California in 1935 when C.S. Noble saw a farmer using a blade-type cultivator that sliced through the soil just below the surface. Noble returned to his farm and built the first Noble blade and invited Palmer out to launch it. This, said Palmer, was the answer, though it was still only a rough idea. Noble's huge blade seemed to work but it had a number of obvious defects. It was hard to keep in the ground and it nudged the weeds instead of breaking them out of the soil. As a result of the helpful advice Noble got from Lethbridge and Swift Current he put his blade through a whole series of modifications, perfected it and set up an implement company to build and market it. The Experimental Farms got behind it and recommended its use without reservation.

Meanwhile, the idea of plowless fallowing spread all too slowly. The instinct to plow and cultivate ran too deeply in too many farmers for them to completely embrace the idea of not plowing and not cultivating. Rough-looking fields had long been known contemptuously across the prairies as "Indian summerfallowing." It was only as the terms used to describe the operation changed that its virtues became generally accepted. Summerfallowing was a word so closely associated with bare black soil that "plowless fallow" was soon displaced by the term "stubble mulch." That was both more accurately descriptive and generally acceptable.

But even "stubble mulch" wasn't right, as Palmer discovered one day on a field trip into the Kindersley area where Ted Everest had organized a huge field day at the Experimental sub-station. After the meeting a farmer approached Palmer and asked him to come over and look at his summerfallow. He had adopted the stubble mulch idea but his summerfallow was an unholy mess.

With a couple of hundred farmers following along, Palmer and Everest did as they were asked. At his farm, the farmer waved his arm at his summerfallow and said:

"Look at that mess. What am I to do with it now?"

Palmer thought for a moment before replying.

"What would I do if I were you?" he said. "I'd go into my bedroom and thank my God that I was such a good farmer. You've got a beautiful summerfallow."

The farmer was almost struck dumb with disbelief. He pointed again to his field.

"But it looks terrible. It's a trash heap," he protested. "It's covered with Russian thistle and weeds and you can't see the stubble for the weeds."

"Well," said Palmer, "what are the weeds doing? They are holding your soil. And they are dead so they are not using up your moisture. You got them in good time in the spring and you've got a beautiful summerfallow. You are a very good farmer indeed!"

Obviously, there was a problem with terminology. Because they were using the term "stubble mulch," which reminded them of "dust mulch," the farmers expected something nice and neat and tidy in the form of stubble. With anything else the field look ragged, a trash heap.

"What we must do," Palmer said to Everest, "is find some

term that will reconcile the farmers to unsightly looking fields as long as the soil is held down."

"Well all that trash certainly holds the soil so why don't we just call it trash cover?" Everest suggested.

A more inelegant term could hardly have been devised yet it was so completely descriptive of precisely the sort of thing that was required that Palmer decided to sponsor it. He talked it up around the Lethbridge station without engendering much enthusiasm, except from local wags who christened him "Trash-Cover Palmer." However, at the next soil drifting control meeting he unveiled his slogan for wider consideration. Again it aroused more opposition than support, but the quality of the support tilted the scales in Palmer's favor. Dr. Archibald himself came out strongly in favor of it and that settled it. "Trash cover" and "trash farming" got into the vocabulary and spread far beyond Canada's borders.

So, in fact, did the work the Canadians had done on soil drifting control. Coupled with the ground-breaking research at Swift Current, the accomplishments of the farmers of Alberta, and the leadership of Fairfield and Palmer at Lethbridge the basic data needed to beat back the desert within the Palliser Triangle were obtained. Long before the PFRA was in being, Dr. Archibald and Dr. E.S. Hopkins in Ottawa had pondered the wisdom of collecting all the available knowledge about wind erosion into a single government bulletin. The people of Alberta, by 1934, had been living with blowing soil for 25 years. Drouth and wind erosion had depopulated a third of the settled area of Alberta. Yet those who remained in the big wind country had gradually by their own genius and exertions tamed the wind and brought it under control, at least in part.

The need to make this knowledge available to the people of Saskatchewan and Manitoba was becoming increasingly urgent. So the task of putting a pocket-sized encyclopedia together was delegated to Asael Palmer, Sidney Barnes and Dr. W.S. Chepil. The latter was a young scientist who had been placed in charge of the soil drifting and erosion control studies at the Regina sub-station. He brought to the job a splendid scientific training, dedication and an unmatched imagination. It was Chepil who took over the soil studies at Swift Current after Sid Barnes's death and built the PFRA soils laboratory at Swift Current. Chepil's endless pursuit of the wind across the Regina plains led him to the idea of building a portable wind tunnel to study the effect of air currents on growing plants at close range. His first effort after he moved to Swift Current was like something out of a Rube Goldberg cartoon, a square tube 50 feet long and about four feet across. The wind was created by a propeller mounted in an old circular saw axle. Power was supplied from a pulley attached to the drive shaft of an old Chevrolet engine mounted crosswise on a truck chassis. On the top of the tunnel were glass windows through which gauges and thermometers could be read and the action of the wind on the crops closely observed. Unhappily the portable tunnel proved impractical in its field tests. But when Chepil moved it inside the Soils Laboratory, the fundamental research he was able to do on wind and soil earned him an international reputation.

Most of the scientific back-stooping material for the pamphlet was supplied by Barnes and Chepil. Palmer did the writing and Dr. Hopkins supplied editorial direction. The booklet was entitled "Soil Drifting Control in the Prairie Provinces" and it was one of the most successful pamphlets ever published by the Department of Agriculture. It ran through four large editions from 1935 until 1946 and found its way into the agricultural and research laboratories of the world. How solid the foundation was of the soil drifting control program is illustrated by this fact—in the 11-year interval between the first and the fourth edition there were no changes in its fundamental concepts, only refinements of its suggested methods.

The booklet ran to 40 pages, which included much statistical information. Not only did it summarize the best, most effective cropping practices to avoid the danger of soil blowing, it outlined the emergency steps which would be required to bring the land back under control after serious drifting had occurred.

It was a complete handbook. There were chapters on the causes of soil erosion, on the damage caused to the land, the farm homes and the economy, on crop rotations, protection of farmsteads and a statistical summary. The entire booklet was written and largely assembled by Asael Palmer on the train between Lethbridge and Ottawa. There is considerable significance to that fact. It indicates how clearly people like Palmer understood the problem, how carefully they had considered cause and effect and how sure they were of their ground. That in itself raised a very interesting and important question:

With so much known, with so much information available to the farmers of Western Canada, how did prairie agriculture get itself into such a mess?

The answer is many sided. One aspect of it is to be seen in the reaction of Dr. Hopkins to the first reading of Palmer's draft manuscript. Hopkins was then Dominion Field Husbandman and Dr. Archibald's deputy and ultimate successor. The first response Palmer got from Hopkins was that it was too strongly worded, too positive in its statements of fact and worst of all it was "the government telling farmers how to farm." But Palmer, who was living with the blowing dust all the time, insisted that the situation was so critical that the booklet had to be positive.

"If we know what to do, we have to tell the farmers because we cannot solve our problems if we don't. And if we know what to do, and we do, the farmers are entitled to that knowledge!"

Still unconvinced, Hopkins decided to take it to Dr. Archibald and, as was happening with such frequency in those years, Archibald took the responsibility, made the decision and ordered that the pamphlet be published.

The pamphlet did in fact run counter to the philosophy of the Experimental Farms. Their function was to investigate the problems of agriculture in the general areas in which the farms were located. Once the problems were solved, the solutions could be made available to farmers through the Provincial Governments, through the farm press or through gatherings of farmers at field days on the farms or at illustration stations. It was no part of their function to launch propaganda campaigns to force farmers to farm properly. They did not go blundering around the country looking for mistakes to correct. They went when they were invited, or not at all. If the farmers chose to ignore their advice it was no concern of theirs for they respected the rights of the farmers to do things in their own way. So the research scientists, by inclination, training and Experimental Farms policy, tended to regard their task as completed when the results were obtained and made available. Ultimately their results could be filtered down through the alert and eager top 10 percent of the farmers who constituted a sort of intellectual elite in their communities. They were always looking for better ways of doing things. When the better methods were used by the leading farmers, the rest would gradually follow suit.

But while there was much validity to this explanation, it covered but part of the question. The Experimental Farms and illustration stations were too few to be reached by more than a small part of the population. The influence of the Experimental Farms on the farm community immediately surrounding the stations was always apparent. Within a radius of 20 miles of Morden, for example, there were fruit trees growing in every farm yard. Fifty miles away they dwindled off into nothingness. Clearly, there was a lack of communication between the Experimental Farms scientists and the mass of the farmers in the dust bowl. Gordon Taggart recognized this in 1934 when he was advocating the appointment of trained agricultural scientists in each municipality to give advice and assistance to the farmers. Ultimately this idea became translated into the agricultural representative branches of the prairie Departments of Agriculture—the Ag. Reps. But in the 1930s there was a communications gap that existed until the PFRA came into existence and the containment of the blowing dust became a national crusade. Once Ottawa gave the order, the Experimental Farms superintendents and their staff took off in a rush to make up for lost time. They went everywhere the dust blew, made speeches, organized listing bees, set up seed depots, supervised the mixing of grasshopper bait, and helped convert and repair farm equipment. They ate when they could, slept where they could and when they could. They choked in the dust with the farmers on the land, sharing each problem as they became part of the solution.

And, retrospectively at least, they loved every minute of it, remembering it with relish as long as they lived.

CHAPTER SIX

The Romance of
Crested Wheat Grass

*I*t is doubtful whether within the whole of our literature a single tale has been told with an agrostologist as the hero; and still less is there likely to have been one glorifying a grass seed. This chapter is, then, an effort to redress the balance, for few Canadians have ever played so large a role in changing the face of the earth as Dr. Lawrence E. Kirk, and few seeds of grass have ever been so face-changing as the crested wheat grass he developed at the University of Saskatchewan.

Lawrence Kirk's involvement with crested wheat grass began with his graduation from the University of Saskatchewan in 1916. He worked for the next year in the Forage Crops Laboratory while obtaining a further degree as a bachelor of agricultural science for which he was gold medalist. The Forage Crops Laboratory had been established at Saskatoon in an effort to find grass that would make better hay and pasture than the famous prairie wool which originally covered the Palliser Triangle. While the early ranchers swore by prairie wool as an ideal all-purpose pasture grass and hay grass, the scientists thought otherwise. They found several types of grass that would yield better than prairie wool in years of adequate moisture. But they could find nothing comparable in dry years or in cold winters. Too often if it would survive the drouth it would winter kill, and if it would survive the winter it would die out in the hot, dry summers. Or they found that such grasses as western wild rye and brome grass produced well in the years immediately after planting, but both crops dropped off sharply as the grass got older. Some grasses were difficult to germinate, others, like red top, germinated easily but died out too quickly.

So it was that the settlers in the Palliser Triangle were plagued with recurrent livestock feed shortages almost from the first days of settlement. In the dry years when crops were light the hay crop was also likely to be a near failure and pastures were overgrazed. In many respects the search for a better grass that would be both winter hardy and drouth resistant became the most pressing problem of prairie agriculture. The lack of adequate forage made all the other problems of a pioneer agriculture ever so much more aggravating.

The story of crested wheat grass goes back to the closing decades of the last century, when North America turned to Russia and China for the fruit, flower and vegetable seeds that would survive the frigid, dry climate of the Great Plains. Settlers from the east who brought from home seeds of their ornamental shrubs and fruit trees found that none would survive in the harsh climate of the northern plains. The horticulturalists and botanists turned to Russia and China for hardy specimens which they thought might adapt to North America. Expeditions were organized to go to Siberia, Manchuria and the steppes of European Russia to collect botanical specimens. These expeditions, and the co-operation between Russian, American and Canadian scientists that followed, provided much of the foundation stock for horticulture on the Canadian Prairies. Their origins still survive in the names of many of our plants. We have Russian olive, poplar and caragana; Siberian larch, crabapple and dogwood; Chinese elm and hawthorn; Manchurian lilac; Amur maple, crabapple and honeysuckle; Ural spirea and Hopi crabapple. There was also Russian wild rye and Russian rye grass. Most of all there was Russian crested wheat grass.

The first samples of crested wheat grass were imported

into the United States in 1898 and were tested experimentally at various stations in the Dakotas and Montana. This grass was native to European Russia and was first cultivated in the Volga region east of Saratov, an area that was quite deficient in rainfall and where the soil was low in organic matter. The Americans found that crested wheat grass did very well in their own areas of low rainfall but the reports of these experimental results were filed and forgotten until the University of Saskatchewan came upon them and imported some seeds from the United States in 1915.

Saskatchewan in 1912 and 1913 had experienced very severe drouth within the Palliser Triangle. There had been a good deal of soil blowing. Overgrazed pastures had been taken over very largely by pasture sage. The need for a drouth-resistant grass that could survive the Palliser winters became increasingly urgent. Nothing, however, was done with the crested wheat seed from the United States until the following year. By then Lawrence Kirk had been taken on the field husbandry department which was headed by Hon. John Bracken, later Premier of Manitoba. Kirk came across the crested wheat seeds in a package of envelopes while cleaning out a drawer of the desk allotted to him. Bracken recalled having obtained them from North Dakota and suggested that Kirk plant them and see how they turned out. They turned out better than anything had turned out before, though it took a decade and a half to be able to say with complete authority how well. By then the university had thousands of grass plants growing in its experimental plots. Each plant was carefully numbered and its performance recorded. Every time a new strain was developed which looked promising it was carefully nurtured in the hope that it would prove to be a winner in the winter-hardy, drouth-resistant sweepstakes. The tedious business of breeding and crossbreeding and performance testing expanded every year.

The first planting of the crested wheat grass was undertaken with what could be best described as restrained hopefulness. It was not cultivated in Russia but the grass had performed well in the American nursery test. The performance had been well documented but nothing further seemed to have been done about it. Had the grass, despite its early promise, developed some later defects which caused further tests to be dropped? At the very least, Saskatoon would supply the answer to that question. So Kirk added a few more feet of rows in the experimental grass plots and seeded the first planting of crested wheat grass. After they started to grow they were watched with the same attention paid the other plants. The first results were disappointing. Because his original supply of seeds was so limited, Kirk was overcautious, even overprotective. Special care was taken in preparing the soil. The seed bed was worked up to a fine tilth. The seed that was produced was carefully harvested and the process repeated again and again. If the grass had not turned out to be so completely winter hardy, the experimenters might have been discouraged and perhaps have discarded it, for it seemed to do poorly otherwise. Its winter hardiness was so outstanding, however, that it got a second and third and fourth chance. It was only then that it was discovered that crested wheat grass thrived on adversity and couldn't stand prosperity.

"We lost four or five years in our testing before we discovered that this was a grass that had to be treated rough," Dr. Kirk recalled.

Only the minimum moisture was required to get the seed started. Then it did best when it was left alone by both man and nature. It could fend for itself in the struggle for survival with annual weeds. When its top turned brown and seemed to die in mid-summer, its root system was going deeper and deeper in search of moisture. It took a great deal of restraint on Kirk's part to leave it alone for, when the weather turned hot and dry, it turned brown and was the deadest-looking grass imaginable. Without water it stayed dead looking throughout the summer. Then, when the fall rains came, it came back to life and by the following summer took care of most of the annual weeds with which it had to compete. All this, however, took years to determine. Kirk, soon after he became settled into his work, decided to look around for more seed. He wrote to the United States, and to Russia which, in 1918, was deep in the throes of its revolution, a fact which was lost on Kirk. Ignoring the revolution, he wrote to the Department of Agriculture of the Government of Russia. He explained, in English, that he was engaged in a study of Russian crested wheat grass under field conditions in Western Canada, and that he was quite short of seed. He asked if the Russians could spare any further samples for his experiments. The Russian revolution was then at its peak, soldiers and revolutionaries fought in the streets, warring armies laid waste the countryside. But inside the Russian Department of Agriculture the scientists went on with their work and so, apparently, did the postal service. Kirk's letter found its way by some miracle to someone who could read it, then to someone who could do something about his request. One day, in the usual mail, Kirk got another package of envelopes from Russia containing samples of various strains of crested wheat grass.

These along with the increase he had obtained from his original plantings were seeded into his expanded experimental plots. By now he had harvested enough seed to try to expand his seed production by planting a half-acre of it in a separate plot. He got an excellent catch. That winter he went off to Moose Jaw to take charge of an experimental school for farm boys the Government of Saskatchewan had established. When he got back to Saskatoon 10 months later, he discovered that somebody had plowed up his half-acre grass crop. Fortunately, the original seed plots were still producing, so it was comparatively easy to replant the larger area. From the way the crested wheat plants were developing, Kirk and his associates suspected that they were behaving better in Canada than they had in the United States. Cooler and drier Canadian summers seemed more favorable to its growth. As the dry years descended after the First World War, Kirk became convinced that in crested wheat they had a grass with a future in Western Canada.

By the mid-1920s, additional supplies had been obtained from the United States so that the Forage Crops Laboratory had more than 1,000 separate strains of the plant identified and growing under test conditions. It was important, however, to expand the testing areas. Seeds were distributed to all the prairie Dominion Experimental Farms and when the Range Station was established at Manyberries crested wheat was among the first grasses planted there. Before the project was 10 years old, Kirk had proved to everyone's satisfaction that crested wheat grass was superior to all other grasses in winter hardiness and resistant to drouth. Seeded with a nurse crop or without, selected strains of crested wheat could match the hay yields of brome and western rye grass in normal years and substantially out-produce either in dry years. And it would apparently live forever.

There was more to the story than simply growing grass and correlating results. There was an aesthetic aspect as well for as Kirk watched his grass grow his eyes were forever seeking out the best-looking strains. Because of crosspollination new strains were constantly appearing and Kirk was continually on the lookout for the leafier and lusher-looking plants. One day his eyes lit on a plant that stood out from all the rest. It was bushier, leafier, greener. It was certainly the leafiest type yet seen. For some years they had been concentrating on saving the seed from the leafiest strains and in this particular plant they seemed to have hit the jackpot. It was fine-stalked and coarse-leaved, precisely the sort of plant that would yield the most hay and do the best as a pasture grass. Its seeds were carefully harvested and reseeded; but with everyone's fingers crossed. It was a beautiful specimen, but would it not disappear in field production in the endless process of crosspollination that was characteristic of the grass? They sent some of the seeds off to the cytologists for a careful look at the cell structure. It was discovered that this was a plant that would breed true because it was self-pollinating and would reject the pollen from all other strains.

The news could not have been better, and when the grass

was eventually put on test its performance was outstanding. The more extensively it was tested the better it performed. Even for farm lawns and rural golf courses, where water was not available for either lawns or fairways, the grass formed a uniform non-tufted and permanent turf. Curiously enough, crested wheat grass would not thrive under artificial watering. Nor did it do well as a forage crop except under the semi-arid conditions which prevailed in Western Canada. That was why its range of adaptability seemed confined to the Great Plains of North America and the steppes of Russia, where similar conditions of soil and climate prevail. Dr. Kirk named it "Fairway" and it was without doubt the finest strain of crested wheat grass ever developed. The next step was to get it out to the farmers for experiments in their pastures and hay fields. The yield multiplied quickly and Kirk and his people were on the point of starting to distribute it in the spring of 1925 when the warehouse in which it was stored burned down.

Fortunately for everybody, there was enough seed around to start over. It was fortunate, too, that Dr. S.E. Clarke had been convinced of the virtues of crested wheat grass when he became the agrostologist at the Manyberries Experimental Farm. This farm was established in 1925 as a rangeland experimental station to specialize in the problems of range management in the dry belt of southern Alberta and Saskatchewan. As it was orientated toward the ranching industry, one of its problems was to discover the most economical use of rangeland and the best grasses with which to reseed areas which had been overgrazed or which had been plowed and abandoned. Clarke became the "Johnny Appleseed" of crested wheat grass. Wherever he went he carried samples with him. In 1928, Clarke broadcast a mixture of crested wheat, brome grass, sweet clover, alfalfa and western rye grass into an abandoned field that was covered with weeds. He ran a disc over it to cover the seed. Three years later only the crested wheat survived and it was flourishing while all the other grass, and the annual weeds, had disappeared.

More striking, perhaps, were the comparative tests of

grass and legumes which Dr. Clarke made in large plots in rows spaced three feet apart. No intertillage was given in any of the test plots and all were overgrown with weeds except the spaces between the rows of the crested wheat. This was a clear indication of the fact that crested wheat was using up all the moisture and would leave none for the weeds. All this was predictable from the study of the root structure of the grass which Dr. Kirk and his assistants were making at Saskatoon. Crested wheat grass roots went down to a depth of six feet on occasions and the drier the summer the deeper they went. The importance of Dr. Clarke's experiments lay in the fact that he could use them to demonstrate the worth of the new grass to the ranchers in their own environment. He got his results under conditions that prevailed over most of the short-grass rangeland.

Extensive tests were carried out on the Scott Station and G.D. Matthews field tested it over the vast area between the South Saskatchewan and North Saskatchewan Rivers. One of the earliest reclamation projects was launched on a section of abandoned land near the station. So badly eroded and blown out was this land that working it with a wheeled tractor was impossible. Only a tracked type could overcome the deep sand drifts and the deep soil blow-outs. The results achieved by seeding crested wheat into weed patches at Scott were spectacular and it proved its worth at illustration stations all across the southern part of the Scott territory. In the northern area, however, where the rainfall was better, brome and alfalfa proved more satisfactory, a fact that corroborated Dr. Kirk's early finding—crested wheat did best under the worst conditions. The Scott Station also did extensive experiments on the grass mixtures and found that even in the drier parts of its district the addition of alfalfa to crested wheat helped both crops. Perhaps most important of all were the discoveries that the Scott Experimental Farm made on the value of phosphate fertilizers for all crops growing north of the South Saskatchewan, including crested wheat grass.

It was at Scott that the idea of adapting soil-listing techniques to create artificial snowdrifts was first tried. They invented snow scrapers that farmers could use to create drifts up and down their fields to trap the snow and keep it on the land until it melted in the spring. They discovered, too, that eaten-down and worn-out pastures could be quickly rehabilitated by discing, harrowing and seeding into the unplowed sod early in the fall. But regardless of the seeding methods used, crested wheat grass out-performed both brome and alfalfa by substantial margins.

The extent to which the Dominion Experimental Farms co-operated in the testing of crested wheat grass is illustrated by the fact that Morden published its first report of its tests in 1928. Then Brandon, Indian Head, Lethbridge, Scott and Swift Current checked in. At Saskatoon, Dr. Kirk had been mainly concerned with beefing up the production of seed, and the search for new and better strains. He had determined that maximum production of seed was obtained if the seed was planted in rows three feet apart. But for pasture and hay production, should it be seeded in closer rows? How much closer in southwest Saskatchewan, in western Manitoba, in southern Alberta? The Experimental Farms made it their business to get the answers to these questions for their areas so that the farmers and ranchers in the vicinity could reap some practical benefits from using the new seed.

The first thing to discover, of course, was the best time to seed it. Was the fact, for example, that they could not get a catch of crested wheat seeded on drifting land because it needed a nurse crop, or because it was being seeded at the wrong time? At Manyberries and Swift Current they made seedings once a week between early April and late November. They even seeded it into the snow in the winter. Then there was the problem of how deeply to seed it on the various types of soil. And how far apart the rows should be in good soil and poor soil, and how thickly in the rows.

Answers came not in weeks or months but in years. But they came nonetheless. Trial and error demonstrated that, to control drifting soil, a fast-germinating grain like spring rye had to be sown to hold the soil. Then the crested wheat could be drilled into the grain or the stubble. Or it could be drilled right into the vast fields of newly sprouted Russian thistle that came up so quickly when the rains came back. It was trial and error, over many years, that led to the conclusion that crested wheat grass was of much greater value mixed with other grasses than by itself in the drier regions of the Triangle, and that its worth as pasture grass exceeded its worth as a hay crop. Its habit of growing best in the early spring and late fall made it ideal pasture for the early calf crops. But when it turned brown in summer it made poor summer pasture, so Russian rye grass, or brome or alfalfa added to crested wheat provided the summer pasturage. Alternatively, livestock could be concentrated on crested wheat pastures in the spring and fall and allowed to run on the native prairie wool in the summer.

There can be little doubt that the whole Community Pastures program was made possible by the ability of crested wheat grass to take root and prosper on abandoned land once the soil blowing was stopped. All the sidelines experts had been talking for 20 years about putting the unsuitable land back to grass. They made it sound very easy indeed. The truth was that getting any kind of grass to germinate and survive in the hot dry summers of the drouth years was exceedingly difficult. Nor would the native grasses come back of their own accord. Instead it was the tough annual and hardy perennial weeds that captured the wasteland and made it useless for pasture—weeds like buckbrush, pasture sage, stinkweed, povertyweed, toad flax, wild rose, Canada thistle. Between the South Saskatchewan and the Missouri there was grave doubt that the prairie wool could ever re-establish itself in competition with the weeds which were fierce competitors for the available moisture.

Many of the native grasses were growing either near the northern limits of habitat or close to the southern limits. Some did very much better 500 miles south, others did better 300 miles north. This meant that surviving was difficult for these marginal grasses under the best of conditions. Under the worst of conditions which prevailed within the Palliser Triangle, the northern limits of growth of some types would be pushed south and the southern limits of the others would be pushed north, leaving a weedy wasteland in between. Without the development of crested wheat grass it would have been difficult, and very costly indeed, to put the millions of blowing acres in the south back to pasture. Left to its own devices, nature would have provided some sort of cover for most of the drifting areas. But it would not have been the kind of cover which would have been of much use to the farming or ranching community. The latter had already learned the bitter lesson of what happens to once-good pasture when overgrazing allows pasture sage and buckbrush to take over.

Meanwhile the success which Dr. Kirk was having at Saskatoon caught Ottawa's eye and in 1931 he was hired away as Dominion Agrostologist. Part of the consideration he exacted from Ottawa was that the Dominion would take over his forage experiments at Saskatoon and finance the subsequent development. Soon after going to Ottawa he was invited to the Third World Congress on Genetics which was being held in Ithaca, New York. There he met Russia's most famous botanist, the celebrated N.I. Vavilov, and the talk turned immediately to crested wheat grass. Kirk reported the success that Canada was having with the Russian grass and Vavilov was so interested that he detoured home by way of Ottawa to pick up some samples of the Fairway strain to take back with him.

Vavilov told Kirk that his country boasted of the world's greatest living expert on the grass, a scientist who had studied every detail of its growth for 20 years, and had done nothing else. He had collected all his data into a book which the Government had published. But nothing had come of either the book or the studies. It was the American experience all over again. However, the conversations with Kirk had so kindled Vavilov's interest in the grass that he promised to send Kirk a copy of the book. Then, he said he was going to set a program in motion to collect all the various grass seeds and follow Canada's example. He said that what he had learned from Kirk convinced him that Canada had provided the clues that would enable Russia to solve some of her own dry-land problems. Vavilov's stature was indicated by his election as president of the next World Genetic Congress which would be held in the United Kingdom. Before it was held, however, he had fallen victim to the Stalin purges and was never heard from again. The book he sent Dr. Kirk was probably his last connection with the outside world.

The departure of Dr. Kirk for Ottawa to take charge of the Dominion Government's grass experiments all across the country did not interfere with the progress of the crested wheat experiments. Trueman Stevenson, who had been Kirk's assistant, was placed in charge of the Forage Crops Laboratory and when Kirk returned to Saskatoon in 1937 as Dean of Agriculture, Stevenson was moved to Ottawa. Progress with the development of seed supplies and the utilization of crested wheat was very slow during the depression in Canada. Small two-pound samples were distributed to farmers in the hope of getting them started in seed production. But little came of this and when the PFRA was formed and began the wholesale distribution of seed for erosion control after 1936, it had to rely mainly on the American suppliers. As a result of the publicizing of the achievements at Saskatoon with crested wheat grass, the Americans rushed into seed production much earlier and in a big way. It was not long before the United States had enough seed on hand to reseed millions of acres of wind-blown land and several carloads were made available to the PFRA.

Nothing comparable to the Fairway strain was developed there, however, and the seed imported by the PFRA was all of the standard variety. But it was used far and wide all over Western Canada to reseed the eroded soil once the soil drifting was stopped.

The idea of importing huge quantities of ordinary crested wheat grass seed from the United States while the obviously superior Fairway strain was not being produced in quantity in Canada offended Kirk's notion of the fitness of things. One day in late fall after he had become Dean of Agriculture, he went over to the Forage Crops Laboratory and picked up a couple of pounds of Fairway seed. Then he drove out to the farm of James Rugg at Elstow, 25 miles east of the city. He handed the package to Rugg.

"Here Jimmy," he said, "I want you to take this and seed it exactly as I tell you. Then I want you to handle it exactly as I tell you to. There is going to be almost unlimited demand for this seed for many years to come. If you will follow my instructions, this seed can become the basis for the best and most profitable crops you will ever grow."

Out of that conversation a new industry was born for Saskatchewan—the commercial production of crested wheat grass seed. Rugg had the good sense to take Kirk's advice and he never looked back. When other farmers saw his success with Fairway crested wheat grass, they too went into the business. It was not long before a farmer in the Battleford area struck it rich with a quarter section of crested wheat seed. Crested wheat became not only the savior of the soil of the Palliser Triangle, it was a reliable cash crop for hundreds of farmers in the years that followed the drouth. And it was this grass, millions of pounds of it, which the PFRA used to reseed more than 260,000 acres of once wind-blown land within the Palliser Triangle between 1937 and 1941. The AIA members themselves were able eventually to get 50,000 acres of land into production of seed which they could use to reclaim their own once-marginal wheatland. And not only the marginal land of the Palliser Triangle. When Dr. Kirk later embarked on an eight-year appointment with FAO as chief of the plant production branch his experience with highly adaptable crops like crested wheat and other grasses and legumes found application in many under-developed countries. It only went to show what could happen when a dedicated scientist fell in love with a blade of grass.

G.D. Matthews said:

Dr. Niels Hansen was professor of horticulture at the University of South Dakota when he went to Russia and brought back the crested wheat grass seed that was the foundation for all our developments. After he retired in 1937 he was retained as professor emeritus and it was in this capacity that he heard about what we were doing and came up to see for himself.

I picked him up in Saskatoon and drove him out to see the way crested wheat was growing on our new Community Pastures. He was absolutely goggle-eyed as I drove him past mile after mile of crested wheat pastures. He just couldn't believe what we had done. When he went back to the States he wrote an article for The Country Gentleman *on the world's biggest Community Pasture that covered over a million acres in Canada.*

We spent the rest of the summer answering letters from farmers all over the United States wanting to know how we had done it and all the details.

CHAPTER SEVEN

Birth Pangs of the PFRA

etting the Prairie Farm Rehabilitation Act onto the statute books was easily done in the winter of 1935. The Liberal members of the House of Commons usually were eager to impugn the motives of the Bennett Administration on any money bill for they regarded all proposed new expenditures by the Government as part of a public works pork barrel devised to win the next election. But on the vote to set up the PFRA the Liberals were fulsomely approving, for, if there were to be any political dividends from the legislation, they wanted to be sure to collect everything that came their way. Yet while the bill sailed through the House of Commons, translating the law into action turned out to be an adventure in frustration undreamed of by any of the sponsors of the legislation.

Hon. Robert Weir could have been under no illusion that the rehabilitation of prairie agriculture could be achieved easily or quickly. As a Saskatchewan farmer first and Tory Minister of Agriculture second, he was as familiar with the nature of the prairie crisis as anyone. Despite the urgency of the situation, however, it is doubtful if any kind of a gigantic crash program could have been pushed through the House of Commons, even if anyone had been able to devise such a program. The Commons was becoming restive with the seemingly never-ending appeals from Saskatchewan for assistance. Not many took time to study the situation, and the widespread, if superficial impression was that Saskatchewan was a rat-hole down which millions of dollars taken from eastern taxpayers were being dumped. Anything that resembled a crash program, moreover, would have set off the Liberals in full cry, baying charges that the Tories were trying to buy their way back into power in the impending election.

In the establishment of the PFRA all the emphasis was on the individual farmer and the provision of individual assistance to help him solve his problems. The PFRA was to *help* farmers to control soil drifting on their land, *help* them to construct dugouts to catch the spring run-off waters for their livestock, gardens and household use, *help* them to build stock-watering dams, *help* them to regrass their land and even, on occasion, *help* them to move to more suitable land. Viewed objectively, the PFRA might have appeared more like an educational program than a great crusade to save the whole of the Palliser Triangle from what appeared to be inevitable destruction. Perhaps it was designedly so for the measure went safely through the House without antagonizing the easterners or arousing the Grit politicians from the West. The long-range nature of the undertaking was underlined by the way it was to be financed. It was allocated $750,000 for the year 1935 and $1,000,000 a year for the next four years. Plans for spending the money were to be worked out by an advisory committee composed of representatives of just about everybody with a stake in prairie agriculture.

The first committee was made up as follows:

Dr. E.S. Archibald, director of the Dominion Experimental Farms system, chairman; Dr. E.S. Hopkins, Dominion Field Husbandman, Ottawa; J.R. Girvin, farmer, Medora, Man.; Olaf Nylund, farmer, Shaunavon, Sask.; Leonard Koole, farmer, Monarch, Alta.; P.C. Colquhoun, rancher, Maple Creek, Sask.; Rueben Gilchrist, rancher, Wild Horse, Alta.; F.J. Freer, representing the mortgage companies, Winnipeg; B.P. Alley, Canadian Bankers Association, Toronto; Dr. W.J. Black, Canadian National Railways, Montreal; E.W. Jones, Canadian Pacific Railway, Calgary; J.H. Willis, Government of Manitoba, Winnipeg; A.M. Shaw, Government of

Saskatchewan, Saskatoon; O.S. Longman, Government of Alberta, Edmonton.

As a board of directors composed of experts in every facet of the drouth problem, it was one which would have been hard to beat. Solving the drouth problem was no less important to the railways, banks and trust companies than it was to the farmers themselves or to the Provincial Governments who were primarily concerned with their care. But the person more important than all the rest put together was Edgar Archibald who spearheaded the campaign to bring the PFRA into existence and was the driving force that eventually got it functioning. The act was scarcely through the House before he was at work devising the skeleton of the organization he would need. It was no accident that this organization would be drawn overwhelmingly from the technically expert personnel of the Dominion Experimental Farms.

It was undoubtedly the Experimental Farms people who were responsible for knocking Hon. Robert Weir's big demonstration farm schemes on the head. One of the primary objectives of the PFRA, as Mr. Weir explained it, would be to show farmers how to combat the drouth by setting up demonstration farms on a township basis. PFRA would take over a township—23,040 acres—and put the latest farming methods to work to demonstrate to the farmers how they could survive and prosper. There would be one such township farm established in Manitoba, three in Saskatchewan and one in Alberta. The proposal was so completely impractical, so devoid of relationship to the job at hand, that it almost stirred up a revolution when it was sent out to the Experimental Farms. It was conveniently filed and forgotten.

The Experimental Farms suggested as an alternative the establishment of a system of district experimental sub-stations. The Government would select 30 or 40 successful farmers scattered thinly over the entire Palliser Triangle. It would subsidize these farmers to let the Experimental Farms experts plan their cropping systems and procedures for them. The purpose would be to experiment with new methods and equipment; and to demonstrate to the other farmers in the surrounding countryside how wind erosion could best be prevented and the maximum profit earned by dry-land farming. In effect the township plan was broken up into small pieces and scattered around to where it would do the most good. There had been a great many small demonstration plots and strips established on private farms in prior years. This would be an attempt to conduct the demonstrations on a farm-size scale, on farms of no less than 600 acres in area.

Within a matter of a very few weeks after the legislation was passed, the framework of the PFRA organization was worked out. It would function mainly in two divisions: water development and cultural practices. But regardless of its form, the heart of the PFRA was the Experimental Farms system during its formative years. In his organization of the PFRA, the first important practical step that Dr. Archibald took was to set up a "committee of Divisional Specialists" which held its first meeting at the Clinic Building in Swift Current on July 8, 1935. L.B. Thomson had been moved from Manyberries to Swift Current as superintendent of the Experimental Farm to succeed J.G. Taggart when the latter became Minister of Agriculture in Saskatchewan. He carried the ball to the new committee for Dr. Archibald, spelling out for its members how they and the committee were expected to function.

Each of the six members of the committee was an outstanding authority in his field. W.L. Jacobson, the irrigation specialist at the Lethbridge Experimental Station, was also secretary of the main PFRA water development committee; A.E. Palmer, the assistant superintendent at Lethbridge knew more about soil drifting than any other Canadian. Norman Ross, the superintendent of the Forestry Station at Indian Head, was an authority on tree planting on the Great Plains. Dr. S.E. Clarke was the expert on forage crops. Sidney Barnes, the field husbandman at Swift Current, was the expert in soil research and soil surveys. Farm implements were the special field of H.J. "Shorty" Kemp, the assistant superintendent at Swift Current.

The function of this committee was to be twofold. Its experts were to make their knowledge and advice available to all the Experimental Farms within the Palliser Triangle in areas in which problems in their specialities had developed. They were also expected to take the leadership in solving the problems that had arisen everywhere as a result of the drouth and blowing topsoil. For example, Palmer, who was elected chairman of the committee, would be responsible for getting strip farming extended to all soil erosion areas, for expanding the system of trash cover cultivation and for devising cover crops where trash cover could not be maintained. Dr. Clarke was expected to co-operate with the forage crop experiments then in progress on all stations, carry the information from the stations to the reclamation areas, to the individual farmers and co-ordinate the forage experimental work of all three Prairie Provinces. Kemp was to expand his experiments with farm machinery to discover the best methods of maintaining trash cover, preserving lumpy surfaces of plowed ground, seeding grasses, handling cover crops and harvesting hay. In between times they were expected to carry on their usual duties at their home bases. Small wonder that the minutes of the first meeting noted that the members were to keep the secretary advised of their movements, wherever possible.

Getting even the rudiments of the main PFRA organization together was a slow process in 1935. Fortunately the atmosphere of crisis that had blanketed the country in 1934 had lifted with the greatly improved moisture conditions that prevailed in 1935. Yet, though the atmosphere of crisis had lifted, it had not been completely dispelled. It was replaced, rather, with a feeling of uneasiness that perhaps things were much worse than anyone suspected. The rains came back in the spring of 1935. The crop got away to a good start. But the rains did not stop the dust from blowing and there were days in western Saskatchewan when it blew much harder after the rain than it had before.

It had been very generally assumed that there was nothing wrong with the country the rains would not cure. Well, it had rained and the blowing dust was still prevalent. Nevertheless, the federal election campaign, which monopolized public attention throughout the fall, tended also to divert interest from the urgency of the problem in the dust bowl. The PFRA became established in Medicine Hat with Ben Russell as chief consulting engineer and its various committees hammered out a program. It would proceed at once with the construction of stock-watering dams and garden-watering dugouts on individual farms within the dust bowl area. It would launch a counterattack on the blowing soil.

The ink was barely dry on the plans, however, before the embryo organization was in trouble. It was flooded with requests from farmers for stock-watering dams and farm dugouts. The digging of dugouts in family farms to trap run-off water in the spring for household use and garden irrigation had been started by the Government of Saskatchewan in 1933. Its Water Resources Branch had supervised the work of surveying and laying out the dugouts, but with only half a dozen crews to send into the field the work had fallen far behind in the branch. Thousands of inquiries came in, and a few hundred jobs were completed. When the PFRA came into existence the farmers bombarded it with applications, but it had neither the staff to process the requests nor the people to supervise them. The province turned its engineering and surveying crews over to PFRA and a stepped-up campaign got under way. PFRA agreed to help pay the cost of digging the dams with a subsidy of three cents a yard, up to a limit of $75, to finance the excavation. The theory was that the $75 would cover the out-of-pocket expenses of the farmer to the extent that he brought in outside help for the project. Unhappily, the PFRA struck a second snag immediately. Priority was given to farmers in the driest parts of the drouth area. These were the farmers who were least able to do the work. Because of the chronic shortage of feed, the farm horses were too badly out of condition to be able to do a hard day's work. The dugouts had to be long, wide and deep—150 feet long, 60 feet wide and 12 to 14 feet deep—to catch enough water to last a year and overcome evaporation. The best-conditioned team of horses in Saskatchewan driven by a well-conditioned farmer, would have been hard put to get that job done. The bonedry subsoil would have required a lot of heavy pick and shovel work to loosen the soil. Moreover, to excavate, even farmers with horses or big enough tractors had to have something to hitch onto and the dump-scoops or Fresnoes were few and far between. The wonder was not that they only managed to get 49 dugouts finished in 1935. It was that 49 farmers had been able to complete the job with the dearth of equipment that was available.

The original dugout building program was indicative of the gulf that separated the thinking of Eastern Canada from the reality of the crisis within the Palliser Triangle. There was still an idea abroad that the problem could be solved by an elaborate, forced draft sort of self-help campaign. The grandiose scheme of the township demonstration farms was based on the assumption that if the farmers knew what to do about the dust storms they would be perfectly capable of taking the necessary action. If the farmer would get to work on the excavating the Government would tell him where to dig and give him a three-cent-a-cubic-yard subsidy to do the digging.

The problems that arose in connection with reclamation were far more complicated, and complicated in a way that was to bedevil the organization for the next two years. In southwestern Manitoba the soil was drifting badly in the Melita district over an area of several thousand acres. It was the type of drifting which the PFRA was established to control, and it was on land that would require extensive rehabilitation before it would be safe to farm again. The PFRA tried to get permission from the owners to take over the blowing farms and turn them into a reclamation project. The owners had long since abandoned the farms, but would give no assurance they would not move back and break the soil up again as soon as the soil blowing had been stopped.

Eventually PFRA was able to get control of 1200 acres and it became its first Reclamation Project, getting under way the following year. North of Regina, in the badly blowing Craik area, W.H. Gibson of the Indian Head Station was able to get control of 1,000 acres which he seeded to barley. It failed to catch, but in the fall of 1936 he seeded it to fall rye, which did catch and he was able to cut it the following spring and leave the stubble to hold the land. A start was made on two other Reclamation Projects in the Cadillac-Kincaid dust bowl, but little progress was made in either place.

In southeastern Alberta, the PFRA got off on the wrong foot in another direction. One of the major categories of water development was to be the damming of small streams as stock-watering reservoirs. The first project undertaken was on the Wildhorse creek near the United States border. The creek was dammed but when the snow melted the following spring the flood carried out the dam. It was rebuilt in 1936, went out again and was then abandoned for good. In one of the truly arid spots of Alberta there had not been enough water in Wildhorse creek to dampen the soil when the dam was being built. Thus it could not be compacted sufficiently to resist the pressure of the water when it came. As a dam, the Wildhorse project was a washout, but as a legal precedent it was important to Canada. The construction of the dam was approved by the International Joint Commission on the principle that the country in which a river rises has a right to control the river within its territory. This principle was enunciated by the United States in justification of construction of irrigation works on a Montana river flowing into Alberta. The Wildhorse dam confirmed it and it was later to be used against the Americans with effect by General A.G.L. McNaughton in connection with the Canadian legal position on the Columbia River.

In the fall of 1934, the Saskatchewan Legislature enacted the Land Utilization Act which was almost identical with legislation passed in Alberta in 1926. It gave the province power to withdraw land from cultivation and bring it under the control of the Government. The Government immediately instructed its municipalities to take inventories of the lands within their borders to determine which areas should be removed from cultivation. Saskatchewan thus had put itself in a position where it could legally take control over its problem land. But even in 1935 there was no clear-cut idea abroad as to what would have to be done with the badlands once the soil drifting was stopped.

Advice was not hard to come by. Putting it back to grass, was a most popular nostrum. But as Gordon Taggart pointed out to a meeting of the PFRA advisory committee, getting grass to grow in the Palliser Triangle was a most difficult accomplishment. He cited experiments over an 11-year period where germination had occurred only three times. There were those who urged the farmers to get out of grain and into livestock. But it had been demonstrated time without number that livestock producers fared worse than straight grain farmers during much of the dust bowl era. Nevertheless, some solution to the agricultural problem had to be found that would not completely depopulate the country. In the conversations that took place more and more consideration was given to the idea of turning the reclaimed badlands, if and when they were reclaimed, into emergency feed-producing land for the livestock industry. It was out of these conversations that the idea evolved of establishing Community Pastures somewhat similar to the one the province had established on the famous old Matador Ranch.

While the preliminary organization and planning were going on the federal election campaign ran its course and when the Liberals took over Hon. J.G. Gardiner resigned as Premier of Saskatchewan and became Federal Minister of Agriculture. The PFRA became his main concern. One of his first acts was to bring in John Vallance, who had lost his Commons seat in the Kindersley constituency in the 1935 election, as director of rehabilitation. Vallance knew Saskatchewan like the back of his hand. He did a tremendous amount of work as contact man with the farmers and helped to get the new organization staffed and in business. Mr. Gardiner, during the next year, spent almost as much time in

Saskatchewan as he did in Ottawa, and was in fact on a tour of the dust bowl in July 1936 when the heat wave was at its worst. It was as a result of this tour that the dugout building program was revamped to make it more workable. Mr. Gardiner later explained it to the House of Commons in these terms:

"We were trying to persuade the people in that area to dig dugouts in order to have water, and when I went there I found very few of these dugouts being made. The leader of the opposition said that when he went and viewed that country last year it created in his mind a depressed feeling. The Hon. Member for Rosetown-Biggar (Mr. Coldwell) has made a similar statement. I must say that when I went and looked at it in the first week of July last year, having gone over the area at the same time of the year for the past five or six years, it created an even more depressed feeling in my own mind. And I began to wonder just why those people would stay there year after year and face those conditions continuously. And the only answer I could get was the answer that occurred to myself, that it was the experience between the nineties and the present time that induced them to believe that they were doing a service to themselves and the country by remaining there. When I went to an individual farmer and suggested that a solution to his problem was to dig a dugout to catch the spring run-off water so he would have a water supply for his cattle, he said:

"'You show me a spot 60 feet long and 40 feet wide and tell me to take a team of horses I have no oats to feed and a scraper and dig a hole 12 feet deep, and say you will give me 3 cents a yard for every yard of earth I dig!'

"When the farmer made that statement to me I realized the thought that would have run through my mind as a farmer if the proposal had been put up to me. If I worked every day of the year from beginning to end it would have been difficult to dig that hole. If I worked at it only on such time as I could spare from farming I would not have been able to dig it at all.

"At a meeting I held I called attention to an experience I had had in Ontario—when farmers want to thresh a crop they get about a dozen of the neighbors in and spend a day threshing that crop; then they go to another neighbor's and do the same thing. I asked why they didn't do the same thing here. The chairman replied:

"'I'll tell you what we will do, you make that 4½ cents a yard and that will cover half the cost of digging that hole. We will dig the top half and you will not have to pay us anything. Then you bring in a drag line and dig the bottom half and that 4½ cents will pay for it and we will dig those dugouts!'"

After the meeting the farmers went out and organized themselves into a committee and the PFRA agreed to just that kind of a program and it ultimately became the basis on which more than 14,000 dugouts were built during the next six years. Instead of individual farmers struggling to gouge out their own water holes with make-shift equipment and undernourished horses, a new service industry developed. Small contractors, farmers in some cases, acquired drag lines and moved into communities where half a dozen dugouts were on order. They could do the job for six farmers in a matter of days when it would have taken individual farmers months to dig their own dugouts. The subsidy which would have gone to the farmer covered the cost of the completed job.

It was out of the meeting-attending, the conferences and the brainstorming through the heat of the summer of 1936 that he was eventually led to the conclusion that the PFRA had to be widened, its sights raised and its goals extended to include not only Community Pastures building on a gigantic scale, but the Federal Government also, through PFRA, would have to come in and take over the reclaiming of perhaps 2 million acres of ruined farm land in Alberta, Saskatchewan and Manitoba. It was to make this possible and give PFRA a third dimension—land use on top of water development and cultural practices—that Gardiner introduced his amendments to the Prairie Farm Rehabilitation Act in 1937. The disaster had gone far beyond anything that could be cured simply by rehabilitating the individual farms. It was the country itself that was being destroyed.

But all this was to come later. What was required mainly in 1936 was vigorous and constructive action to halt the blowing dust, for soil erosion had come back worse than ever after the 1935 respite. The groundwork for this campaign had been laid in 1935 by the Committee of Divisional Specialists. The committee met frequently trying to devise practical steps which could be taken, first to stop the blowing dust, and then to get the land back into production.

Stopping the blow was perhaps the least of their problems. Measures to prevent wind erosion had been perfected in both Lethbridge and Swift Current. Because of the strong winds in southern Alberta, wind erosion there had been a far more serious problem much earlier than in Saskatchewan. At the time Saskatchewan was setting up its commission to investigate drouth conditions in 1918, the Board of Trade in Lethbridge brought William M. Jardine to town to a symposium on wind erosion. Mr. Jardine was an outstanding American authority on dry-land farming and later became President Herbert Hoover's Secretary of Agriculture.

Mr. Jardine explained to the farmers of southern Alberta how the farmers in Kansas and Nebraska had used listing shovels to prevent soil drifting. The listers were foot-wide, heavy V-shaped blades which were attached to the arms of duckfoot cultivators, or to specially designed machines. The tools threw up large furrows which, when plowed crosswise to the wind, stopped the soil blowing. Alberta farmers on the light soil that was subject to blowing imported a number of listing machines and the Massey-Harris company laid in a large supply of listing shovels for attachment to its own cultivators. However with the turn into the 1920s the weather became damper in the Lethbridge area. Strip farming came in and it seemed for a time as if blowing soil was to become a memory. The listing machines were abandoned in the fence corners and the shovels gathered dust in the Massey-Harris warehouse.

Meanwhile the farmers on the land and the Lethbridge and Swift Current Experimental Farms had come up with enough information to make dry-land farming without wind erosion possible. Strip farming had been well developed, trash cultivation was being perfected and better tillage machines and methods were being devised. But it was not until 1935 when C.S. Noble developed and perfected his famous Noble blade that the answer to the problem was obtained. And so it was, when Palmer's committee met to exchange information and plan its line of action, the dust bowl was no longer an insoluble problem, in theory at least. The real conundrum was how to go about getting the job done. Both Lethbridge and Swift Current had the equipment and men to demonstrate to the farmers what they could do to save their farms. But these were only a dozen men and half a dozen machines and there were 250,000 acres of soil blowing across other millions of acres of once-fertile land. How to get the know-how from the Experimental Farms to the farmers on the land? And do it quickly, before the country was damaged beyond repair? There was an even greater problem—the lack of equipment in the hands of the farmers which would enable them to get the job done once they knew how. By 1935, the farming equipment of Western Canada was in a sorry state, worn out or broken down often beyond usefulness at all. Few of the farmers would have been able to buy the equipment needed even if they had known what to order.

It was "Shorty" Kemp who came up with the idea that broke the bottleneck. Everyone on the Experimental Farms had become aware, as the depression deepened, of the increasing inquiries flowing into the stations from the farms. Where it had once been difficult to interest the farmers in the results of the stations, they came now in increasing numbers looking for answers to their problems. In every district there was a farmer or two in contact with the stations and it was through these people that the stations were able to extend their contacts with the other farmers. Ottawa had already agreed to set up a network of district experimental sub-stations where local problems could be attacked on a farm-sized, as distinct from an experimental plot, basis. What about getting farmers together into groups either around these sub-stations or with the leading local farmers as spear-heads? Out of this idea came the Agricultural Improvement Associations. Within a matter of months 30 of them were organized in western Saskatchewan and eastern Alberta. For the next five years, the AIAs became the shock troops for the battle to contain and beat back the desert of the Palliser Triangle.

Organizing AIAs became a full-time job for a research officer at each Experimental Farm. In practice, the associations often organized themselves informally around local farm leaders. By 1937, there were 109 organizations in operation with 14,000 members. The numbers do not indicate the extent of the organization of the farmers that developed to fight the blowing soil. In almost all cases there was an unofficial membership that probably doubled the number of registered members.

When an attack was launched on a particular disaster area, a call would go out from the municipal office to the association members. They would round up their neighbors and head for the listing bee. There were times, many times, when more volunteers turned up than there was equipment for them to work with.

Probably never before were the farmers as receptive to anything as they were to the AIAs for they were desperate for help and guidance. Cliff Sherriff of Swift Current, who was assigned the task of organizing the AIAs, once arranged a field day at Cabri, in the heart of a badly blowing region, and brought Palmer out as his main speaker. But before the meeting started, and it was one that jammed the school where it was held, a farmer arose to speak.

"Cliff Sheriff," he said, "I'd like to say something to you before we start. We aren't here today for social talk and we didn't come here just to visit with you. We're here to learn how to control soil drifting. We've got a problem and we want you to tell us how to fix it. If you can't do that, tell us right now and we'll go home. But if you've got any answers for us, if you can tell us anything that will help, we will stay with you till the cows come home!"

They stood and listened and asked questions for two and a half hours in the stifling heat of a Saskatchewan July. That was the attitude of the farmers of the dust bowl, men desperately thirsting for answers to the problems of survival on their land. It was this attitude that made communication easier and the AIA so effective an instrument. The AIA made it possible for meetings of farmers to be quickly organized to which the Experimental Farms scientists could take their equipment for demonstrations. In each group there would be half a dozen exceptionally capable farmers, the acknowledged leaders of their own localities, who could be made into overnight experts on soil drifting control. They became the team captains who organized the listing bees which became so widespread a feature of the struggle against the desert. Looking back on the struggle 30 years later, Dr. Archibald summed it up this way:

"It was really the farmers themselves who got the job done. I never ceased to be amazed at the wonderful co-operation we got from the western farmers in those years. All we had to do was ask and they would come from miles around to help. And it wasn't always simply a matter of us telling them what to do. They had ideas of their own, and they thought nothing of driving 15 or 20 miles to Swift Current or Lethbridge to see what "Ace" Palmer or L.B. Thomson thought of their ideas. Of course they had confidence in our people. The farmers knew that they were working as hard as it was humanly possible to solve their problems. But without the marvellous co-operation of the farmers everywhere we could have accomplished very little."

The ideas the farmers brought to Swift Current kept Grant Denike and his engineering assistants on a 16-hour day during those dust bowl summers. The conversion of vague ideas into farm equipment was a slow, laborious and often painful process. Getting an idea to work at all could take weeks and then evaluating the results could take years. What worked one place failed in another or like the one-way, equipment that seemed at first glance to be the answer to the problem turned out on test to have built-in defects that made it more dangerous than advantageous under certain conditions. The search for a practical one-way that would accommodate to the uneven surfaces of Saskatchewan and work the heavy straw into the soil without burying the stubble became an endless obsession to the University of Saskatchewan engineering faculty as well as the Swift Current engineers. What made the search doubly frustrating was the fact that while the testing and evaluating of equipment could take years, the blowing soil kept emphasizing that time was running out for prairie agriculture.

While the AIAs were in the process of being organized Massey-Harris cleaned up its Lethbridge warehouse and came across the long-forgotten listing shovels. Palmer bought the entire 200 sets and distributed them far and wide through the new organizations. At the same time the country was scoured for the long-forgotten listers which were de-rusted and put back into working order. The Swift Current Station sent down to the States for more equipment and by the end of 1936 the PFRA had reached a point where it had almost enough equipment to start a major counterattack on the blowing soil. And it was just that, and almost only that, a special-purpose counterattack. There was no point preaching trash farming to the farmers whose land had long since blown bare of stubble and weeds. It was pointless to urge them to adopt cultural practices which would leave the stubble on the surface, when they had no stubble. The first task was to stop the soil from blowing away. Only then could anything be made to grow, and something had to be growing before it would be possible to keep things growing. If seed could be planted simultaneously with the listing and ridging of the fields, well and good. If not, then the first step must be taken alone for the destructive power of the wind had to be contained.

In 1936, no discernible lines of responsibility or authority divided the PFRA from the Experimental Farms. The latter became largely deserted as all the top people spent their time helping the farmers on the land with money supplied by the PFRA. L.B. Thomson at Swift Current became the driving force of the whole campaign. He was everywhere at once, urging his people to greater and greater effort. When they ran out of equipment they adapted what was available to their needs. Old moldboard plows were resurrected. The moldboard was removed and the blade used to gouge deep furrows in the soil. Alternate discs were removed from one-ways and the machine was converted to a lister. Sometimes seed boxes were attached to the listers and the bottoms of the furrows were seeded to fall rye or to grass. Even the seeders themselves were converted into listers by removing two out of three discs and angling the draw.

Through the AIAs, great listing bees were organized; when one farmer's field was stabilized the organized farmers moved onto another. When they ran out of gas, Thomson got them some more, enough to finish the job. When they ran out of seed, he found them more seed. When they ran out of energy he found ways of encouraging even greater effort. Certainly greater effort was needed more in some places than in others. There were many areas where the topsoil had been replaced by great sand dunes which defied the listers. This land had to be gone over again and again. On the other hand, it was quickly discovered in some places it was not necessary to list an entire field in order to stop the soil blowing. On such land it was often only necessary to make a couple of passes up and down the windward side of the field in order to settle down the topsoil.

When they had time to assess their results that fall, Palmer estimated that the Massey-Harris listers he had sent out from Lethbridge, plus the work done by the Lethbridge and Swift Current Farms staffs with their own equipment, had settled the soil on 100,000 acres. Yet compared with the land that was blowing that year, and would blow again in 1937, it could only be a beginning. There were too many badly blowing areas too remote from the Experimental Farms for any broad-fronted campaign to be mounted. It was more a matter of locating the very worst of many bad areas and concentrating on them, areas like Melita, Kisbey, Estevan, Ardath, Vanguard, Canuck, Craik, Cadillac, etc.

Yet desperate as conditions became in 1936, the work of the people primarily responsible for getting the campaign launched became increasingly complicated. Thus when L.B. Thomson took some emergency measures south of Moose Jaw late in 1935, a member of the Legislature accused him of destroying land not saving it, and when the soil in another area drifted in the roads in the spring of 1936, the Highways Department blamed the drifting on Thomson and the PFRA. These, however, were inconsequential irritations compared with the handicap of not being able to overcome some of the legal obstacles that beset their paths.

Perhaps the most vexing of all problems was caused by the wind erosion on land that had been abandoned by the settlers but whose title was still in private hands. The Government of Saskatchewan had power to take over abandoned land from the municipalities. But when the land was owned by absentee landlords or mortgage companies, no government had any authority to do anything about the soil that was blowing on it. In Alberta, the Legislature had passed a law making it an offense to permit land to blow, but, as dubious an instrument as that might have been, it did not exist in Saskatchewan.

The PFRA had no authority to spend public money on private land without consent of the owners. Getting such consent could take as much as a year or two. Much of this land could have been seized by the municipalities for non-payment of taxes, even that land whose titles had been taken over by mortgage companies. Some mortgagers followed the practice of allowing tax arrears to pile up to a point in time just short of the tax sale deadline. Their hope was that they would eventually find a buyer who might assume the liability for back taxes. While they waited, they rented out the land to whomever would try to put a crop in. There were farms in the dust bowl on which a succession of farm families had gone broke.

Even the good farms fell behind in taxes and there was a universal disinclination on the part of municipalities to take over land for tax arrears. To do so would set the law of diminishing returns in motion. The more land the municipality owned the less money would be collectible to pay for community services. As long as the land was up for grabs, somebody might take it over, get a crop and clear up the tax indebtedness. Inasmuch as it was producing no revenue anyway, whether on or off the tax rolls, it might just as well be left on the rolls. Moreover, if the municipalities did take title to the abandoned farms they would at once face demands that they take action to stop the soil from blowing on them. Most municipalities had enough trouble already without buying more on that score.

In one aspect, the creation of the PFRA became an embarrassment to the Experimental Farms experts because it forced them to completely recast their thought processes. For five years their Experimental Farms had been starved for money and their own salaries had been cut. The economy wave that began in 1930 had permanently settled over their lives. They became conditioned to thinking twice, thrice or even four times before asking for money to spend. Then, out of nowhere came a fund of $750,000 for the first year and $1,000,000 a year thereafter which they were required to spend on reclamation work on the prairies. The money was hardly voted before the urging started for them to get on with the job of spending it.

There can be no doubt that the Bennett Government hoped, as all governments have always hoped, that their largess would enhance their stature in the eyes of the electors. The Bennett Government, in the summer of 1935, could have done with a good deal of stature enhancing. Unfortunately, nobody in the Government, or out of it, appreciated the magnitude of the organizing job that had to be done before the money could start flowing into circulation. In fact, it was well into the mid-summer of 1938 before PFRA was shaken down into an operative organizational form. The one man whose mind seemed to adjust more quickly to the new conditions than anyone else's was L.B. Thomson. To his field lieutenants, Grant Denike, P.J. Janzen, Kemp, Sheriff and many others, Thomson had a clincher for every argument:

"Look. You go out and get the job done. It has to be done and that's that. I'll find the money, some place. We'll get the work done and I'll find some way to pay for it."

For people whose whole careers had been spent in doing everything through the proper channels and in the proper way, Thomson's disregard for red tape was far from contagious. To some, it must have seemed like taking their careers in their hands to follow Thomson's lead, but most of them gulped, got busy and hoped that everything would work out for the best.

An example of the problems that confronted Thomson was the shortage of grass seed that developed. The new crested wheat grass that Dr. L.E. Kirk had developed and Dr. S.E. Clarke had taken under his wing had become a vital instrument in the long-range struggle against drouth and blowing soil. There was far from enough to go around. Thomson found a good supply of crested wheat in the United States and bought tons of it. How was it to be distributed? If he had followed channels it would have had to be from Swift Current, to the Saskatchewan Government, to its relief agency, to the municipalities, to the local councillors, to the farmers. That was how all relief had to be handled. Thomson and Palmer worked out a system of distributing it directly to the farmers by mailing it out to the members of the AIAs in 10-pound bags. At that time nobody had any specific authority to go around organizing AIAs and still less to use the associations to deliver grass seed to the farmers. But in 1936 the PFRA got 500,000 pounds of grass seed distributed and into the ground where some of it, miraculously considering the conditions, found moisture and germinated.

Russell Sheppard said:

In my last year in high school, I came down with a tubercular bone infection and was hospitalized for a long time. When I got out of the hospital, I was not eligible for relief of any kind because I could not work and I was too old to be qualified as a dependent child. The solution to our problem was suggested by my uncle who proposed that I come out and live on the farm with them.

So I spent most of 1934 with my uncle and aunt. Unhappily, they had even less to eat than people on relief in Edmonton. We lived for most of that year on potatoes. The crop had been good and they had a great unsaleable surplus. So we had potatoes varied with eggs, varied with an occasional chicken that had stopped laying, and potatoes varied with potatoes. There must be a hundred ways of cooking potatoes and my aunt tried them all. Some of the leafy weeds made excellent greens and my aunt used to mix some of the spicy weeds in with the potatoes.

You would think, under such conditions, you'd get to hate potatoes, to lose your appetite at the mention of the word. But I never did and in fact I recovered my health that summer on an unbroken diet of potatoes, eggs and milk. We weren't the only ones who went short on food. All over eastern Alberta there were people living the same way. But the food we missed never did us much harm and it was only rarely that you ever met anybody who worried about his health.

Land blowing out of control produced black blizzards, which eroded the barren fields and destroyed the crops growing on better soil. *Courtesy Glenbow Archives/NA-2496-1*

Dunes drifted around deserted farm buildings and abandoned machinery as farm after ruined farm was left to the wind and a sea of sand and dirt. *Courtesy PFRA/7085*

The Cadillac reclamation area before regrassing. *Courtesy PFRA/25960*

On the move from Morse, SK, to Carrot River, SK, 1934. An estimated 247,000 people left the Prairies in the period 1931 to 1941. *Courtesy Saskatchewan Archives Board/R-A4287*

Many men simply jumped a freight train, their belongings on their backs, and left the Prairies during the Depression. *Courtesy Glenbow Archives/NC-6-129556*

Three shoemakers on arrival in Hudson Bay Junction drove 300 miles from southeast Saskatchewan. *Courtesy Saskatchewan Archives Board/R-A15459*

Bennett Buggy in the Montmartre district of Saskatchewan, circa 1930.
Courtesy Saskatchewan Archives Board/R-A19945

Many farmers had to rely on relief trains from the East to keep them alive.
The queue of horse-drawn wagons is waiting for the arrival of the relief
train. *Courtesy PFRA/22150*

Farm machinery lies half-buried in drifted soil. *Courtesy PFRA/13119*

Courtesy PFRA/22211

An early blade-type cultivator at the Lethbridge Research Station, circa 1933. *Courtesy PFRA/33652*

Farmers were offered a subsidy of three cents per yard to dig their own "dugouts." Hard, dry subsoil often made the job almost impossible. *Courtesy PFRA/4718*

A listing demonstration at an AIA meeting. AIA listing bees became important weapons in the fight against soil drifting. *Courtesy PFRA*

An early Community Pasture fencing party in central Saskatchewan. *Courtesy PFRA/4715*

A grass-seeding operation on an abandoned farm in southwest Saskatchewan. Grass was seeded directly into the weed cover. *Courtesy PFRA/7043*

Left to right: M.C. Smith, Dr. L.B. Thomson, G.N. Denike, and Dr. J.G. Taggart. *Courtesy Saskatchewan Archives Board/R-B9312*

CHAPTER EIGHT

The Fruit Fell from the Money Tree

hen the PFRA advisory committee got down to business in Regina on May 6, 1937, there was a new air of urgency to its proceedings. The near rainless fall and snowless winter of 1936-37 were punctuated by intermittent dust storms that turned what few snowdrifts there were from white to black. The spring run-off scarcely dampened the surface of the soil and the dust began to blow early, strongly and frequently. When Dr. E.S. Archibald arose to review the events of the previous year his report was far from exuberant. It was now two years since his colleagues had hatched the idea of a Prairie Farm Rehabilitation Administration for the Hon. Robert Weir and the Conservative Government. At the end of two years the PFRA was still struggling to be born, although those who were seeking to hasten its birth were at least more fully aware of the extent and the complexity of the problem than they had ever been before. J.G. Gardiner and J.G. Taggart already knew the south country farm by farm for they had made safari after safari across it during 1936. L.B. Thomson and Dr. Archibald criss-crossed their paths and Jack Vallance, who was the nominal head of PFRA, was everywhere that summer.

Yet while the winds were unabating and the dust was blowing worse than ever in the spring of 1937, a look back on 1936 revealed that it had been a year of many notable accomplishments. A total of 43 district experimental substations had been established to demonstrate methods of soil drifting control and water conservation and some very satisfactory results had already been obtained. Three Reclamation Stations had been established. Thirty-two grass seed and seeding stations were in business, five tree-planting associations had been set up and 39 Agricultural Improvement Associations were in action. Rust, drouth, hydrometric and economic surveys were under way and the water development program was now in high gear. The small water-projects could report impressive results. Of the 5,900 applications that had come in, 2,506 had been approved of which 1,823 were actually completed. These included 1,014 farm dugouts, 668 stock-water dams and 141 individual irrigation schemes on the creeks and gullies of the three Prairie Provinces.

Two large irrigation projects were being completed at Val Marie and Eastend in southwest Saskatchewan. Storage reservoirs would provide water with which 100 farmers could irrigate 80 acres of hayland apiece and solve the permanent shortage of cattle feed that existed in that area. The ill-starred Wildhorse dam in southeastern Alberta, which had been built in 1935 and had gone out with the first flood of 1936, was rebuilt. When it failed to hold the second time, it was abandoned for good, but it taught the dam builders how not to build dams, and the lesson was well learned.

Behind all this was an immense amount of organizational work. The Experimental Farms at Lethbridge, Swift Current, Indian Head and Scott took on deserted looks as their research scientists were conscripted for field work among the farmers. The situation was most apparent at Swift Current, Scott, and Indian Head because these stations were the command posts for the whole Saskatchewan operation. By the late summer of 1936, the disappearance of the staff from Swift Current reached such a point that the Civil Service Commission in Ottawa became concerned. The paper work got far behind and the Commission sent an investigator out West to find out what everybody was working at. To him the Saskatchewan problem had nothing to do with wind, drouth or grasshoppers. The Civil Service "Saskatchewan problem" centred on the people not doing the work they had been hired to do and were paid to do. Research scientists were hired to research, not to go traipsing all over the country at government expense, making speeches and organizing farmers into anti-erosion task forces.

The Civil Service sleuth was fuming and fretting around the Swift Current Station one day when H.A. "Herb" Purdy blew in from parts unknown for additional supplies. Purdy was a holder of a master of science degree from the University of Saskatchewan who had been given a temporary appointment the previous year as a cereal researcher, at 36 cents an hour for a 55-hour week. He had barely got his experiments organized before L.B. Thomson fingered him for emergency field work. He was put to organizing AIAs, running summer camps and winter short courses, supervising erosion control crews, judging junior seed crops and helping to distribute emergency grass seed.

"But this," protested the investigator, "is extension work! This is work the Province should do, and must do! This is education! Education is a provincial responsibility! You have no business running around the country! There is no authorization for you to incur travelling expenses!"

Purdy's answer was the only answer the investigator ever got from anybody:

"You'll have to see L.B. Thomson about that. He is the officer in charge and I take my instructions from him."

This was the reply that was eventually to so frustrate the investigator and confound the investigation that the whole matter was quietly filed and forgotten. Thomson was the one who caught the vision of the PFRA idea best of all, and once he set out in pursuit of the vision not even the sacred rules of the Civil Service Commission were allowed to get in the way.

The truth was, of course, that it was only through the marshalling of all the manpower available on the Experimental Farms that a start on organizing the counterattack on the desert was possible at all. The Experimental Farms had been starved for funds for five years. Staffs had been cut, salaries were cut and capital budgets were drastically pared. For Thomson and the Experimental Farms scientists, the PFRA appropriation was manna from heaven. It could be used to buy the huge quantities of seed needed to tie down the topsoil once the blowing was stopped. It could be used to buy badly needed equipment for the Experimental Farms, equipment needed for emergency treatment of the rapidly multiplying critical areas. It could be used to build and equip a Soils Laboratory at Swift Current which Archibald and Taggart had been trying to obtain for almost a decade. In it a wind tunnel could be built to document scientifically the conclusion reached in the field studies set up by Sidney Barnes and W.S. Chepil. But in the beginning only L.B. Thomson fully appreciated the opportunities which the creation of PFRA was opening for his fellow scientists. He immediately saw, moreover, that PFRA funds would enable the Experimental Farms researchers to launch massive field tests all over the Palliser Triangle, to evaluate under farm conditions the theories they had grown on the experimental plots at the stations. The PFRA money could provide for tests of equipment, cultural practices and seed varieties. There was now money for equipment, for seed, and for the hiring of help. But as Asael Palmer has said:

"It took months for us to become acclimated to the new conditions after so many years of financial stringency. But Thomson twigged at once and could hardly contain himself."

In 1936, the PFRA spent a total of $228,046 on small water-projects and $434,000 on the larger schemes. But as sizeable portions of both sums were re-voted from the year before, the organization fell far short of spending the $1,000,000 which had been budgeted for it when the PFRA was established. This was surely the crowning irony of the depression—a government organization, in a period of financial famine, being unable to devise ways of spending the money appropriated to it! During the May conference, when the delegates became bogged down in fruitless discussion of irrelevancies, it was Dr. Archibald himself who brought the discussion down to earth again:

"We have 6,000,000 acres of land out of control and we are talking only about a few thousand. We have $2,000,000 waiting to be spent and the question we have to answer is: How do we spend it?"

It was far from an easy question to answer, even for a group as large or as representative as that gathered at Regina for that meeting. Mr. Gardiner had expanded Mr. Weir's original advisory board of 13 to more than 86. The PFRA was beginning to get an organization fleshed out. In addition to Vallance and Russell it had recruited W.L. Jacobson as its irrigation specialist, S.F. Arthur, G.A.D. Will and Mark Mann for senior administrative positions. Mr. Gardiner headed a group of 14 top officials from his own department. Saskatchewan sent a delegation, headed by Premier W.J. Patterson, which included four cabinet ministers, three deputies and half a dozen expert advisers. Alberta had three officials, headed by Hon. Lucien Maynard, the Minister of Municipal Affairs. Manitoba, whose Government was lukewarm toward the PFRA and stone cold toward Mr. Gardiner personally, sent only Hon. D.L. Campbell, the Minister of Agriculture. The representation of the railways, insurance and trust companies was expanded to include agricultural experts and representatives of more than a score of individual companies. There were nine representatives of the municipalities of the three provinces.

Obviously, here was a sounding board equal to the needs of the occasion, if that was what the organizers of the gathering thought they needed. But while getting control of the drifting topsoil was still the top priority of the PFRA the thinking of Gardiner, Taggart and Archibald was beginning to move much further afield. It was true, as Archibald had said, that concern seemed too concentrated on small problems when 6,000,000 acres were out of control. L.B. Thomson had explained that it had taken one of his crews 10 days to bring 400 acres in the Cadillac district under control. Someone had wondered out loud how long it would take, at that rate, to control 2,000,000 acres.

The minutes of the meeting do not record any answer to the question. Nevertheless the field work that had been started in earnest in 1936 indicated what the answer would be. As previously mentioned it was not a question of bringing every one of the 2,000,000 acres under control by working on each acre. Rather it was a matter of spot-treating critical areas within the large expanses of blowing soil. A couple of passes with listing equipment on a stretch that would encompass only 10 or 15 acres might stop the soil from blowing across 40, 50 or 60 acres. Soil blowing off a few knolls might unsettle several hundred acres. By concentrating on the main trouble spots the whole farm might be stabilized. There were, of course, many thousands of acres affected by wind erosion which would take concentrated work over many weeks, even months, to stabilize.

The problem was not what to do but rather it was one of knowing where to start; the task was so vast, so many-sided. It was one thing to hand the PFRA a couple of million dollars with which to rehabilitate the West, it was another very different thing to spend the money within the framework of the laws of property. Between the money, and the objective, government officials would have to move onto private land, stop the soil drifting, reseed it, and bring it back into production. Then what? Turn it back to the private owners to begin the cycle all over again? If not, was the Government to expropriate all the abandoned private land to take it permanently out of cultivation?

Instead of trying to rewrite the laws of property and find neatly packaged long-term solutions, the PFRA in the beginning made its rules up as it went along. It searched out the worst blowing, abandoned land scattered across the Palliser Triangle and, where possible, leased it from the owners for 25 cents an acre per year for five years. These leased areas were dubbed Reclamation Stations and task forces from the Experimental Farms moved in with government-owned machinery and equipment to stop the soil from blowing.

The process quickly transformed the Reclamation Stations into hurry-up experimental stations. It was not enough simply to stop the soil from drifting with the equipment the Experimental Farms had rounded up. It would have to be stopped with the kind of equipment that could be gathered up and put into operation on the farms. It cannot be emphasized too strongly that, by 1936, the farmers in the Palliser Triangle were worse off for equipment than for anything else. They got relief livestock feed, relief seed, relief fuel, relief food and relief clothing. But only in the most desperate circumstance could they get more than makeshift repairs for their equipment. If the nearest blacksmith could not fix it for a maximum cost of $2, the chances were that it went unfixed. Swift Current, Scott, Lethbridge and Indian Head each had half a dozen tractor-powered cultivating units with which to attack the worst blowing areas. But it could only be through their AIA, or individually by the farmers on their own farms, that the monumental problem of controlling erosion would be attacked on the millions of acres that were affected.

The first Reclamation Stations were established in 1935 on some of the worst drifting land within the Palliser Triangle, at Melita, Manitoba, and at Cadillac, Saskatchewan. On the Cadillac Station, for example, there were stretches where the land was drifted to a depth of four and five feet. South of Ponteix, it drifted so badly across Highway 13 that the worst drifted stretch of road was abandoned. Peter Janzen, who was in charge of the project, managed to get the whole section, highway and all, seeded to spring rye. After the crop came up the Highway Department was invited back to reopen the highway. Over much of Saskatchewan it was as common for farmers enroute to town to become trapped in soil drifts across the roads in summer as by snowdrifts in winter.

Perhaps more important than the Reclamation Stations, however, were the Experimental Farms Sub-stations which were set up during 1936. The plan was very simple. Farmers were asked to place their farms under the direction of the PFRA supervisor who would lay out a wind-proofing plan for them. In return for co-operation, the farmers were each paid $600.

The task of organizing the sub-stations fell to Herb Chester of the Lethbridge Farm. A great many sub-station contracts were signed in the early winter of 1936 so that when spring came the Experimental Farms crews could get onto the blowing land quickly. Once the soil was stopped blowing, field days were organized and the farmers from miles around were invited in to see what had been accomplished.

The sub-stations had one very great advantage over the Reclamation Stations when it came to demonstrating the effectiveness of erosion control measures. The sub-stations were still being farmed, though with great difficulty in face of the drouth and blowing soil. The Reclamation Stations, of course, were located on abandoned land on which nothing was growing. Thus the farmers who came to the sub-station demonstration could see conditions much like ones they had on their own farms and have the effectiveness of the recommendations demonstrated for them. It was while their interest was highest and their attention sharpest that Sherriff or Chester, or Purdy or Janzen moved in to get an Agricultural Improvement Association organized. And of course the best propagandist for the AIA was L.B. Thomson himself whose faith in the future of the Palliser Triangle never wavered. For Thomson, soil conservation was a religion that generated an unmatched missionary zeal.

A farm meeting without L.B. Thomson was almost unheard of, for he would drive all day and half the night to get to one. There was the day in July 1937 when Herb Purdy recalled getting a call from Thomson asking him to get a car and call for him at 4 o'clock the next morning. They drove from Swift Current to Regina, over the rough gravel highway and through the dust, for a PFRA meeting that lasted most of the day. Then they headed for a farm meeting in Meyronne in the heart of the southwestern dust bowl. They got there just before dark and Purdy ran the meeting till Thomson finished his supper. Then Thomson spoke while Purdy ate. They got back to Swift Current just before dawn with over 450 miles of gravel and dirt road travel behind them. No one could keep up with Thomson for long, but his non-stop effort was illustrative of the intensity of the personal drive which was so characteristic of the people who fought the dust and wind throughout the Dirty Thirties.

In their first offensive against the blowing soil, particularly on the Reclamation Stations, the Experimental Farms people tried everything and anything. They listed the blowing sand in the spring, summer, fall and winter and kept track of results. Sometimes they had to go over the same fields several times within a matter of days. They listed it over wide stretches and over narrow stretches with varying widths of unlisted strips in between. As has been noted previously, they tried modifications of every kind of cultural equipment that turned up. Between the ridged areas, and into the bottom of the furrows, they planted everything that might grow. They experimented with sudan grass, corn, sunflowers, wheat, oats, rye and once even tried growing hemp until the RCMP pointed out that hemp growing was illegal in Canada.

The value of such experimenting, of course, lay in the authority it gave the experimenters when they came to advise the farmers what was likely to work when their land had reached the disaster level of that in the Reclamation Stations. Nobody could have worse land, or worse blowing soil than was to be found on the Melita, Estevan, Cadillac, Kisbey and Aylesbury Reclamation Stations. By using every crop imaginable, every cultural practice imaginable, and every modification anyone could think of to all the available machinery, they quickly acquired the answers to the problems particularly relevant to the areas in which the Reclamation Stations were located. They could help the farmers through their AIA to tackle their own problems and back their suggestions with a solid body of fact. They could show the farmers how to modify and utilize their own equipment. That was what the campaign to control erosion had to rely on—the equipment the farmers had regardless of how badly worn it happened to be, and the efforts of the farmers themselves to save their farms.

Trying to bring the Cadillac desert area under control

taught the Swift Current team several lessons in a hurry. The first they learned from trial and error. It had been generally assumed that the best chance of getting something growing in the sand of the Cadillac area was to seed spring rye as early in the season as possible. In 1936 each time the land was seeded the wind either buried the seed or cut off the seedlings at the surface with a sand-blasting action. After each disaster they went back and reseeded it. Then P.J. Janzen decided to stand their accepted theories on their heads. There was usually a period in June when the wind stopped blowing for a while. Instead of rushing onto the fields in early spring, they waited until June, when the soil had warmed up and the wind had subsided for a while. If they seeded when the soil was warm and germination would be rapid, perhaps the crop would be able to advance sufficiently in the calm period to withstand the wind when it started to blow again. They tried it and it worked.

Having grown nothing for seven years, the Cadillac soil had some moisture reserves, as much as this sandy light soil ever could store up. That was enough to get the rye started. The ensuing heat and drouth quickly stunted its growth, but the winds were tamed in the area where the rye was growing. They were to discover, too, as their experiments continued, that spring rye had one tremendous advantage as a means of combatting soil erosion. It was prodigious in its production of volunteer plants. It reseeded itself, and often with better results than when the seed was drilled into the ground. Over a good part of the Cadillac project, the rye that was sewn in 1936 obtained a catch of sorts. It was allowed to ripen and reseed itself in 1937 and in the following year the grain was three feet high on land that had been blowing desert 24 months before. The work on the Reclamation Stations, however, was also marked by disappointment and misadventure. The soil blowing on the Mortlach project was sufficiently controlled in the fall of 1936 that a good catch of fall rye was obtained. Several hundred acres of greenery were too much of a temptation for the farmers in the district. They opened their gates and turned their famished cattle into the fields, nullifying the year's work.

Within a year after they had moved in, M.J. Tinline's crew from Brandon had the Melita project well in hand. The soil blowing was pretty well stopped in 1937 and the land was being put back into experimental crops as quickly as conditions allowed. W.H. Gibson's team from Indian Head had the soil at Aylesbury under partial control and the Kisbey project was in hand. Swift Current reported the Mortlach project going well even though slow progress was being made at Cadillac. Lethbridge had stopped the drifting at Youngstown and Hutton. Given sufficient equipment and supplies, there was confidence among the higher field command that they could neutralize the destructive force of the wind. But what next, after the dust storms stopped?

It was the "what next?" which concerned Gordon Taggart and the Saskatchewan Government and had been since before the PFRA was established. At the Regina conferences in 1937, Mr. Taggart came back to the question many times. True, the land could be reclaimed and restored to grass. But Saskatchewan as a great cattle-raising province was already having doubtful second thoughts about the worth of cattle raising in the south country. Already plans were far advanced to move out 100,000 head of cattle for which there would be no feed available. Since the drouth began, many millions of dollars had been spent on emergency livestock fodder programs; not in just one year but in almost every year. Huge quantities of hay had been moved in 1931 and again in 1933–34, and in 1936 the Government had subsidized the marketing of tens of thousands of head of starving cattle. Clearly the growing of feed for livestock would be essential if the people were to be sustained on the land. Unless its productivity could be restored, the wasteland of the Palliser Triangle would become a dead weight upon the economy of the entire area. The best use Taggart could suggest was for the Government to take over the land and convert it into Community Pastures for the people still surviving in the general vicinity.

The wholesale removal of the people from the south country could not be contemplated, Taggart insisted. Already, by 1936, more than 7,000 families had migrated to the north and many of them were worse off than they would have been had they stayed where they were. The Government had been forced to inaugurate a comprehensive relief and resettlement scheme to move many of these people for the second time. Obviously the submarginal lands had to be utilized. It was inevitable that some people would have to be moved. Some 200 or 300 families had already been moved to as far away as the Maritimes and British Columbia. But there was no future for a depopulated Saskatchewan. The Saskatchewan Government had asked the municipalities to make land inventories and turn whatever submarginal abandoned land there was back to the province.

Legislation to enable Saskatchewan to take over submarginal land had recently been enacted, and the Government was moving as quickly as possible to remove it permanently from cultivation. But there were serious difficulties. The municipalities were quite reluctant to have too much of their land declared submarginal for fear that it would destroy them. After the dust blowing was stopped, the task of recreating a viable agricultural community within the Palliser Triangle would remain. The steady drift of population out of the Palliser Triangle and out of Saskatchewan was already undermining the social organization of those who were left. The schools, roads and hospitals, rudimentary as they were, could not be adequately maintained by a steadily declining population.

Simply to return the wasteland to grass and go back gradually to a cattle economy would solve nothing for the municipalities. There was no future for them as ranching centres. The Government might keep the land out of grain production to prevent the recurrence of the dust bowl and lease it out to ranchers, but this would provide no tax revenue for the municipalities. And even if it was converted into Community Pastures for the benefit of the local residents, it held little attraction for the municipal officials. They could not see how they could attract more people to help share the tax load that way. And more people was the universal need of all the municipalities. In the end, however, it was as a straw at which they grasped for survival rather than as a panacea for their problems that the municipalities embraced the idea of Community Pastures in their midst. They could become, at very least, a primitive type of crop insurance. On them all the farmers who could run a few dozen head of cattle in the summer could obtain some cash income when their grain crops failed.

Gardiner and Taggart had discussed the "what next?" question many times during the visits of the former to Regina. During his first years as Dominion Minister of Agriculture, Gardiner spent almost as much time in Saskatchewan as he did in Ottawa. He probably had more information at his finger tips about conditions inside the Palliser Triangle than any other Canadian. His frequent on-the-spot investigations took him into southern Manitoba and Alberta as well as Saskatchewan. Gardiner's own farm near Lemberg was on the fringe of the Triangle and he had solved his stock-watering problem, in part, by eavestroughing his barns and diverting the downspouts into cisterns. Gardiner was a convinced believer in mixed farming and a practicing cattle feeder. Thus when the Saskatchewan Minister of Agriculture suggested the creation of Community Pastures in those areas where the wind erosion was worst and most extensive, he got a receptive hearing from the Dominion Minister of Agriculture. From the two ministers, the Community Pasture discussions spread out in all directions. By the spring of 1937, the idea had become very much like the weather, everybody was talking about it but nobody could figure out how it could be done. The Regina conferences in May and August did that.

The May conference instructed the PFRA to take a survey of possible Community Pasture sites in Saskatchewan and report back to the next meeting in August. A start had already been made in planning the assembling of land for reserve pastures and Community Pastures. In some areas the municipalities had actively pushed to turn abandoned land into feed banks. In others they had held back. But getting something organized, and immediately, in view of the impending critical shortage of both pasture and livestock feed, became imperative. So George Will was instructed to complete his survey with all possible dispatch. He found a baker's dozen of possible pastures, but there were vexing problems with most of them. There were 48 sections in the Mariposa Municipality that could be assembled into a pasture. It would carry 1,200 head of cattle for the 100 farmers in the surrounding district. But much of it was so badly drifted it would have to be fenced off and regrassed before it could be used.

The best immediate prospects for Community Pastures turned out to be in the Saskatoon area along the northern edge of the Palliser Triangle. Five locations were picked and the work of laying out the water holes and surveying the fence lines for the 30-section Dundurn pasture got started early in the summer of 1937 so that it would be available for pasture for 600 horses that winter. In the Usborne Municipality there was a block of 83 quarter sections that would pasture between 1,000 and 1,200 head of cattle for the 300 farmers in the area. All that would keep it from being organized was arranging to take over 30 quarter sections of privately owned land with it. As it turned out, the Usborne land was the medium of a crash program launched late that summer to provide a pasture that would carry 1,000 horses through the winter.

The Rural Municipality of Estevan petitioned the Government to establish two Community Pastures. One block contained 125 quarter sections and the other 46 quarters. There were 42 farmers inside these areas and surveys indicated that roughly a quarter of the land was unsuitable for grain growing. The operators inside the pastures would have to be moved out but unfortunately there was little land available onto which they could be moved, if they could be convinced they should move.

In the nearby Municipality of Coalfields, 85 sections of

land in the middle of the municipality had been designated marginal by the municipality but only 15 sections were in the hands of the Government. The balance was in the hands of private interests and negotiations with them would have to be completed before anything could be done. In central Saskatchewan things were more favorable and pastures capable of carrying 1,500 head of cattle in the Brokenshell Municipality and 1,200 head in the Laurier Municipality were found to be capable of being put into operation by the coming fall.

All but one of the pastures suggested in the Will report were eventually completed. However, before anything could happen, something had to be done to ensure that the Community Pastures and other projects undertaken with federal funds would become permanent establishments, that they would be operated efficiently and be used by the farmers of the locality. The first step in that direction had to be to sort out all the legal complexities of the problem. The setting out of adequate legal safeguards for the future of the Community Pastures was of utmost importance to Mr. Gardiner. If title was left in private hands the whole objective of the Community Pastures could be defeated if private interests decided to pull out of the scheme. Strong management would have to be provided to ensure the proper operation once the pastures were established, and before the project would reach maturity no one could guess how many millions of dollars of Federal Government money would have to be spent. Because the entire PFRA program would be staffed by the federal employees, both Gardiner and Dr. Archibald believed it essential to place the pastures under federal control. But leading the three Prairie Provinces over that hurdle proved to be a more than passing difficulty.

For the provinces to turn the land back to the Federal Government was unpalatable on two grounds. They had only recently acquired title to their natural resources, a title withheld by Ottawa from the date of their entry into Confederation in 1905 until 1929. To return to Ottawa the lands used to establish Community Pastures would be turning back the

clock. A much more satisfactory arrangement for the provinces would have been for Ottawa to pay to establish the
pastures and other works and turn the management over to
the provinces. This argument had gone on intermittently
almost from the time Gardiner and Taggart had launched
their first Community Pasture trial balloons. But by the
summer of 1937 the need to get something started had become so clamorous that Saskatchewan gave in. It agreed to
acquire the land required for Community Pastures and deed
it to the Dominion so that the PFRA could get on with the job
of putting the pastures together. Alberta, however, refused to
either deed or lease its land to the Dominion. Thus it stayed
out of the project completely though Manitoba eventually
came in with Saskatchewan.

There was a lot more to the land titles difficulties than the
willingness or unwillingness of various governments to co-operate. There was the disheartening discovery, during George
Will's investigations on the spot, that the submarginal land
was often scattered all over a municipality in quarter- and
half-section parcels. In order to put a Community Pasture
together a solid block of 10 or 15 sections was needed.
Interspersing the badly blowing land was often somewhat
better land on which farmers were still living. The Saskatchewan Land Utilization Board was gathering up all the abandoned and submarginal land it could, but it was having
difficulties putting sizeable spreads together. An example of
the "speckled" pattern in the best spread it had located was in
the Mariposa Municipality. There were 187 quarter sections of
submarginal land in two townships. Of this the municipality
had taken title to only 29 quarters. There were still 120 quarters
in tax sale, there were 22 quarters with the taxes paid up, the
Crown owned 16 quarters. Within this area there were only 14
resident farmers, of whom 6 owned their land, 5 were leasing
and 3 were simply squatting. Before a Community Pasture
could be established, title would have to be obtained for the
187 quarters and the residents convinced they should move
out. And how could all this be done when no one could say

with any certainty what a Community Pasture was and when and how it would be established?

Tempers frayed like collars in the stifling heat of that Regina August. Gardiner in particular seemed completely out of sorts. He was impatient with Provincial Governments who were unwilling to compel those in receipt of relief to co-operate with the Government in its effort to get its pasture and water projects into operation. He snapped at the Saskatchewan representatives for not cancelling a handful of grazing leases in the Frenchman River area where a few ranchers were holding up developments that would provide 30,000 man-days of labor for the population on relief there. A spokesman for the Land Utilization Board complained that the individual mortgage companies refused to negotiate. A spokesman for the mortgage companies said no one company could afford to deal unless it knew what its competitors were being offered. He criticized the Government for not doing a collective deal with all the mortgage and land companies. A representative of the municipalities complained that nobody was trying to sell the Community Pasture proposition to the municipalities and suggested a better publicity campaign. No one, said Gardiner, could give the projects publicity because it would trample on somebody else's toes.

There was no doubt that there was a great deal of confusion abroad, in the country as well as around the conference table in Regina. An army of employees of the Experimental Farms were out driving tractors on Reclamation Stations, organizing meetings, distributing seed and tillage accessories. The attention of the farmers everywhere was focussed on their efforts. But when the farmers themselves became interested in investigating the Community Pasture idea, the Experimental Farms people usually referred them to the PFRA office in Swift Current. Unhappily, the PFRA had no authority to negotiate for Community Pastures. That had to be done with the provincial authorities, up through the Department of Agriculture to the Land Utilization boards. And in Saskatchewan, the latter body was still not equipped to do anything except acquire title to land. The run-around was maze-like in a labyrinth.

However, when matters threatened to get out of hand in Regina, Dr. Archibald was able to intervene with the suggestion that some committees be appointed to work out solutions. The next day the committees were back with reports that were to lay the basis for the Community Pastures project along with an ambitious water development program. Certainly, before the Community Pastures program could become effective, some way had to be found of getting control of a great deal of the land that was still in private hands. Some of the farm families inside potential Community Pasture blocks had not had a crop for six or seven years. Each year they had obtained relief seed with which to put in their crops. The crop failed and they would be kept for the rest of the year on relief. Some of these people were still the theoretical owners of their farms, though they might be five or ten years in arrears in taxes. Should compulsion be exercised to force the people living on relief to co-operate in the establishment of Community Pastures? Everybody was for compulsion, but who wanted to do the compelling? Certainly not the municipal secretaries, the hardest working and most put upon officials in the country. There was, moreover, an almost universal lack of public sympathy in the West regarding foreclosures of any kind, for taxes as well as for non-payment of debts.

Relief families were not the only cause of difficulties. The mortgage companies who kept turning over tenants on submarginal lands also contributed. The idea of inviting so many representatives of the mortgage companies to Regina paid off in these discussions. For many, it was their first intimation that such problems existed. No one had ever connected their submarginal investments with submarginal farms, submarginal people and submarginal areas. It became clear very quickly that once the mortgage companies, the railways and the Hudson's Bay Company became acquainted with the nature of the problem of land ownership the PFRA would be able to count on co-operation from that side of the fence. It was the mortgage company representatives who suggested that exchanges might be made of privately owned land inside Community Pastures for municipally owned land outside the pastures, and that private owners might be prepared to lease the land to the PFRA for a 21-year period. The bankers' representatives urged the PFRA to get its Community Pasture plans in concrete shape so that a series of meetings to clear away obstacles could be arranged with government officials, banks and trust companies in Winnipeg, Regina and Edmonton. Obviously, there was no lack of willingness by the representatives of the banks and mortgage companies to help get the PFRA pastures into operation as quickly and as efficiently as possible.

Every aspect of Community Pasture establishment was examined and discussed at the August meeting, and eventually the meeting got around to definitions. What, in fact, was a "community" pasture and how were the pastures to operate? The farmers had been told generally what the PFRA Community Pasture program would be. A pasture would be established by taking over a great block of marginal land, fencing it, cross fencing it, digging water holes, building stock-watering dams, installing windmills and stocking it with the required number of bulls. But who was going to be able to use it? How many cattle could one farmer put into it? Who would hire and fire the pasture foreman and fence riders? Would it have a permanent staff or would the farmers who put cattle into it be required to do part of the work? Who would be responsible for calving, breeding, branding, castrating and dehorning?

As Mr. Gardiner told the meeting, a great many concrete answers would have to be provided, and policies for the operation of the pastures would have to be worked out long before they went into operation. L.B. Thomson, who had been in Montana investigating the organizational techniques of grazing associations, discovered there were no two alike. Mostly they tended to function under committees made up of the ranchers who used the pastures and the usual practice was to charge one fee that included monthly use, bull services, fence maintenance, etc.

But nowhere could Thomson or anyone else find an example of spectacular success which would touch the spark of enthusiasm to the tinder of necessity. Every pasture seemed to have problems of its own, the commonest of which was a lack of business-like operation and management. Committees seldom functioned the way they were expected to function. The willing horses had to carry most of the load and what was everybody's business was nobody's business, two cliches which Thomson heard again and again. The only way in which the new ventures could avoid the mistakes of the past was to get off on the right foot with a strong central control of the operation. This, of course, was essential for two very good reasons. The entry of the Government of Canada into the farming business, which in fact was what was to take place, created great political hazards. The whole nation, and particularly the anti-western politicians of Eastern Canada, would be forever peering over Mr. Gardiner's shoulder and breathing down his neck. Public money would have to be carefully expended, and a wary eye would have to be kept on vested interests which might become vocally unhappy with the existence of the Community Pastures. The second reason was perhaps more basic. Community Pastures would have to demonstrate to the surviving farmers in the areas in which they were located that it was worthwhile first to stay farming and second to take maximum advantage of the opportunities which the Community Pastures offered. The big advantage, of course, was that the farmers could convert to grain growing a good deal of the land they previously had to keep in pasture for livestock.

The fatal defect of land settlement policy within the Palliser Triangle had been to settle too many people on too little land. Quarter-section and half-section farms were simply too small to yield a profitable living to the settlers over any lengthy period of time. Part of the blame, of course, lay in horse-power farming. The more land a farmer had the more horses he needed; the more horses he had the more help he had to hire, and the greater the acreage he must have in pasture and feed. The Community Pastures, in a real sense, would enable the farmers to take an important step toward expanding their cultivated acreage in the direction of a more economic farm unit. In order to achieve maximum usage of the pastures immediately, the fees charged the farmers who used them would have to be set low enough to make them attractive.

The Government of Saskatchewan had a hand in two Community Pastures. The Matador Ranch was operated by the Government with fees sufficient to pay for running expenses and rebuild the fences at the end of 20 years. This worked out at 40 cents per head per month and $1.50 per head for bull service. The Department of Natural Resources also operated a pasture, charging 8 cents per head per month exclusive of operating and maintenance, which was taken care of by the users. For the PFRA pastures, deciding on the fees to be charged was akin to picking a number out of a hat. The number turned out to be 35 cents per head per month.

A committee composed of L.B. Thomson, O.S. Longman, Prof. J.R. Ellis, R.W. Neely, J.A. Rose, R.W. Hanham, G.A.D. Will and Jack Byers was set up to work out the rules and regulations that would govern the pastures. Their code of rules provided that all farmers who were land owners in the pasture area, or who had been moved out, or who lived in the vicinity determined by the carrying power of the pasture, would be eligible to use it. They would elect a Board of Directors who would advise the Government on matters of administration and fix the fees in conjunction with the Government. They would choose which beef breed would be used in the pastures.

The PFRA, however, would keep the operation of the pastures in its own control. Each pasture manager would be chosen by the Superintendent of Community Pastures, and would be a permanent government employee.

N.K. Neilson said:

We depended on the radio for everything. We had no electric power, of course, so our radios were battery sets. There were two sets of batteries. One was a storage battery like they had on cars or tractors. The other was four dry cells made into one. Radios were hard on batteries so when the battery ran out of juice, we scrounged an old car generator. Then we whittled a propeller out of a piece of 2" x 6" and attached it to the generator. The next step was to attach the generator to the top of a pole, and connect the lead wires to the battery. On a windy day that propeller whirled so fast it was just a blur and in a matter of three or four hours the battery would be fully charged.

The Great Hunger–
Livestock Branch

he late Joseph Stalin once remarked, during the
Second World War, that there was nothing so powerful as the logic of things. It was the logic of things
which continually drove the people who were struggling with
the desert in the Palliser Triangle to slash and bulldoze their
way through the legal underbrush to the heart of their problem. And each cut that was made through red tape and
precedent soon became a well-travelled path over which they
moved toward new natural and economic ambushes which
required new slashings and bulldozings. Thus the emergency
measures taken in 1931 and 1934 by the Conservative Government to overcome the livestock feed crisis became the settled
policy of the Liberal Government in 1936 and 1937. These
policies involved the shipping in of food and fodder for
people and livestock and the subsidizing of railway movement
out of the stricken areas of both. But the problem in 1937
suddenly had become so critical that the precedents previously established offered no hope for solution. As had
happened before, the emergencies came upon them so suddenly that there was no time for casual debate or the niceties
of parliamentary procedure.

In the first week of June the crop once again looked as if
the turn out of the drouth had been made at last. By the last
week of June even the most inexpert optimist had to write it

off as a total failure. When the blistering sun and abrasive winds produced the worst crop failure Saskatchewan had ever experienced in a matter of days there was no time for a special session of Parliament or democratic debate. There was barely time for the passage of orders in council and the signing of Governor General warrants for as many millions of dollars as would be needed.

It was the compulsion to deal with the temporary, periodically erupting crises that delayed the frontal assault on the long-range problems which were at the bottom of everything. Until the economic and natural viability could be restored to the Palliser Triangle, there would be dust storms, grasshopper plagues, sawfly, cutworm and rust infestations following one another with almost seasonal regularity. But treating the immediate crises became so time consuming that the long-range measures essential for permanent solutions tended to get shunted aside. Then, in the summer of 1937, the very magnitude of the disaster shook down all the problems—short range, medium range and long range—into one all-encompassing hopper. The logic of things as they were in Saskatchewan that summer provided the impetus the directors of the PFRA needed to find the way out of the legal entanglements that had stymied the establishment of the Community Pastures.

The ill-concealed impatience of Mr. Gardiner with the Regina discussions that summer was understandable. He had toured Saskatchewan and Alberta in the last week in June and watched the crop disappear before his eyes. Then he had gone back later with Hon. Norman Rogers, the Federal Minister of Labor, to inspect a country in which nothing grew for miles on end, where there was seldom a haystack to be seen, where the cattle bawled hungrily in pastures eaten down to the roots. An already well adjusted and efficient relief system would take care of all the needs of the destitute people, as it had done since the depression began. But in 1937 the big problem was not people but livestock.

To find out the magnitude of the problem, the Saskatchewan Government, at Gardiner's urging, organized an emergency census to count the livestock and come up with an estimate of the fodder shortage that faced the country. The survey revealed that to bring 1,440,000 head of cattle in the Palliser Triangle through the winter would require that at least 1,000,000 tons of hay be imported and distributed and a whole series of other emergency measures would have to be taken. To bring the farm horses through, it would be necessary to build a number of emergency pastures. The PFRA field staffs redoubled their efforts to find areas suitable for pastures, even though the directors were still arguing over the legal aspects of the problem. For Norman Rogers, the idea of building Community Pastures at least had this merit: In a country of complete devastation and unbroken stagnation, it would provide employment and some cash income for a near-destitute farm population. When the question of voting emergency finances came before the Federal Cabinet, Gardiner had a powerful ally at his side in the Minister of Labor.

In the livestock disaster in the making in the summer of 1937, Gardiner saw the final confirmation of the thesis he had been espousing for many years—there were far too many cattle on the farms in Saskatchewan. Until the land could be made to support the cattle population it was tragic lunacy for the farmers to try to keep so many. The economics were hopeless. At a time when cows might bring less than $15 a head, what was the point of paying $12 a ton freight for hay costing $7.50 a ton to give to farmers on relief to sustain the $15 cows over a single winter? There was no point, except that the farmers and the cows were there and the cows would die without winter feed.

The cows were there because the farmers during the depression had been listening to the advice of the experts who said that the solution of their problems lay in mixed farming. With the collapse of wheat prices, they were told they would be much better off with a few cows, pigs and chickens than relying only on wheat for their income. Such advice sounded so reasonable that a livestock population explosion developed. In the drouth area of Alberta, 490,000 head of cattle in 1931 increased to 620,000 in 1935, and in the dry belt of Saskatchewan the increase was from 726,000 in 1931 to 833,000 in 1935. All this took place at a time of record low livestock prices, and despite the fact that the Canadian Government had to provide $7,017,000 in relief feed for livestock in 1931–32 and almost $4,000,000 in 1934–35.

While more than three-fifths of the Palliser Triangle is in Saskatchewan and less than two-fifths is in Alberta, the proportion of the relief supplied to Saskatchewan was much larger. In most years the drouth in Alberta was confined largely to the southeastern regions where the big ranches and sparse population were located. Much of the increase in livestock numbers was on the ranches for the simple reason that the prices offered at the stockyards often barely covered the cost of freighting the animals to market. The ranchers were able to keep their steers at home and let them graze for another year while they waited for prices to improve, a process which resulted in overgrazed ranges and hungry cattle. But when farmers reached the point where they had no more feed, they had no such choice. Their cattle had to go to market. However, there was usually enough feed grown in Alberta outside the Triangle to meet the needs of most of Alberta. It was not until 1937 that the drouth really blanketed the Alberta side of the Palliser Triangle the way it covered Saskatchewan. During the winter of 1937–38 the Federal Government assumed the cost of providing direct relief for livestock within 300 municipalities in the two provinces at a cost of $20,000,000.

In the most critical years, the Federal Government had previously come to the aid of the provinces with both financial and fodder assistance. It bought and shipped in 141,000 tons of hay in 1931, over 100,000 tons in 1934–35 and 50,000 tons in 1936, mostly for Saskatchewan. These were the years in which drastic action had to be taken. In the years between, periodic local and regional shortages were quite common. At such times southern Saskatchewan farmers travelled north to bale straw from crops grown in the park belt and Alberta farmers went as far north as Edmonton for feed. Despite moderately severe feed shortages most of the time, the cattle population kept steadily increasing. Despite the Government assistance there was frequent disruption of the livestock trade by sudden large flows of starving cattle to market. This traffic not only helped to keep livestock prices depressed, it impeded the movement of higher quality animals through the packing plants. It was costing the packers more to kill and process the cattle than they could get for the meat so they simply refused to handle any more canners and cutters at any price. The Dominion Government stepped in with an emergency policy to solve the problem. It undertook to pay the farmers 1 cent a pound for their cattle and to pay the packers 1 cent a pound to do the butchering. The packers, therefore, got the cattle for nothing plus a penny a pound bonus to put the animals out of their misery.

A second step taken by the Government was to pay half of the freight to any Ontario farmers who would buy feeding stock on the Prairies and move the animals east. In 1936, this subsidy took care of about 35,000 head of cattle while the packers' subsidy got rid of another 19,000. That year the United States market was reopened and 100,000 head went south through the usual commercial channels. Government bonusing also got the export trade restarted to the United Kingdom.

When Messrs. Gardiner and Rogers made their 2,500-mile tour of the Palliser Triangle it became apparent at once that the country faced a crisis of historic proportions. Cattle numbers exceeded the number the country could feed in a normally dry year. There was nothing normally dry about 1937. By the last week of June, there was scarcely a blade of grass growing anywhere within the Palliser Triangle. Calculating how many tons of hay would have to be imported was a futile exercise. The 1,000,000 tons of hay that were needed might just as well have been 10,000,000 because it would not be available anyway, anywhere on the continent. There was a few thousand tons surplus in British Columbia and there had been a good crop in Minnesota and North Dakota. The agents of the Canadian Government went south of the line and bought all the hay that was available but it would be far from enough. The railways volunteered to move whatever feed the Government needed at half-price and the hay buyers turned to Eastern Canada to line up what supplies they could.

As summer edged toward fall, the shipments of canners and cutters to market swamped the abattoirs again. As Jack Byers put it, inelegantly but accurately, after a visit to the Canada Packers plant in Winnipeg:

"If this keeps up they'll be in blood and guts up to their hips next week!"

In 1936 the Federal Government had established a temporary cattle storage yard at Carberry, Manitoba, in an effort to achieve a more orderly flow of the distress cattle to market. In 1937, the flow reached such a volume that it quickly flooded the Carberry yards at a time when the Government was beginning to bring a new policy into effect. The new policy recognized that it would not be enough to take a few thousand head of distress livestock off the market; or even tens of thousands of head. The cattle population of the Palliser Triangle had to be reduced by hundreds of thousands and within a matter of a very few weeks. The alternative would be to condemn perhaps 300,000 cattle to death by starvation. There was no way in which sufficient quantities of feed could be found for them and transported to them. The crisis, moreover, had developed at the worst possible time. The big movement of prairie cattle to market comes normally in the fall months. Handling the normal 500,000 to 600,000 head of finished cattle taxed the capacity of the stockyards and abattoirs at the best of times. If another 300–400,000 head were pushed in on top of the normal flow the physical facilities would be strained far beyond capacity.

The first step taken by the Government was to place an arbitrary limit on the number of animals any farmer on relief would be allowed to keep over the winter. Farmers and ranchers who had the resources to buy their own feed were excluded from the scheme and could keep all they wanted to. Families of five on relief were allowed to keep up to four cows and nine horses. Larger families could keep an extra cow. But everyone who wanted the Government to supply the feed for their stock had to bring their livestock population to within those limits.

The announcement of this scheme spread havoc among the farm population and ranching industry for it was assumed at once that the movement of cattle to market in the numbers needed to achieve this reduction would destroy the price. Governments were accused of trying to denude Saskatchewan and Alberta of this livestock to avoid the cost of providing relief feed. The response was unfriendly but the fear of the farmers was somewhat relieved by two other developments. One was the announcement that the Federal Government would absorb all freight charges and pay the farmers the Winnipeg price for their cattle at point of shipment. Then to facilitate the handling of the out-flowing cattle, the Government set about building one of the world's greatest feed-lots and community pastures at Carberry, Manitoba.

Government agents went out to buy all the barbed wire and fence posts required to fence and cross-fence 130,000 acres of good grassland south of Carberry. Jack Byers, who had spent a lifetime raising cattle in Saskatchewan, and who was a former president of the Saskatchewan Stockgrowers and Dominion Livestock Commissioner, was placed in charge at Carberry. O.S. Freer was handed the job of organizing the assembly points for the cattle in Saskatchewan and Alberta. He also had the job of hiring and dispatching the Government experts who would grade the cattle when the farmers brought them to the assembly points. The canners and cutters that year were still being marketed under the previous arrangements, though the price to the farmer was increased to 1¼ cents a pound. All other classes were bought on grade.

Unhappily for Byers, the flow of cattle to market began to hit Carberry long before he had got his pens, holding yards or pastures properly fenced. So in the first weeks of the scheme many thousands of good feeder steers had to be sent directly to the packers for there was no room for them in Carberry. The job of fencing the huge Carberry pastures went on from dawn to dark. As quickly as the 50-man crews could string the fence around one pasture cattle would be turned into it. Nobody stopped to count the number of post-holes dug at Carberry that fall, or the miles of wire that were strung. The numbers would have been immense. In addition to the fences, crews of carpenters worked on double shifts to build the corrals, holding pens and chutes required to segregate the incoming cattle into the various grades. The mere task of sorting up to 2,000 cattle a day into stockers, feeders, butcher steers, good cows, canner cows, baloney bulls, etc., required a high order of skill, judgment and physical endurance.

In the beginning the establishment at Carberry had only two basic purposes. The first was to reduce the flow of the cattle to a volume which the packing plants could handle with efficiency. The overflow was to be diverted into the pastures until the movement from the farms slackened a little. Then the animals could be moved out of the pasture to keep a constant flow to the packers. The second objective was to use the grass reserve at Carberry to fleshen out some of the better grade of feeder steers that the farmers were being forced to liquidate to get their herds down to size.

It was not long before Jack Byers came up with a third and, to him, more important goal—to unhorse the packers and commission men who he was convinced were profiteering on the prices they were offering the Government for the cattle. Byers not only confessed to all the normal prairie farmer prejudices against the buying side of the livestock industry, he had a few special prejudices of his own. One was a life-long distrust and a cordial dislike of all commission men. At first the cattle in Carberry were disposed of by the tendered bid system. The commission agents came out, looked over the cattle and made an offer to buy what they wanted at a price the Government could accept or refuse. The umbrage that

Byers took at this system could only be described as wild Irish. He set about to confound the commission men and packers.

Without telling anyone, Byers built a huge system of pens into which the cattle could be carefully sorted for sale by auction. His next step was to hire a team of auctioneers to work in shifts. Then he sent agents far and wide to urge buyers to come to Carberry to get their beef needs at his auction sales. He even invited the packers and the commission agents. The Carberry pasture became the site of the biggest non-stop cattle auction Canada had ever seen and the reaction to it fluttered the political dove-cotes in Ottawa. The livestock men accused Gardiner of trying to drive them out of business, which was the first Gardiner knew of what was going on at Carberry. When he did find out, he backed Byers to the hilt and for the remainder of the operation, the livestock all moved out of the Carberry yards under an auctioneer's hammer.

Jack Byers's next brainstorm was vetoed by the Minister of Agriculture, however. At the tail end of the big run there was still a lot of grass left at Carberry and Byers proposed that a herd of the best animals that could be selected be wintered at Carberry and sold the following spring. The idea might have had more merit if the cattle had been coming off the ranges where they had learned to rough it from infancy. Instead they were farm cattle which had been accustomed to stand in the yard and wait for their owners to throw the feed to them. Gardiner's judgment was that such cattle could never stand roughing it through the bitter Manitoba winter.

In addition to the packers, eastern farmers were large patrons of the Carberry sales. They took their purchases home to Ontario, where, if they kept them on feed for three months, the Government refunded them half their freight costs. Under this half-freight policy, the Government moved 70,000 cattle through the Carberry yards to Ontario. Under its emergency purchasing policy it bought and sold another 90,000 head. Marketing through normal channels of trade increased substantially and more than 275,000 head were exported to the United States, more than double the exports for 1936. Jack Byers's auction sales system at Carberry enabled the whole Government cattle-buying program to be operated at a loss of only $430,000 or an average of about $3.80 a head. And it was all done without destroying the price structure for beef which, by that time, was slowly improving. Perhaps improving was too strong a word for what had happened. The farmers might then count on getting $25 up to even $30 for good steers on the farm, which was $25 or $30 more than they had been worth a couple of years before. But the weight of numbers, and the poor quality, half-starving animals still brought the average price for Palliser livestock down below the $20 level for 1937.

Despite the herculean effort that was made to reduce the cattle population, there would still have been a monumental disaster in the West that year without an unexpected assist from nature. The rains came back over millions of acres in western Saskatchewan and Alberta in the last half of July, long after all hope for any kind of crop had evaporated. Within a matter of days, most of eastern Alberta and western Saskatchewan turned the lushest green anybody could remember. The whole country was covered with a thick blanket of Russian thistle, from the seeds that had been collecting for half a decade. The farmers turned their cattle into the fields. They rushed out with haying equipment to put up the green thistle for winter feed. And not only to the fields; Professor J.W.G. MacEwan, who was head of the animal husbandry department at the University of Saskatchewan, got harvesting crews organized on the vacant lots in the city of Saskatoon. Through their efforts enough Russian thistle hay was put up to bring the university's fine experimental herd through the winter. Across the Triangle, Gardiner later estimated that the farmers had managed to harvest between 100,000 and 200,000 tons of Russian thistle hay. It wasn't much, as quality went. But it provided a little nourishment and some roughage and enabled the farmers to use to better advantage whatever low-grade grain the Government was able to make available.

During the winter of 1937-38, the governments were able to move in and distribute almost 400,000 tons of hay in Saskatchewan and Alberta, and individual farmers and ranchers brought another 70,000 tons. For sheer weight and numbers of cattle and fodder moved, it was the greatest operation of its kind ever undertaken in Canada, and it was carried through successfully. There were few cattle losses that winter directly as the result of famine. The thousands of calves that died in southern Alberta in late March 1938, following the winter hurricane, were the victims of the wind and snow, not hunger. The whole operation, moreover, was carried to success without the breath of scandal attached to it. Here and there, claims were made that people who were not entitled to it got free feed from the governments. But when these cases were investigated and the facts were dug out, little more than picayune errors of judgment were made to stick.

The emergency program undertaken to save the Palliser cattle population from extinction had another more permanent effect. It got the Community Pastures started. Without the emergency, another year at least would have been lost before the crossing of the t's and dotting of the i's could have been completed on all the legalities. After all, they were still drafting motions at the Regina meeting in August. They were good motions, which would go a long way toward breaking through the legal fog that had been so frustrating. But there would still have been parliamentary debates and inter-provincial conferences ad infinitum. The terrible emergency of 1937 gave everybody not only an excuse but a real justification to get out and get at it.

Archibald, Thomson and Taggart had all been convinced from almost the inception of the PFRA that something like a Community Pastures program would have to be devised. One of the first concrete steps taken in its first year by the PFRA was to set up a warehouse in Regina in which it started storing barbed wire and fence posts in anticipation of approval of Community Pastures. It even hired a small crew to build cattle squeezes that would one day be needed for inoculation, branding and castrating when the projects eventually got under way.

An immense amount of "getting ready" work was also undertaken on the Experimental Farms and in the fields. A new Soils Research Laboratory was built at Swift Current with PFRA money. It also financed new programs of soil surveys at the universities, bought erosion control equipment and distributed it to the Lethbridge, Swift Current, Indian Head, Scott and Brandon stations.

One of the factors which helped the desert-making force in nature to gather in the immense stretches of the Palliser Triangle was the lack of power on the farms. Nine-tenths of the farms within the Triangle were still dependent upon horses and the tractors then in use were iron wheeled and low powered. Once the technique of ridging the fields to stop the blowing had been developed, the job of making the ridges was often too much for the out-of-condition horses or wheeled tractors. If the farmers had been able to ridge the edges of their fields when the soil first started to blow, whole sections on the leeside of the ridges would have been held in check. But like the forest fires, the dust storms built their own gigantic momentum and it was this momentum that spread destruction far and wide. Then, even to have to plow deeply enough to work up a five- or ten-rod wind-and-dust-breaker strip was too much for the kind of power the average farmer had at his disposal.

Once the situation got out of hand and the topsoil was turned into drifting sand dunes, the most powerful wheeled tractors available sank to their hubs in the sand. The most important make-ready step the PFRA took was to buy two dozen Caterpillar tractors and distribute them to the Experimental Farms. The "cats" could ride across the surface of the ridges and pull the listing equipment. The Experimental Farms all rigged up lowboys which they could haul behind the big trucks, and they owned the only big trucks outside the cities. When new emergencies developed, as they did continually, they could move their equipment to the critical areas quickly. Once the soil blowing was stopped, the local farmers could be hired to seed between the ridged strips. Their horses had enough power to pull the Dempster seed drills which the PFRA also bought for the Experimental Farms.

Another important "getting ready" step was the arrangement made between the Dominion Department of Agriculture and the Department of Mines and Resources to borrow its fleet of airplanes to make an aerial survey of the Palliser Triangle and 20,000 square miles were photographed the first year. Printing and classifying the pictures was an immense task but the aerial survey provided the engineers with information on possible dam sites and water holes that might otherwise have taken many months to obtain. PFRA money also financed comprehensive soils surveys and land use investigations by the universities and provincial soils scientists. Economic investigations were started into the relationship of mortgage debt to farm failures. Small armies of provincial engineers moved across the Triangle surveying future stock-watering dams and water holes and bossing the construction of PFRA farm dugouts.

One of the oldest amenities projects of the prairies was given a massive shot in the arm. That was the tree-planting program centred around the Indian Head Forestry Station and the Morden Experimental Farm. Thomson had shown at Manyberries what could be done with irrigation to turn the stark farmsteads of the bald-headed Prairies into oases of beauty. Manyberries's buildings became hidden in quickly growing trees and its yards became lush orchards and gardens.

It was not enough, in Thomson's or Archibald's minds, to simply save the soils of the West. Life had to be made livable on the farms of the Triangle. The only fact that the West would not let them forget as they travelled the country together was the stark unattractiveness of the farm surroundings. No wonder people were deserting in the uncounted thousands. Living on the average farm even in years of good crops had little to recommend it. The answer as they saw it was beautification of farmyards with trees. Not trees to cure the blowing dust—there was ample evidence on 10,000 farms that trees themselves were the first casualties of the extreme drouth—but trees to encircle gardens which could be watered from the farm dugouts. They would get the dust blowing stopped, but that had to be followed by the improvements to the farmsteads that only trees could provide.

Even while the dust was still blowing in areas of almost total crop failure, gigantic new tree-planting projects were launched. It was no longer simply a matter of shipping out trees to the farmers to plant willy-nilly. The trees were taken out by government crews and the farmers were hired to plant them under direction. Nor was it confined to farmyards alone. Between Conquest and Rosetown, hundreds of miles of trees were planted in rows 30 rods apart. The farmers were hired to cultivate around them and protect them from weeds and the result was the growth of a vast tree farm in the midst of the arid prairie.

The "getting ready" process involved endless travel, endless planning and endless conversation, of which conversation was probably the most important. Wherever their paths crossed, the people from the Experimental Farms stopped to compare notes, problems and solutions. Already the first results from the work done on the Reclamation Stations at Aylesbury, Melita and Kisbey were beginning to appear and the success of the emergency measures taken was beyond all doubt. Agents of the Saskatchewan Government were in personal contact with the municipal officials to sell them on the wisdom of getting behind the Community Pastures idea, and they were making headway. On the Community Pastures front, by the summer of 1937, everybody was poised at the "Ready!", waiting for the signal to go.

However, even if by some miracle all the vague plans for the setting up of Community Pastures could have been realized overnight, little assistance would have been given to the solving of the main problem of 1937. In everybody's thinking, the essence of Community Pasture planning was to reclaim marginal land and turn it into pastures; land that was blowing, weed infested, abandoned and useless. There were vast stretches of such land between Boissevain and the Rockies, in 2,500-acre, 5,000-acre and 25,000-acre blocks. But instant fencing and cross-fencing of these blocks would not have converted them into instant pastures. This land was worse, in most cases, than the pastures the animals were already in. To have turned the hungry surplus cattle into such "pastures" would have condemned them to die of hunger and thirst.

Nevertheless, interspersed within the blocks of marginal land were some rather large pockets of good land that had been abandoned. It was on this land that attention focussed as possible winter pasture for the farm horses which would not be needed until spring. In these poor-land, good-land localities most of the farmers were on relief and had been for some years. So the federal ministers reasoned that, as they would be keeping the people anyway, they might as well try to get something in return for their money. That something could be Community Pastures built as make-work relief projects. Happily enough for once, money was no impediment to such an undertaking. There was far more than enough to finance the fence building in the PFRA's unspent appropriation. There was more money in the Federal Emergency Relief Fund established in June. There was even money enough for the pasture project in Mr. Rogers's own unemployment relief appropriation. The situation, surely, was without parallel in the history of Canadian Government financing!

How the accountants eventually sorted it all out does not matter. What does is the fact that someone in authority, probably Dr. Archibald or Gardiner, passed the word quietly in July of 1937 to get started building pasture fences and let the bookkeepers and lawyers sort out the accounting fine points and legal technicalities. Raymond Youngman, who had been hired on the year before as a squeeze-builder in the Regina warehouse, put aside his hammer and saw and took off for Watrous and Dundurn to get the fence building started. As quickly as the posts, wire and staples were obtained, crews were hired from the relief rolls and it was not long before money was again circulating in Kerrobert, Yellow Grass, Ormiston, Watrous, Dundurn, Radville, Hardy, Hitchcock and Bienfait. The fence-building farmers were paid 35 cents an hour, worked a 10-hour day and were so starved for work that they provided PFRA with its first public relations problem. A demand arose from those who were not hired that the work be spread around, that a limit be placed on the length of time any one man could hold a job. Except for a few key men needed as straw bosses, the work was indeed rationed and after a couple of weeks, crews were laid off and new crews hired.

On the fence building, everything was done the hard way. Tractor-mounted post hole-diggers had not yet been invented so the holes were dug with picks, shovels, bars and augers. And they built the best livestock fences ever seen in Canada. The posts were treated to last a couple of generations; the fences went up in 80-rod sections to maintain tightness and, instead of the usual three wires, five strands of wire were used. They were as calf-proof and cow-proof as any barbed wire fence could ever be made. As quickly as the cross-fence could be put up, crews from Scott, Swift Current and Indian Head moved in to reseed the wind-blown areas with spring rye or crested wheat grass. The fence building went on far into the winter for not even the bitter cold of Saskatchewan could chill the enthusiasm of the farmers for the Government's 35 cents an hour. During the fall and winter they dug in excess of 120,000 post holes and drove better than 600,000 staples to hold 5,000 miles of barbed wire.

One of the side effects of the 1937 emergency was the decision to establish at once a couple of emergency pastures in southwestern Saskatchewan. What had happened once would happen again and some foresighted planning was called for. By setting aside 150,000 acres of rangeland near Val Marie, a livestock food bank could be created to draw on during the next crop failure. It would also provide a place where many thousands of cattle could be given temporary pasture. All the attendant experts seemed committed to the theory of reserve pastures; but the idea barely survived the fencing at Val Marie. Once the pasture was there, the pressure to use it became irresistible.

At the very beginning, however, the administration drew a rude rejection from Alberta to its proposal that the latter turn over its submarginal land for the purpose of setting up Community Pastures. The new Social Credit Government of Premier William Aberhart had been angered mightily by Ottawa's disallowance of some of its legislation and was embroiled inwardly in embittering debate over Social Credit doctrine. It was in no mood to invite the Federal Government to come into Alberta to operate any Community Pastures on land it would be compelled to lease to Ottawa. Though the Alberta representatives took an active part in the PFRA meetings and were free with their suggestions and advice, they remained mere spectators for as long as they attended. Alberta, of course, welcomed the spending of federal funds on irrigation projects and stock-watering dams. Indeed much of the agitation for such developments as the St. Mary's River dam came from Alberta. But its opposition to federally operated Community Pastures remained adamant. Nevertheless, the Lethbridge Experimental Farm was as active as any in the crusade to stop the dust bowl in 1937, but its work was confined mainly to the immediate problem—getting something growing to stop the soil blowing without regard to the conversion of the land to permanent pastures. There was, indeed, very little practical difference between the anti-erosion campaign on the land marked for Community Pastures and on the other land.

In any event, nobody had much time during the last half of 1937 to think much about short-term versus long-term objectives. The big rains of late July had given the west country a chance to harness the wind. By this time the organization and indoctrination of more than 14,000 members of the Agricultural Improvement Associations network were well in hand. Indoctrination, indeed, was an instrument of organization. Farmers were attracted to meetings with movies and slides and became subjects of personal contact by the Experimental Farms personnel. The big rain brought a redoubling of effort both by the AIAs and the Experimental Farms personnel to get something planted into the Russian thistle. All the crested wheat grass seed that had been stored and bagged at Swift Current, Lethbridge, Scott and Indian Head was shipped out to the AIAs. More seed was imported to supplement what was now being grown locally. From the few hundred bushels that had been distributed to the farmers less than five years before, more than 500,000 pounds of seed were harvested in Saskatchewan and Alberta in 1937 before the drouth destroyed the grain crops. Every truck in working order that could be hired was pressed into service to move grass seed and rye out of the farms.

The Experimental Farms crews and the farmers themselves ran their seeders from dawn to dark. In the Scott area a new wrinkle was added to farming when Doug Matthews got his staff to rig up some headlights on their tractors so they could work all night. This innovation was quickly adopted by the other stations. It made it possible to get thousands of additional acres seeded to grass and fall and spring rye, and it helped spread the idea that the Experimental Farms directors had become mentally unbalanced by the dust and wind. The idea of seeding grass into weeds and expecting it to grow was crazy enough, but sneaking up on the weeds at night had to be just plain laughable!

And people laughed, and scoffed, and impugned motives. The kindest thing some of the doubters in Kerrobert had to say about the whole operation was that it was just a Liberal political dodge to enable the party to repay its supporters with some cash patronage. The grass wasn't expected to grow, they said, because the only thing wanted was a harvest of more votes for Jimmy Gardiner. In the Radville area, the scoffers outnumbered the believers by ten to one. But Roe Foster and his crew from Indian Head were able to get several thousand acres seeded to crested wheat grass in what would soon become a big Radville Community Pasture. Three years later every scoffing farmer in the district was mobilized to cut and thresh the bumper crop of grass seed that filled ten freight cars and overflowed into an abandoned school building. Though it perhaps did little good in 1937, the Experimental Farms all had potent arguments with which to counter the scoffing. One answer was to take the doubters to the plots sewn on the farms three and four years before, and to point to the grass that was growing where it had been seeded into the weeds. The other answer was the faith that the farmers were building up in the AIAs, faith that sprang mainly from the common touch of the experts who went out to talk to the farmers' meetings.

The Agricultural Improvement Associations were one of the good ideas that emerged from the dust bowl. They were successful because the people who went out from the Farms could give their advice in terms the farmers understood. They could do so because they had learned by doing. They were able to convince the leaders of each of the associations of the wisdom of their suggestions and once the farm leaders were convinced the rank and file usually fell into line. It took time and proof.

"It wasn't enough for us to go to a meeting and just tell the farmers to take out every second disc when they were seeding into weeds," G.D. Matthews recalled. "We had to show them how to do it. So instead of the usual extension bulletins written by specialists, we drew pictures and maps for them."

Perhaps the quality that brought the Government employees and the farmers closest together was the spreading recognition by the latter of the dedication of the former. The Scott Station, for example, distributed rain gauges over a wide area between the two Saskatchewan rivers. It was early recognized that one of the troubles the Palliser Triangle was having was rain at the wrong time, rather than a shortage of overall precipitation. So the Scott idea was to take quick advantage of summer and late spring showers. When the showers measured a half-inch, the gauge watchers were instructed to phone Scott at once and it would send out a fleet of trucks with spring rye to seed the ground while the moisture was there. Thousands of acres were seeded this way in 1936 and 1937 and some good catches were achieved. The only greenery to be seen in the Kerrobert area was on several thousand acres of rye growing inside the newly strung fences of the then-being-created Community Pastures. To the farmers in the area that term had not yet been defined, and the land on which the grain was growing was abandoned wasteland. With starving cattle at home the temptation was too much. Long before the rye was ready to cut, they invaded the pasture and began harvesting it for green feed. They were literally pulling it out by the roots when the Experimental Farm people discovered them. They could not be persuaded to desist until Doug Matthews himself came out to reason with them.

"Let it grow. Let it grow," Matthews pleaded. "We'll give it to you. It will be yours for the taking. But don't cut it till I tell you because we must leave the stubble on the surface so we can seed grass into it. We've got to have the stubble or the soil will blow again." It was hard advice to give farmers facing a winter without feed for their livestock. It was even harder for them to take; but they took it.

Trying to contain and beat back the encroaching desert became such a challenge to the personnel of the Experimental Farms that they were all soon spending more time on the road than travelling salesmen. They travelled to the AIA meetings by car, truck, farm wagon, sleigh, horseback and in the cabooses of the world's slowest freight trains. They came early and they stayed late for it was not uncommon for a farm meeting to start in the early afternoon and go on until midnight.

Though the fence crews were able to get almost 180,000 acres in 16 separate pastures enclosed in 1937, the real work of turning the fenced acres into effective pasture did not get started until the following year. The acreage enclosed in 1937 had a potential capacity for between 6,000 and 7,000 head of livestock. That, surely, was an eye-drop compared with the possible 500,000 cattle being carried through the winter on emergency relief feed after the forced exodus. The actual number of livestock that were carried in these pastures—mostly farm horses—did not exceed 3,000.

In any realistic sense, the forced draft fencing of Community Pastures did nothing to alleviate the fodder famine. But it did get the Community Pasture program started, and that was the main thing. That winter representatives from PFRA spent a good deal of time in the localities adjacent to the pastures getting the farmers organized into pasture associations, explaining the way in which the pastures would operate, drumming up enthusiasm for them and, above all, discussing what was to be done about the people who had been fenced off inside the pastures.

In almost every pasture there was a farmer or two located on some better land inside the area that was being fenced. It would obviously be better if the fenced-in farmers could be moved out. To get them out would require that another farm as good as the one he was on be found for them, and that they be given some incentive to move. Unhappily the authorities had not yet found a way of getting these farmers to move, either by threat or cajolery. The alternative to moving them out was to fence around their lands and down whatever road they used to get in and out of town. It meant, literally, that the farmers inside the pastures would be fenced out of the pastures, until such time as the policy makers could find a solution for the problem.

Before the fenced-in areas could become Community Pastures in fact an immense amount of work had to be done. The newly seeded areas had to be fenced off to protect the new grass from the cattle, if they got a catch of grass. And there were areas, particularly in the southeast, which had to be seeded again and again before the grass would grow. The Indian Head crews working in the southeast, which missed most of the rain, ran into problem after problem. Straw had to be spread on the soil to keep it from blowing then slow progress had been made in seeding because of the hardness of the ground. When they did get a catch the grasshoppers all but cleaned out the newly sprouted grass. On pastures in other areas, water holes had to be excavated or wells drilled before grazing would be possible. Once the water holes were in they had to be fenced and windmills and troughs installed to keep the cattle out. Corrals and shelters had to be built for the bull herd, the bulls had to be bought, houses for resident foremen had to be reconditioned. But most of all, before the pastures were put to use there had to be a botanical survey, acre by acre almost, to determine their present and future carrying capacity.

From the day that the idea of Community Pastures was first discussed back in the winter of 1936, L.B. Thomson had harped on the need for a botanical survey. To Thomson and G.D. Matthews of the Scott Station and Ace Palmer and Gordon Taggart, the creation of Community Pastures would enable the livestock industry to take a giant step forward by the application to the beef industry of the knowledge gained in 10 years of research at Manyberries. Thomson had been the original superintendent at the Manyberries Range Station. After he moved to Swift Current he was succeeded by Harry Hargrave, a son of one of Alberta's oldest ranching families. The Manyberries Station was established in 1927 to study the problems of raising cattle on the arid ranges of the Palliser Triangle. Like the other Experimental Farms, it had come up with solutions to a great many of the problems, economic as well as natural.

Manyberries was able to establish the importance of scientifically located and constructed water holes to the carrying capacity of pastures. When it was established on 18,000 acres of short grass prairie, the Manyberries spread contained but a single water hole capable of supplying the water needs of only 100 head during the summer grazing season. The progressive construction of 28 dams and dugouts not only increased the year-round capacity to 300 cattle plus 500 sheep, it provided for over 300 acres of land that could be flood irrigated for the production of hay. In the process, a great deal of most useful information was acquired about the best way of building dams and dugouts.

Studies by Dr. S.E. Clarke definitely established the superiority of crested wheat grass, and crested wheat and alfalfa mixtures, over the native prairie wool for both pasture and hay cropping. On the short grass range, livestock owners could count on making 18 pounds of liveweight gains per acre on steers on the native grass. When they substituted 25 percent of the acreage to crested wheat grass with 75 percent in native grass, the gains doubled to 35 pounds. When a 100 percent combination of crested wheat grass and alfalfa pasture was substituted, the gains were 60 pounds per steer per acre. Coupled with such results, Manyberries was able to show many other things. Overgrazing a pasture for a prolonged period would cause the deterioration of the quality of the breeding stock as well as the pasture. Contrary to the universally accepted theory in the moister areas of the country, it was demonstrated that it was better to continuously graze cattle on the range instead of rotating them from one pasture to another. All these results were capable of working the most profound changes in the economics of livestock production in the Palliser Triangle, and everybody was eager to put their ideas into practice on Community Pastures. But the best use of all this information could only be made following a thorough botanical survey of the pastures.

A botanical survey would indicate the exact condition of the native grasses. One of the most strikingly successful experiments at Scott had been the eradication of pasture sage, the bane of the ranchers' existence, with crested wheat grass. A botanical survey would show whether the native grass could be left to recover by itself while more urgent work was done, whether pasture sage was enough of a menace to justify immediate reseeding, whether it would be safe to pasture cattle on the grass while new pastures were being seeded.

So it was that, hard on the heels of the fence builders, teams of specialists went from the Experimental Farms to map the new pastures, quarter section by quarter section. It was these maps, correlated with the aerial pictures that had been taken, which would dictate where the cross-fencing and water holes would have to go, where there would have to be accelerated efforts to control soil drifting.

In retrospect, all this may appear but elementary good sense. But in the context of 1936-37-38 only the persistence of Thomson and Archibald was able to carry the program through. As far as overgrazing was concerned, Thomson need not have worried for there was little threat of that during the first years of the Community Pastures program. In 1938, there were 189,800 acres of pastures in operation on which there were only 3,227 head of cattle, or one head to 58 acres. The following year the pastures expanded to 612,300 acres which carried 11,534 head or one to 53 acres.

The grass that was seeded into the weeds in 1937 germinated and grew in 1938 and was ready for pasturage in 1939. And the organization of the grazing associations, it may be repeated, took time, and many of the farmers near the pastures by 1938 had no cattle to put into the pastures. It was not until the Second World War, with rising farm incomes and a return of the good crop years that the pastures began to achieve their full potential.

But a start, a big start, was made in 1937, not only in getting the Community Pastures in business but in controlling the drifting soil that was turning the Palliser Triangle into a desert. The Experimental Farms crews and the farmers working under their supervision had managed to list and seed almost 65,000 acres out of the 250,000 to 300,000 acres that were completely out of control. The rains had given the erosion fighters a powerful assist and tens of thousands of additional acres were seeded to grass that fall where the Russian thistle was providing the ground cover. The struggle was by no means over, but a great deal that was good and constructive had been harvested from the crop failure of 1937.

Dan Cameron said:

I was teaching school at the Cold Creek Colony southwest of Rockglen and used to hitch rides into Moose Jaw to see my folks. It was as common, in those days, to get caught in silt drifts on the highway as it was to be caught in snowdrifts.

The Mounties used to say that they were busier gathering up people who had been driven insane by the depression than in chasing crooks. There was one occasion when I was getting a ride back to school from Moose Jaw and we were stopped by the Mounties. They were searching for a farmer who had disappeared. His section-and-a-half farm had once been excellent land but it had grown no crop in five years. The day before the Mounties stopped us, people going past had noticed this man driving his binder up and down a field in which nothing but stunted Russian thistle was growing. He had stopped and shouted to one of them:

"Look at this for a stand of wheat! If it will go a bushel, it'll go 50 bushels to the acre! Best crop I ever saw! Best crop I ever saw!"

The Mounties had come to take him away but he was nowhere to be found. His wife hadn't seen him since the day before when he had gone to the barn after breakfast.

CHAPTER TEN

Fleshing the Bones of the PFRA

O n a slight switch of the Churchillian phrase, the year 1938 was both the beginning of the end, *and* the end of the beginning of the campaign against the dust bowl. It marked the definite, incontrovertible change in the weather. After the great, land-saving rain storms of August, the normal fall rains returned to most of the Palliser Triangle in 1937. Good winter snow and timely spring rains got the wheat crop off to a healthy start even on land that was eroded badly from the previous years.

The struggle to get the badlands back to grass, to get the thousands of small pockets of drift-prone land back under control would take another five years. For the last three years there had been a frantic race against both time and the weather. The year 1938 removed the urgency of the time element by dampening down some of the worst drifting regions and this made it possible for the whole reclamation project to proceed in a more organized, even thoughtful, manner. There was still an immense amount of work to be done, both on the part of the farmers themselves and their scientist-helpers. But enough progress had been made to engender confidence that ultimate victory over the destructive forces in nature was assured. The beginning of the end was in sight.

For the PFRA itself, it was only the end of the beginning, a period in which it had rattled around like a skeleton without skin, bones, muscle or a definable function or purpose. In essence, the PFRA was little more than a catch-all label to encompass the activities of half a dozen armies of technicians and theoretical scientists who were paid by the Government to do something else, some place else. The PFRA functioned more like a volunteer fire department trying to bring a raging prairie fire under control than a government bureaucracy.

In 1936, when the Civil Service Commission sent its investigators out to see what was going on at the Experimental Farms, nobody gave the probers or their questions more than perfunctory attention. Who, the investigators wanted to know, authorized researchers in forage crops, botany, plant pathology and genetics to go rushing around the country fighting grasshoppers and plowing soil and succoring starving livestock? All these things were Provincial Government responsibilities. The concentration of so much federal personnel and the spending of federal money in these fields could not be justified or excused by anything in the Civil Service code. But at the very height of the crisis, when more soil was blowing than ever before, when a new plague of grasshoppers had suddenly blown in, nobody had time to answer stupid questions. The earnest probers were treated as the volunteer fireman would have treated curiosity seekers—abruptly.

The problem of jurisdiction and propriety nevertheless remained and when winter came in 1937–38 the problem came forcefully to roost on the desks of Gardiner, Archibald and Dr. G.S.H. Barton, the Deputy Minister of Agriculture. From its birth, the PFRA had been little more than an off-shoot of the Dominion Experimental Farms Service. When the PFRA was established in 1935, the only large body of people capable of doing anything about the drouth emergency were the people on the Experimental Farms.

Because the drouth was regarded as a temporary emergency, ad hoc steps were taken to deal with it. Thus it was assumed that, when the drouth was overcome, the organization itself would disappear. That assumption was inherent in the legislation that established the PFRA for it was only given a five-year lease on life. Because it was to be so short lived there had been no compulsion to set up a permanent organization. As a body involved in a transient situation, it seemed logical enough to confine the function of the PFRA to providing the money while the Experimental Farms people did the thinking, organized the work, and then went out and got the job done.

It was a highly irregular way for government agencies to be doing things. And not only financially. No one was really in charge of the PFRA's day-to-day operations or responsible for its actions. In practice, the people in the field did what seemed reasonable until something that involved policy came up. That had to go to Ottawa to Gardiner, Barton or Archibald. This, of course, caused delay in matters which should not have been delayed, cluttered the files with paper and disrupted accounting procedures.

To revert to the volunteer fire-fighting analogy, while the firemen were manning the hose nozzle, they had no time to worry about who was supplying the water or manning the pumps. It was an understandable attitude but it caused administrative chaos and a nightmare for the bookkeepers. In the end the bookkeepers had to be satisfied or they could have derailed the entire operation by shutting down the flow of funds. In that event, there would have been painful embarrassment for both the politicians and the senior departmental officials. In fact, neither Gardiner nor Archibald had any reason for not wanting to get everything sorted out and regularized. Both had been forced to spend so much time on PFRA that other duties had to be neglected, other work put aside. But until the weather broke neither had the time needed to put an organization together because, until the PFRA had been in operation for many months, no one had a very clear idea of the form the organization should take. Certainly the organization that emerged in 1938 bore little resemblance to an organization that would have been set up in 1935.

In any event, the first order of business at the March 1938 meeting of the directors of PFRA was to give it a regular organizational form so that it could have a life of its own. As a first step, it had to be divorced as far as was practicable from the Experimental Farms Service, in the best interest of them both. Important work on the Farms was falling behind and it was now becoming clear that the course on which PFRA was embarked would take many years to complete and hence, would have to have its own permanent captain and crew.

For the first three years of the existence of the PFRA its handful of employees were recruited mainly from the scattered personnel of the old Dominion Reclamation Service. The Federal Government operated the Reclamation Service prior to the transfer of the natural resources to the Prairie Provinces in 1930. This branch had been responsible for a great deal of water development and research, particularly in Alberta. With the transfer of the resources to the provinces its function disappeared and the Reclamation Service was abandoned. Some of its employees retired, others transferred to the Provincial Governments or to the Dominion Experimental Farms Service. It was this group of dispersed experts that the Weir Government drew on in the first months of the PFRA.

Ben Russell and Charles Moore were brought back as consulting engineers. W.L. Jacobson, an outstanding irrigation expert who had gone to the Lethbridge Experimental Farm, came back as secretary of PFRA and irrigation specialist. Moore was not only an engineer but a successful rancher in the driest part of Alberta, near Seven Persons, where he had been imaginatively successful in catching and holding the moisture that fell on his ranch. After the 1935 election, Jack Vallance, a farmer turned Liberal politician who had been defeated in the Kindersley constituency, was made de facto head of the organization with the title of director of water development. The first PFRA office was set up in the Medicine Hat post office in two rooms in 1935. It was moved to Swift Current soon afterward and then was moved again to the McCallum and Hill Building in Regina in 1938.

The first step taken in 1938 was to appoint George Spence

as the operating manager of the PFRA. Spence was a dry-land farmer and a Liberal politician like Jack Vallance, but he was a man of somewhat wider experience. He had been Minister of Public Works in the Gardiner Government in Saskatchewan where he had built up a reputation as a tight-fisted and efficient administrator. It was through his department that most of the dam building and dugout excavating was being done. He therefore had an intimate knowledge of PFRA affairs, a better knowledge, in all likelihood, than anyone else. He was given the title of Director of Rehabilitation.

Under Spence were two main departments. Vallance was in charge of one as superintendent of water development, and O.S. Freer the other as superintendent of land utilization. Freer was also a farmer and rancher and his work as the organizer of the collection of the distress cattle in 1937 made a deep impression on Gardiner, who, recognizing these accomplishments, insisted that Freer be placed in charge of the Community Pastures development. Under him were George Will as senior officer in charge of development and Mark Mann, senior officer in charge of administration. Ben Russell was named senior consulting engineer under Vallance; James Mutchler was appointed senior survey engineer; S.H. Hawkins was a senior construction engineer; and Jacobson was named agricultural advisor on all small projects. Over on the left side of the organization chart, and still under Dr. Archibald, was the cultural branch headed by the Experimental Farms superintendents. They would carry on as directors of the soil-saving services and continue their efforts to reclaim the Palliser Triangle with listing machines, nurse crops and crested wheat grass.

From a practical viewpoint the entire campaign of 1938 went on very much as it did in 1937, but at a greatly accelerated pace. George Spence fleshed out the clerical staff of PFRA and recruited a permanent staff of young accountants, lawyers and engineers who would ride herd on the details and paper work required by Ottawa. Within a year Spence had put a permanent staff of 175 together of whom a third were graduate engineers and technicians. There was, however, a great deal more to the developments of the winter of 1937-38 than a mere desire to arrange the affairs of PFRA for the convenience of the bookkeepers. When the time limit was removed from PFRA and its organization was established on a permanent basis it gave recognition to the fact that the rehabilitation of Western Canada was no longer a one-shot, short-range undertaking. It would take years, not just one herculean effort, to solve the problems of soil erosion and grasshoppers. This conclusion, however, had not emerged full blown from the minds of the Ottawa deep thinkers. Rather, it had come in part out of the soil of the Palliser Triangle, out of the reaction of the people on the farms to the first efforts of PFRA. A separate and distinct organization of PFRA was necessary because the people had seized the germ of an idea that was PFRA in the beginning and had run off with it.

The many-sided exertions of 1937—the tackling of the distress cattle problem, the multi-fronted campaign to fence the Community Pastures and give agriculture a new direction, the construction of the farm dugouts and small dams and stock-watering projects, caught the public imagination. Why not capture and harness the run-off water from the Cypress Hills? Why not build a water storage facility in the Pembina Mountains of Manitoba? Why not dam the St. Mary's River in Alberta and duplicate the success that irrigation had achieved around Lethbridge? Why not dam the Natukeu Creek at Vanguard in the heart of the dust bowl and irrigate the land? And what about the towns and villages? Why not create domestic water supplies for the small towns by damming creeks and rivers? Why not pump the water out of the South Saskatchewan above Elbow and divert it down Thunder Creek to Moose Jaw? So great did the volume of requests for help from the towns and communities become that Dr. Archibald had to recall the attention of the directors to the fact that the PFRA was primarily concerned with rehabilitation of prairie agriculture.

As for farmers themselves, the best indication of their

attitude was in the statistics. At the tail end of the worst year ever recorded within the Palliser Triangle the PFRA had 1,000 applications on file from farmers who wanted help to be resettled elsewhere, and 5,000 applications from farmers who wanted dugouts or stock-watering dams built on their farms.

An important contributing factor in the maintenance of morale was certainly the many projects into which the PFRA subsidies nudged the farmers. They were dragooned by the thousands into the spreading of grasshopper bait; they were hired to help list and seed the thousands of acres being worked on Reclamation Projects and on Community Pastures; they were hired by the many hundreds to help build the Community Pasture fences; they were hired to truck supplies around the Triangle, from grasshopper bait to relief feed to fence posts and barbed wire. In the wooded areas work was provided in cutting and treating of fence posts. All these projects, whether they got work on them or not, focussed their attention on "next year" and underlined the official position that there would be a next year. They spelled out the conviction that, while the country seemed headed downhill to destruction, trying to save it was still worth the effort.

To the impoverished farmers, the PFRA people must have seemed to be grasping at straws, but the straws of encouragement for which they grasped had substance if not much size. For one thing it was demonstrated beyond all doubt by the end of 1937 that even the worst blowing land could be saved and reclaimed. The Melita project which had been listed in 1936 grew a crop of rye of sorts that fall and a catch had been obtained in the grass strips planted in 1937. So well had the emergency measures worked on those two sections of sandstorm blistering at Melita that, in the spring of 1938, plans were being laid for a whole series of new experiments in grain and forage production. The 800-acre spread at Cadillac was well under control with a crop of rye and was being reseeded to grass. A quarter section at Meyronne that had been regarded as hopeless was within sight of being reclaimed. So was the 950-acre project at Aylesbury, and the 765-acre project at

Kisbey. The smaller reclamation acreage at Hutton, Alberta, and the 320 acres at Youngstown where the blowing was extreme in 1936, were back in grass in 1938. Even the big Mortlach project, where two sections had blown out very badly in 1936, was on its way back into grain production and hayland. Compared with the 300,000 acres that were completely out of control, these were indeed small successes. But they were fortuitously spotted across the Palliser Triangle so that they could be used to demonstrate to the doubters what could be done.

It was these successes that made it possible for the field workers to go out in 1938 with renewed hope and to expand the organization of the Agricultural Improvement Associations. More and better equipment was continually being obtained so that greater headway could be made with the anti-drifting campaign on both private farms and on the new Reclamation Projects. Only in the southeast of Saskatchewan was there little progress to record. Around Estevan the crews from Indian Head had to go back over the drifting land again and again. The rains that fell elsewhere missed Estevan. High winter winds blew out newly establishing cover crops. Yet even in the Britannia School District, where the blowing and drifting reached its very worst, the countermeasures taken were eventually effective and the land was brought back into production.

In one way the Reclamation Projects were even more important than the Community Pastures—they demonstrated to the grain growers that efficient management of the soil could reclaim some of the worst blowing soil for grain production. There was an illusion abroad that putting the land back into grass was a simple, nothing-to-it proposition. This led to the idea that regrassing was an act of surrender to the elements, and a concession that once-fertile wheatland would never grow wheat again. The Reclamation Projects demonstrated, in so many cases, that the abandoned and soil-drifted farms could be brought back into grain production once more. If it could be done on the land at Melita, Kisbey and

Mortlach, there was still hope for so much of the erosion damaged land that was still being farmed. Later, George Spence was to become the eloquent advocate of putting this land back into crested wheat grass, simply to restore its fibre and fertility. But even without anything else being done, the Reclamation Projects demonstrated that the damaged soil could still produce stands of grain.

Long accustomed to preparing for the worst all the time, the conservationists both in and out of the PFRA were well organized to take full advantage of the improved moisture conditions in the spring of 1938. The grass seed was all in the farmers' hands. The AIAs had by now pinpointed most of the drift-prone fields within the Triangle. Most of all, the farmers were preparing to put in their grain crops with more confidence than they had had in years. With the good fall rains, winter snows and spring rains they could once again concentrate on getting something to grow. And things grew that spring, just about everywhere in the Palliser Triangle. The grain the farmers were able to plant sprang to life even on the soils that had been blowing the years before. On the abandoned land the annual weeds took over as they had taken over in the summer of 1937. It was fortunate indeed that spring that no one could have imagined the blows that nature was planning for later in the summer; blows that would be worse, in many ways, than the crop failure of 1937. However, the forces of nature were staunch allies for the conservationists in the spring of 1938, and they made the most of it.

With the PFRA in business for itself at last, the work of containing the desert was divided between the PFRA and the Experimental Farms staff. The latter henceforth would confine active participation to regrassing the Community Pastures and the Reclamation Stations and helping the individual farmers through the Agricultural Improvement Associations. In all this work the PFRA would supply the material and equipment required. PFRA personnel took over all the water development and irrigation projects. The slow business of having farmers excavate their own dugouts was phased out in favor of mobile mechanized contractors who did the job quickly and more efficiently with drag lines. The PFRA's own engineers were turned loose on big water projects as well as on small water projects. A flood of requests rolled in for water conservation projects and the organization was quickly forced to set up an order of priority as well as a clearly stated policy. Community water conservation projects, for example, had to serve enough members of a community to justify the cost. Thus when the big Cypress Lake project was first suggested to serve a handful of ranchers, Gardiner rejected it out of hand. It was only when it was completely revamped to provide 70,000 acre-feet of water to downstream farmers that it was approved. In no area did the demand for PFRA services explode quite like it did in the Community Pastures development. Only the extreme emergency of 1937 got the project underway at all. But in 1938 the organization was snowed under with Community Pasture proposals.

The PFRA had managed to get 16 pastures on the books as complete in 1937. Yet none of these would reach its optimum usage for several years. They were fenced. The farmers who would use them were organized. Regulations that would govern all pastures were established. Fees were set for the users; pasture bosses and fence riders were hired. Policies in connection with pasture and herd management were worked out. Yet the pastures, from any realistic point of view, were still mainly on paper. They could not reach optimum usage until the fundamental job of reclamation had been done. All the abandoned and wind-blown land within the fences had to be put back into grass, and putting it back into grass was the job of the Experimental Farms. On that count, reorganizing the PFRA in 1938 did not reduce the work of the Experimental Farms personnel. For those at Indian Head and Scott it got much heavier because of the concentration of Community Pastures around them. The regrassing of the pastures, despite the energy expended by the conservationists, went slowly. It was quite common, on the worst land, to have to reseed the same ground several times. Nevertheless on the 16 pastures completed in 1937 almost 20,000 acres were successfully re-seeded in 1938.

While the regrassing was being done on the completed pastures, several armies of PFRA employees were fanning out across the prairies. The on-the-ground surveys of the soils and range were stepped up. An additional 400,000 acres of pasture sites were inspected and assessed. The Government of Saskatchewan asked it to take over 1,350,000 acres of rangeland to be set aside as reserve pastures and fodder banks against the day when a year like 1937 would return. It picked one of these blocks—146,160 acres in southwestern Saskatchewan and put 160 miles of fence around it. It also selected 12 other sites covering approximately 200,000 acres and fenced them in. With the 16 pastures from 1937, this gave the PFRA 28 pastures covering 380,000 acres at the end of 1938. It was also able to select nine additional pastures with almost 300,000 acres on which to work during the winter.

Leaving aside the reserve pasture, the PFRA in a little more than a year was able to take over almost 700,000 acres of wind-blown and eroded farm land and convert it into potential rangeland. But that it was potential more than actual was indicated by the original carrying capacity of some of the pastures. A 23,000-acre pasture at Kindersley would be able to sustain only 200 animals, or one animal to 115 acres. At Coteau the capacity was an animal to 60 acres and in most of the others it was one to 50 acres. Before the potential of the pastures could begin to be realized, a massive program of regrassing was essential. While it went on, the process of taking over more and more submarginal grain land also proceeded until more than 2,000,000 acres were grassed down and fenced out of cultivation for all time. With the regrassing and the development of new techniques in range manage-ments, the carrying capacity of the pastures expanded four-fold—to a point where they could carry one head to less than 15 acres. Ultimately there would be 85 pastures in which 160,000 head of cattle would be grazing for 7,000 individual farmers. Alberta never did come into the Community Pastures although Manitoba did and a dozen were eventually developed in that province.

Once the process of removing the badlands from cultivation started it never stopped. Each year the Experimental Farms crews went out to seed another 25,000 or 30,000 acres, and helped the individual farmers to regrass much more. Each year the climate within the Palliser Triangle improved a little so that the farmers who survived were able to get their land back into production. The demand generated by the war for food pushed up the price of livestock to a point where it was again profitable to raise cattle. With the return of livestock prices to more reasonable levels, the worth of the Community Pastures gained a widening recognition.

In addition to its intensive efforts to nurse the Palliser Triangle back to health, the PFRA brought a whole new concept into the lives of the Palliser people. This was the concept of expending public money for the general improvement of the local farming communities rather than for relief. In no other area was this approach to be seen at work with quite the same effect as in water development. Gradually the people themselves came to see their country not as an arid wind-blown and dust-covered land subject to periodic disasters. Rather it came to be regarded as a well-watered land in which too much of its precious moisture was allowed to fritter away in spring floods and heat-wave evaporation.

Manitoba was the first to recognize the potentiality of small water development. Most of the early works undertaken in Manitoba, with the exception of the Melita project, were in that category. In proportion the Manitoba farmers were the most pressing applicants for farm dugouts and turned first to the drag lines to speed their construction. A whole series of dams were built along the Souris River for domestic, municipal and stock-watering supply. All were of small capacity but all were of great importance to the people of Napinka, Wawanesa, Hartney, Gladstone, Morden and Rock Lake. Many areas of Manitoba with more than adequate rainfall nevertheless lacked good wells for domestic water supply. In the construction of the farm dugouts, filtering beds were often included to provide water for human consumption as well as for livestock.

PFRA money was used in getting some comprehensive small water irrigation projects going in the Swift Current area of Saskatchewan and in the Special Areas of Alberta. The diversion of South Saskatchewan River water into Thunder Creek to supply Moose Jaw's domestic needs was completed. A dozen Saskatchewan communities were provided with adequate domestic water supplies. In Alberta, emphasis was on irrigation, and extensions to several existing developments were undertaken, including the Eastern Irrigation District and the Canada Land Company system.

The water development program, however, was just getting into high gear when the war emergency forced a sharp cut-back in PFRA activities. Many of its key employees enlisted in the services. Its budgets were sharply reduced and instead of concentrating on the handling of emergency conditions, it relapsed slowly into a state of near hibernation for the duration. But not quite hibernation for there were still Community Pastures being built and essential facilities were being provided those in existence. And in Regina, George Spence and his staff were devising and keeping track of a growing number of "shelf" projects. These were part of Hon. C.D. Howe's planning for postwar employment. He wanted the country to be prepared for a gigantic public works program when the war ended to prevent the recurrence of mass unemployment. All government agencies and departments were required to completely detail as many such works as possible and have them "on the shelf" for instant use. Two of the most important projects ever undertaken by PFRA had their origin as "on the shelf" projects.

The first was the St. Mary's River dam which began as an agitation among the farmers in the Burdett area of southern Alberta to get the PFRA to recapture some of the tail water from the Taber irrigation district. They devised a completely impractical scheme and invited George Spence and his engineers to come out and hear about it. Spence disposed of their ideas very quickly, and then suggested they should settle for nothing less than the St. Mary's River project, which would provide enough irrigation water for southern Alberta clear down to Medicine Hat. The rights to the waters of the St. Mary's River, which rises in Montana and flows northeastward into the Oldman River, had been ceded to Canada by the United States in 1921. The International Joint Commission had also decided, however, that the upstream country should have first call on the water of rivers flowing across the 49th parallel. This policy led to an agitation in Montana for the construction of storage dams on the headwaters of the St. Mary's River. Canada was making no use of the St. Mary's water and this agitation showed signs of making considerable headway. George Spence pointed out to the Alberta farmers that unless Canada bestirred itself and put the St. Mary's water to use, the water might well be lost to American interests. Out of the meeting of the farmers at Burdett, a St. Mary's River Development Association was born and as a result the $40,000,000 St. Mary's dam and canal system was one of the first postwar projects to get off the drawing boards into construction.

In those years, wherever he went in the West, George Spence was beating the drum for more and better development and use of resources. That of course included water resources. One of the projects most talked about by Albertans was the famous Pearce scheme to develop the Red Deer River basin with stock-watering reservoirs. The Pearce scheme was always rejected as being too costly. In Saskatchewan, the big dreamers had their eye on the possibilities of damming the South Saskatchewan River to create an irrigated farming centre in the heart of the Palliser Triangle. The South Saskatchewan project was held back by a different reason—nobody could find a place along the river where it was practicable to build a dam. Ben Russell investigated a site north of Cabri but after drilling the subsoil was found to be unsuitable as a foundation for dam building. The next site located was near Outlook, but it too had to be rejected after drilling into the subsoil. Finally it was Gordon MacKenzie, the chief engineer who was later director of PFRA, who suggested a test be made near the Coteau Creek, far to the north of any of the previous locations. It was thoroughly drilled and tested, was found to be satisfactory and the agitation to build the South Saskatchewan River dam was on.

The PFRA engineers made exhaustive studies of the irrigation and power potentialities of the river. Briefs were presented to Ottawa but nothing happened. Not even the persuasive eloquence of Jimmy Gardiner could get it a place on Mr. Howe's shelf. Nor could the spokesmen for the Saskatchewan basin get it much of a hearing in Parliament. The stumbling block was arithmetic, and it remained arithmetic for the next 15 years. It would cost $100,000,000 to provide 500 farmers with irrigation water. Even after a Royal Commission had investigated the project and presented a yes-and-no report, the arithmetic remained the problem. By then George Spence had gone from the PFRA to International Joint Commission as Canadian representative along with General A.G.L. McNaughton.

Prime Minister Louis St. Laurent was immovably opposed to the South Saskatchewan dam and, in one last effort to convince the Prime Minister of its worth, Gardiner decided to throw Spence into the breach. He got Spence to agree, arranged an appointment with the Prime Minister and George Spence carried the message. He avoided arithmetic, concentrated on the economic and social advantages that would accrue to the whole of Western Canada from the dam. He quoted experience from the Lethbridge area to show how the economic effect of irrigation multiplied far beyond the numbers of irrigators. He talked of the recreation advantages that the big lake would have for the farm people of Saskatchewan. In the end it all turned on arithmetic again. Spending $100,000,000 to provide irrigation water for 500 families just was not justifiable, the Prime Minister insisted.

But nobody in Saskatchewan, least of all the farmers of the

Triangle, were prepared to take Mr. St. Laurent's "No" for an answer. They went on talking it up and in the end Mr. St. Laurent's Government went down to defeat. When Prime Minister John Diefenbaker came in, the South Saskatchewan River Project came into existence. It was, of course, the PFRA that built the big dam and it became the organization's crowning achievement. Not only will it supply irrigation water for the country below the dam, and the first reliable source of water the communities 100 miles to the east have ever had, it will provide the very heart of Palliser's Triangle with recreational facilities and social amenities that would otherwise never exist. Like the St. Mary's dam, it will go on generating economic activity within the Triangle for as far ahead as anyone would care to foresee.

And yet, was the harnessing of the South Saskatchewan really the crowning achievement after all? Its completion was surely a far cry from the picayune business of digging water holes on dust bowl farms, which gave PFRA its start. But when history gets around to making its assessment, surely it will not dismiss the farm dugouts and the Community Pastures without a long second look. The dugouts were as inelegant a collection of holes in the ground as ever devised by man. They did nothing aesthetically for the landscape. They were utilitarian in the extreme. Yet, if acceptance is a measure of worth, few more valuable projects were ever devised. From the 49 holes the PFRA was able to complete in its first year, the numbers of dugouts completed on prairie farms doubled and redoubled in the years that followed. The year 1936 saw 858 finished, the next year there were 1,493, in the year after there were 2,745. Construction dropped off in 1939 to 1,023 but jumped to 4,423 the next year. From that time onward, dugout building went on without letup until more than 80,000 of them had been installed on the farms of Western Canada.

In addition to the dugouts, PFRA's stock-watering dam department continued to steadily expand its water storing until almost 10,000 were in place. Its irrigation works proceeded much slower, for the difficulties of teaching new irrigation tricks to old dry-landers was never lost sight of. Nevertheless this too was an impressive accomplishment, particularly in the Saskatchewan side of the Triangle where more than 3,000 irrigation projects were completed. When Manitoba and Alberta were counted in, the total approached 5,000. In its 30 years of existence the PFRA managed to spend $32,859,496 on water development on the prairies. True, it fell far short of what Mr. Gardiner said should be spent— $10,000,000 a year over a five-year period. But it was also a world removed from what the originators of the PFRA had in mind when they launched it in 1935.

In terms of time, effort and money, the Community Pastures were never able to keep up with the development of the small water projects. Yet the impact of the pastures on both the income of the farmers of the Palliser Triangle and on the livestock industry could hardly be exaggerated. The pastures gave the livestock specialists in the Experimental Farms System an opportunity to demonstrate to the farmers the worth of their ideas. This demonstration began with the very inception of the projects.

The Pastures administration managed to steer a steady course around the shoals of controversy between the various purebred beef breeds. They held firm to the need of uniformity of breeds within the pastures so that the cattle that came onto the market from them would gain a reputation for uniformity and quality. The expert eye of the livestock specialists helped to buy the kind of bulls that raised the quality of the progeny produced on the pastures. In the process they saved the farmer patrons the heavy capital cost involved in keeping their own bulls. When the time came when the qualities of the Charolais cattle could no longer be ignored, the PFRA pastures pioneered in using these animals to further improve the quality of the beef herds. And it was the PFRA as well that did a great deal of the pioneer work on a big scale in the breeding of beef animals by means of artificial insemination. But most of all the Community Pastures demonstrated the wisdom of the action taken in 1935 to save the Palliser

Triangle from ruin. The regrassing program that began only to stop the blowing topsoil went on as a justifiable activity for its own sake. From the very first year, when the pastures operated on the basis of one animal for every 58.9 acres, the carrying capacity increased almost unbelievably. Within a decade after getting into business, the carrying capacity was increased to one animal on 21 acres and the carrying capacity was to increase again in the next decade, to one animal to 15 acres.

It took the Community Pastures administration five years to catch up with the demand for pastures that were on hand in the spring of 1938 when the organization took recognizable form. It was not until 1942 that it was able to report 1,000,000 acres behind the fences. Thereafter the expansion went at a slower pace so that at the tenth anniversary there were 53 pastures covering 1,412,000 acres in operation. Eventually those figures would grow to 84 pastures covering 2,325,000 acres in 1965.

In terms of money spent and projects completed the accomplishments of the PFRA are impressive. In terms of the transformation of the Palliser Triangle from an arid, wind-swept and beaten-down countryside into a prosperous country in which the farmers have come to enjoy the amenities of civilized living, the accomplishments are also impressive. But what makes them so is not the sight of the land as it became after everything was done. It is the memory of what it was like before the first halting steps were taken to beat back the encroaching desert in 1935. The Palliser Triangle in 1935 was in truth well on its way to becoming the Great Canadian Desert. It was prevented by the fortuitous combination of the intelligent application of scientific knowledge, the incredible patience and fortitude of the people on the land, the dedication of brutally underpaid employees of the Experimental Farms and other government departments, and a break in the longest siege of atrocious weather since, in all probability, the times of Joseph in Egypt.

W.C. McCargar said:

*I bought a little store in Ernfold in 1933 and in 1934 our town fi-
nanced over $1,600 worth of relief with a single $10 bill. We issued
scrip for relief and the people took the scrip to the stores and got their
groceries. The merchant could pay the scrip for work done and who
ever got it could pay it on his taxes. It worked fine and nobody went
without that winter for want of money. We had $10 when we started
and when the winter was over we still had the $10.*

*I remember getting very angry with one fellow who came into
my store. He had a family of small children and he had earned some
small change somewhere. Instead of buying a quart of milk for his
baby, he bought some chocolate bars. He sat around for awhile
munching candy and then went off. I stewed about him for a long
time. I took a real dislike to him, and I wondered what chance his
family would have with him as a father. They all grew up to be strap-
ping, strong and amazingly successful citizens.*

CHAPTER ELEVEN

The Tragic Trek to the North

T he endless cycle of settlement, unsettlement, resettlement and unsettlement again, which was characteristic of agriculture development within the Palliser Triangle, was by no means a phenomenon of the depression. It had been going on without interruption since the arrival of the first immigrants 50 years before. As each wave of settlers came in, lingered awhile and moved on, the area went through a rudimentary kind of land-use shakedown. Uneconomic quarter-section farms became uneconomic half-section farms, then expanded into economic full-section farms. The passage of years demonstrated to even the most optimistic and ignorant of the settlers that some land just was not suitable for grain growing. This land, by the many thousands of acres, was allowed to go into another cycle—annual weeds, perennial weeds, native grass and sagebrush. Thus when the Dominion-Provincial Land Use Committee in 1946 made its study of 16 municipalities in southwestern Saskatchewan it identified some 26,000 acres as abandoned, most of which had been lying unused and unwanted for 20 years or more. And by 1946, all the land that could be put back into grain production was back in grain production. A great deal of it was unsuitable for that purpose but under the forced draft of war conditions it had been turned back to grain production anyway.

It was the breaking of the settlement cycle at the negative-unsettlement-point which did as much to create the dust bowl and threaten the Palliser Triangle with complete destruction as the drouth itself. Drouth, grasshoppers, rust and low prices drove the farmers off the land. In previous decades, the abandoned farm would have been picked up by a new arrival who would have tried to get it back into production. In the hiatus between abandonment and resettlement it would have gone back quickly into annual weeds. But in the dry years that began in 1929, the weeds did not germinate, uncommonly high winds were generated by the high temperatures, and the topsoil on the abandoned land began to blow.

In the years before PFRA there was not much that the ordinary farmer could do when his topsoil began to blow except let it blow. The body of information being accumulated at Lethbridge, Swift Current and Scott was not widely disseminated beyond the immediate vicinity of the stations. Even had they known what to do, few farmers had the equipment to take the action needed to wind-proof their fields. However, their fields raised crops of sorts even in the early crop-failure years and the growing crops and stubble helped to soften the force of the wind on the soil. If the stubble was not plowed under in the fall it cut down the wind velocity and prevented undue damage by the winter blizzards. Nevertheless, the universal practice of maintaining a black summerfallow throughout the summer was the primary cause of soil erosion and farm abandonment. But in the beginning blowing summerfallow was a local menace, as the high winds blew the soil from the summerfallow with such force that it cut down and destroyed the crops growing on the neighboring fields. It was the abandoned lands that transformed a serious local nuisance into a national disaster.

The surrendered land seldom contained anything to diminish the force of the wind. When the knolls started to blow it was not long before the sharp sand cut down the weeds, polished the fence posts and drifted over whatever was growing in its path. Even the Russian thistle could not match the wind and when it was reduced to a few scattered clumps it became quickly covered with dunes. Within a matter of months, the blowing topsoil from a few acres could unsettle the surface of hundreds of other acres, then thousands of acres and ultimately scores of thousands of acres.

The deserted land was nobody's responsibility, for it still belonged, legally at least, to the farmer who had given up the struggle. The land might be mortgaged for more than it was worth, it might be years in arrears in taxes. The mortgage company might foreclose and take back title to it, or the municipality might take it over for taxes. But until somebody made a move of some kind it really "belonged" to no one, so no one was obliged to take care of it, or do anything about the drifting soil; and no one did. The chances were that neither the mortgage holders nor the municipal officials were even aware of the condition of the land. The only people with any real interest in doing something about it were the neighbors whose own farms were being ruined while they impatiently watched. When the process of ruination was complete, they too would pack it up and move out and the whole problem would be doubly compounded.

The longer a farm remained abandoned the worse the problem became. The MacDougall farm at Kisbey, the Stevenson farm at Melita or hundreds like them could be cited as examples of what was happening. These were good farms with fine big houses, well-built barns and granaries, surrounded by treed shelterbelts. They were as fine an example of good farmsteads as could be found in a day's drive. The MacDougall place had been abandoned early in the depression and the soil began to blow on a small stretch of soil 200 yards from the house. Eventually the blowing area spread until it covered more than 200 acres and the topsoil was drifted four and five feet deep in the farmyard. By 1938 the topsoil was blown off down to the point described as "burnout." The hardpan was so rock hard in the summer that it was difficult to penetrate it in order to get anything seeded. It had to be gone over again and again.

Nor was it alone a problem of the good land of the farms still occupied being ruined by the silt blown in from abandoned farms. The amenities of life of the farmers who remained were also destroyed. The country roads which gave them access to town became drifted into impassability with soil to the height of the fence posts. Thousands of farms in the Palliser Triangle had gone in heavily for planting shelterbelts around their homes and gardens in the years before the big drouth. Within the shelterbelts, fruit trees and berry bushes had been nursed along and prize flowers and ornamental shrubs were grown. When the soil blowing started the shelterbelts provided these better-than-average farm homes with temporary protection. But as the dust clouds became thicker and thicker, the shelterbelts trapped the blowing soil which buried gardens, shrubs and even the trees themselves. In the process the winds turned the farm homes into dust traps. It seeped in around windows, under the doors, came down the chimneys and blew in through the walls. So it was not alone a matter of getting out of the country because the productivity of the land was destroyed; it was also a matter of getting out because life was no longer worth living in the dust that was as omnipresent inside as out, where there was no escape from the nerve-rasping winds.

How many farmers abandoned their farms during the decade between 1929 and 1939—the depression years? No precise answer will ever be possible. There was no massive migration or general exodus; there was only a steady trickle off the farms and into the cities, off the farms in the south into the more sparsely settled areas of the northern park belt; off the farms and out of the province and the prairies. The Royal Commission on the South Saskatchewan River estimated that the prairies lost 247,000 people between 1931 and 1941; that the short-grass country of Saskatchewan alone lost 73,000. It estimated that 10,000 families moved from the farms of the south country into the northern parts of Saskatchewan. The northward trek however would account for only part of the farm abandonment within the Palliser Triangle. Farmers from Saskatchewan also straggled into western Alberta and into British Columbia, farmers from the Manitoba dust bowl moved into the Manitoba parkland, and into the cities. Hundreds of Alberta farm families were moved out of the central border section to better land elsewhere. The only official figures are those of the 1936 census which reported 8,200 abandoned farms within the Palliser Triangle in Saskatchewan, 5,000 in Alberta and 700 in Manitoba. This total of 13,900 farms encompassed almost 3,000,000 acres.

Not all of the 3,000,000 acres were wholly subject to soil drifting. But at least 300,000 acres were described as subject to severe erosion, which could mean that the topsoil had blown off down to the hardpan. In all likelihood another 1,000,000 acres were blowing badly enough to be a menace to the farmland in the immediate neighborhood. The severely damaged areas were not as extensive in Alberta as in Saskatchewan because of the action taken by Alberta in 1920 to depopulate most of the Palliser Triangle within the province. In Manitoba the area affected was comparatively small, embracing about 200,000 acres in the southwest corner. But where it did blow, the soil blew as badly in Alberta and Manitoba as it did anywhere on earth.

In the first years of the drouth—1929 and 1930—the movement off the land was probably not of much consequence. But after the disaster of 1931 it began to build and, as the depression deepened, the people of the Triangle were torn by two contradictory impulses. There was first the urge to "get out while the getting was good" and second the compulsion to put in one more crop, in the hope that the worst was over. In the vast majority of the cases, the second urge proved to be the most compelling, for more people stayed than left. But even those who stayed would yield to the impulse occasionally to take off with their neighbors to look for better land in the north, in Alberta's Peace River block or in the interior of British Columbia. Others, who had come from Ontario or the Maritimes developed a desire to return home. In the first years of the depression, the Saskatchewan Government through its Relief Commission embarked on a modest resettlement scheme. Dry-land farmers from the south, who could find homesteads in the parklands of the north, were encouraged to move. The Government, up until the end of 1934, moved 1,626 families, 2,514 carloads of settlers effects and 1,525 carloads of livestock to new farms. Yet even as it was doing so, the Government recognized that the depopulating of the Palliser Triangle would ultimately do much more harm than good. When the Liberals succeeded the Conservatives in 1934 the northward movement was actively discouraged, but even official discouragement failed to stop it. The numbers of farm wagons seen on the roads heading north increased rather than decreased, despite the fact that there was nothing in the experience of the first migrants to encourage others to follow. Most of those who left the south country were far worse off than those who remained.

Saskatchewan, long before the big depression, had developed a rough-and-ready system for handling agricultural relief. The system was based on the distribution of vouchers which the recipients were able to convert into food and clothing and other necessities at the local stores. In 1931, when the Red Cross emergency appeal brought relief gifts of food and clothing from all across the country, distribution was made through the same system. Basic to this system, however, was the policy that relief was a municipal responsibility. When the farmers got a crop they were expected to repay the municipality for the help received, particularly for feed, seed and binder twine. As long as the farmers stayed on their farms their minimal needs were largely supplied through the relief system. But once they moved off the farm and headed north they went through a vast no-man's-land of red tape. From Climax to Meadow Lake, or from Roche Percee to Nipawin was 300 miles over dirt roads and those who broke down in between acquired the status of Canadian displaced persons.

To become eligible for relief they would have to go back to where they came from. If they could not, or would not, relief could be granted only if their home municipality accepted responsibility for the cost of their care. So there was endless correspondence, endless bickering back and forth, and it all became doubly complicated when the migrants moved from province to province. When the crops failed within the Palliser Triangle, all the authorities, both provincial and municipal outside the area, became alert to the possibilities of new migrations of the destitute into their areas of responsibility. Public notice was served on the people of Saskatchewan to stay out of Alberta and Manitoba. Warnings were issued that no relief would be dispensed to outsiders.

Despite it all the abandonment of farms and migrations went on, without rhyme, reason or pattern. They moved in single families, in pairs or in groups. They moved in one-, two- or five-wagon outfits. They moved in dire necessity or with some of the comforts of the home. They moved almost cheerfully, with signs like "Meadow Lake or Bust" and "Melfort or Bust" crudely painted on the sides of the wagons. Or they moved quietly, almost in the hope no one would see them pass. Sometimes they headed for a pre-determined location which had been investigated beforehand. Sometimes they simply took off and headed north. When Robert Dunsmuir left from Maxstone, Saskatchewan, for the Red Deer country, all his neighbors came around to help him load his wagons. When Alf Murphy and his family gave up after 20 years at Kincaid and moved to Cold Lake, Alberta, they got a send-off from a party of 100 friends, but in the main there were few celebrations. The departing farmers simply sold off what they could not take with them and moved. By the time their decision to move out was made there would usually be very little they would have to move for most of their farm equipment would have been repossessed by the banks and implement companies. Most of their household equipment would have been worn out.

The rudimentary nature of the farm roads dictated that the migrants travel light for they could carry only what the horses could pull over long distances. Yet it was possible for them, with only moderate ingenuity, to travel in reasonable comfort. Tents were often pitched on hayracks. Curved ribs fitted over a grain wagon, and covered with binder canvas or linoleum from the kitchen floor, made a handy sort of covered wagon. Most of the migrants took along a couple of wagons, one for sleeping in and one for household effects. Usually they had an extra team or two of horses tied to the rear of the wagons and a cow or two following along. There were not many as well organized as the S.B. Mackenzie and Alex Duncan combination that left North Portal for White Fox in 1934. They had 4 wagons, 11 horses, 7 colts and 18 head of cattle, including 4 milk cows. They announced that they would milk the cows and churn and sell the butter in the towns enroute to help pay their expenses. That was the summer 5 farmers from Oxbow turned up at Rocanville, 100 miles north, with 65 beehives which they set out while they looked around for new farms.

But for most of the late migrating farmers the farms that they could find were inferior in almost every way to those they had left. The land that was available from the railways and the Hudson's Bay Company, almost without exception, was well treed and required a lot of heavy work to clear for cultivation. They moved in such numbers into the north, however, that it was not long before relief regulations had to be bent double to accommodate their needs. It would have been impossible for them to have established themselves quickly under the best of conditions. In the context of their times it was impossible for them even to achieve a subsistence level. This was demonstrated beyond all doubt by the experiences of the back-to-the-land settlement scheme which was one of the wildest brainstorms of the depression.

When it was almost impossible for the established farmers on good land within the Palliser Triangle to keep off relief, the governments decided it would be the course of wisdom to establish the unemployed of the cities on farms. Urban unemployed with farm backgrounds were encouraged to move onto quarter-section farms located for them by the Back-to-the-Land associations. They were provided with a team of horses, a cow, a pig and some chickens with the idea that they could become subsistence farmers in a few years with assistance from the Government. Saskatoon established a Back-to-the-Land block in the Loon Lake area, Moose Jaw got one going at St. Walburg and another was set up north of Yorkton. The failure rate of all such projects was predictably high and many of the Back-to-the-Land families were still getting relief long after the urban unemployed were all back at work.

The migrants who took to the roads in the earliest years and got settled in the parkland eventually made it back on to their feet. For one thing, they were able to get the pick of the land that was still available. But the good land was gone quickly and by 1934 there was very little left but the bush lots. And it was in the years after 1934 that the migrations reached their peak. One day, between Meadow Lake and Glaslyn, Gideon Matte, the chairman of the Northern Settlers Re-establishment Board, counted 14 migrant families on the move to the north. The Northern Settlers Re-establishment Board had been established in 1935 because the immigration of destitute farm families from the south country was imposing an impossible burden on the municipalities of the north. There were then 6,600 refugee families living north of Saskatoon who were getting assistance. Most of them were on newly acquired homesteads trying to scratch a living without equipment or capital. There were also between 600 and 800 families scattered across the northern fringe of the province who had come north, could find no land, and were squatting on vacant land around the small towns. There were 40 families of squatters on the outskirts of Meadow Lake alone in 1937 and more were arriving all the time. Some had filed on homesteads only to discover that their new land was useless until it was drained. Others came looking for friends who had already given up and moved away. Unable to find land, for whatever reason, they had simply stopped in their tracks along the road allowances. Some picked out a vacant clearing and built a log cabin or shack on it. Others moved into old trappers' cabins, abandoned lumber camps or anything that would give them shelter.

The NSRB not only set about finding land for the resettlement of the squatters but it set up a system of helping the other migrants with loans for horses, machinery, seed, breaking and necessary supplies. The operation of the Northern Settlers Re-establishment Board is not strictly speaking a part of the story of the conquest of the desert of the Palliser Triangle. It could best be described, perhaps, as the gathering up of the human debris that was scattered about by the violence of the storm. The operations of the NSRB did not influence or affect the conquest of the desert except to this extent: The experiences of the refugees from the dust bowl helped to convince everyone on the spot of the madness of the notion that 50,000 farm families could be moved out of the Palliser Triangle and resettled elsewhere. The fact was that the so-called "wide-open spaces" of Western Canada were already too thickly populated for the good of the people or the economy. The bush land that was available in the north was totally unsuited to the needs of the dry-landers. But it was the only land there was and in 1937 Gideon Matte had 800 families on his hands who had to be picked up bodily and moved. They could not be left to freeze and starve in their tarpaper shacks and make-shift log huts. There was simply no choice—the bush land had to be cleared and the squatters had to be moved.

While he was pondering the "how" of the problem Matte happened to be thumbing through a farm magazine and he got an answer to his land-clearing problem. A couple of Alberta farmers had invented a tree-mowing gadget to attach to their tractor. Matte took the picture to the Regina Caterpillar tractor dealer and they, together with an engineer from a Calgary iron works, redesigned and rebuilt the gadget. Several were shipped north and became the tools that got the resettlement started.

The Northern Settlers Re-establishment Board had previously taken on a staff of experienced land men who located about 1,000 quarter sections suitable for settlement. But the resettlement had proceeded slowly with only manpower and oxen muscle to rely on to clear away the trees that covered the land. With the arrival daily of new squatters in the north country, the need for new land on which to settle them far outstripped the supply.

Matte opted for mechanization. He bought tractors to go with the tree mowers and hired crews to clear 30 acres of brush on each of the quarter sections and get it ready for cropping. A number of central camps were established and groups of about 40 squatters were rounded up and converted into work gangs. The first task was to build a log school. When it was finished the men moved into the school to live while they assisted each other in building log houses and barns. With the completion of the houses the families were brought in and the farmers with completed buildings dropped from the work gangs and were replaced by others.

The next step was for the NSRB to supply farm animals and the equipment the farmers needed to get started back in business. When the board was first established in 1935 it decided to go back to oxen for motive power. When Matte took over in 1937 he switched immediately to horse power and later loans were approved for tractors. Though they came from the very bottom of the social and economic scale, despairing, disenchanted and dispossessed, the progress which some of the squatters made was astounding. Encouraged by the NSRB fieldmen to plant alfalfa on their small acreage, many of them got into the alfalfa seed boom and rode it back to complete solvency in short order.

In comparison with the magnitude of the resettlement problem tackled by the Northern Settlers Re-establishment Board in the bush land and muskegs of the north country, the task of moving and resettling the farmers off the Community Pastures was child's play. Instead of thousands, the PFRA faced only a few hundred. Instead of people beaten down to a point where they had simply collapsed in despair, the survivors of the dust bowl were tough of mind and body and better-than-average farmers. They, at least, had stuck it out after most of their neighbors had been driven out.

In the early months of the Community Pastures surveys, there was a good deal of vocal resistance to the idea of moving or being moved. But as the negotiators convinced the farmers of their seriousness the opposition tended to soften. When the government agents produced concrete plans of helping the farmers to relocate, many of them took the initiative in finding new property. Crown land or municipal land was made available to them under what was known as the "short move" policy. The first consideration was that the nearby land to which the farmers would be moved had to be better than their old farms or there could be no deal. Then the government would pay the cost of moving all household and farm equipment and the farm buildings as well, if they were worth moving. Finally they were located in a place where they could become users of the Community Pasture they had vacated. If the original property was mortgaged an arrangement was made to transfer the mortgage to the new property, thus making it an easy matter to switch the original property to the Community Pasture.

The better vacant land in the vicinity of the pastures was all taken up quickly and new areas of settlement had to be investigated. Obviously there was no point in looking very far north. The PFRA therefore turned to some of the fringe irrigation land of Alberta. In doing so it made a complete about face. In the beginning of the PFRA there was a good deal of talk about solving the drouth problems by irrigation. But such irrigation experts as W.H. Fairfield, A.E. Palmer and W.L. Jacobson preached caution. Irrigation was an art that had to be acquired the hard way for it was an axiom of the arid areas that it took two generations to make an irrigator. It was definitely not something that dry-landers could pick up overnight and succeed at. So the original suggestion of immediate embarkation on converting dust bowls into water reservoirs was quietly filed and forgotten.

As the sights of PFRA were raised, however, and it was reconstituted to develop community projects as well as render assistance to individual farmers, irrigation came back into the picture, though it came slowly and with a different emphasis. Gone was the notion of growing specialized crops, truck farming, etc. Instead the emphasis was on flood irrigation of hay meadows, on storing the water released by the spring thaws and using it on comparatively small land spreads that could be easily irrigated. The end objective was to gradually convert the Palliser Triangle from a predominately grain growing economy to a cattle plus grain economy and that could only be done by using irrigation to overcome the constant threat of fodder famines.

Once the idea of irrigation had been resurrected, attention turned naturally to Alberta. The Federal Government had been forced to step into the Eastern Irrigation District of Alberta to finance the reconstruction of some of the main ditches to keep the farmers on the land. In return the PFRA took over 30,000 acres of irrigable land in what was known as the Rolling Hills area and prepared it for settlement of the farmers displaced from the Community Pastures. They were brought into Alberta under what was called the "long move" policy. This was a policy that contrasted sharply with the way in which the original immigrants were settled on the Palliser plains. The early immigrants were brought in by governments, railways, land companies and colonization societies and dumped and forgotten. The settlement of the irrigated lands was a masterpiece of constructive paternalism. And it worked.

The first step was for the PFRA fieldmen to convince a farmer that he should move out of the Community Pasture. When that was accomplished the fieldman took the farmer to Alberta to show him what was available for him. He was offered a quarter section of land on a two-year lease-option-to-purchase plan. If, after two years, he decided to buy, the price was $8 an acre for the irrigable land and $1 an acre for the dry-land, with nothing down and twenty years to pay. The PFRA would buy his old farm for cash less encumbrances.

In practice this usually meant that the price paid was on the generous side, for it was worth a good deal to PFRA to clear all the farmers out of the pasture areas. If they remained, the cost of fencing around them and the disruption of efficiency in using the pastures were considerable. In any event, the uprooted farmers would start life anew with some money in their pockets. The government also undertook to pay the farmers for breaking 100 acres to get the first crop in. The cost would be added to the purchase price of the land, but the payments were made to the farmers in cash. This gave them an assurance of at least some cash income for the first year while they were getting into business.

These farmers too were permitted to tear down all their buildings and homes and take the lumber with them to the new settlement. The government paid for three freight cars of settlers' effects, one of which could be lumber. Passenger fares for the settler and his family were paid and the water development program brought the water to his farm. Perhaps most important, the PFRA arranged to settle a dozen experienced irrigators in the area who could help the new arrivals by both precept and example. It sounded like the best deal the farmers of Robsart, Coderre, Brock, Bracken and Kindersley had been offered when it was put up to them in the late summer of 1938. But when they visited the Rolling Hills country, with its eternal winds and dust, its teeming gopher population, and its total emptiness except for the great herds of roaming antelope, the gloss came off the offer. In the process of inspecting the new land, the guides took the prospects to the irrigated land to the west, where trees were reaching for the sky, the grass was green and the gardens were lush in the moist soil. When they were shown what could be done by the application of water to this soil, a surprising number of the farmers reached for the PFRA application forms. Enough reached, in any event, to turn the railway siding at Scandia, the next spring, into a mile-long junk yard, as settlers' effects were unloaded from the boxcars from Saskatchewan. Despite the help provided by the government, the first year in the Rolling Hills was a nightmare of endless toil. First, a house had to be built with second-hand lumber that slivered and split and cracked. Then the land had to be broken and seeded. Dorothy Daniels, who moved to the Rolling Hills from Robsart, described it best:

> I never served a single meal at one serving that summer. The men worked in shifts around the clock. We had two old tractors and while my husband and father-in-law were eating, my brother-in-law and uncle would be driving the tractors. We didn't even have time to get the roof on our house for a long time. So we had to store our sugar and flour and other stuff under the bed in case it rained.

But there were compensations. When the crop was in and the water was turned on, the whitefish came down with the irrigation water from Lake Newell and the farmers caught them by the tubful. The addition of fresh fish to the diet took a lot of the sting out of the hard work that summer.

Settlement of the smaller irrigation projects that were established in Saskatchewan followed a different course again. Each of these projects was designed to cover 5,000 to 10,000 acres when fully developed. Because most of the land involved lay along old river bottoms, it was frequently badly cut up by the old river courses. In order to prepare the land for easy and efficient irrigation, the PFRA decided to do all the work and take off the first crop itself. It could do it much better and cheaper than the farmers could because the PFRA already owned all the equipment needed. It was new equipment and was far too expensive for even prosperous farmers to buy, and there were no prosperous farmers.

Each project was subject to an economic and land use investigation before the form of agriculture to be followed was determined. At Val Marie, where the surveys indicated the land was unsuitable for cereal production, the settlers moved into the area were encouraged to base their operation primarily on livestock production.

At Eastend, the situation was quite different, even though

both places were in the same general area. The land surrounding the Eastend irrigation dam was for the most part fairly good grain-growing land. So the plan there was to supplement grain growing with livestock and to insure a supply of seed and feed during years of scanty rainfall. The irrigable acreage, therefore, was leased to the surrounding farmers in parcels of from 20 to 40 acres on which they could raise hay for their cattle.

The importance of the PFRA resettlement program lay not in its size and scope but in its lack of either. In the first year of its resettlement operations it managed to relocate exactly 97 families from within its Community Pastures, or about one-eighth of the number of squatters Gideon Matte had to resettle in the bush of northern Saskatchewan. The Rolling Hills project took 38 families, the Val Marie project absorbed 20 and the rest were relocated in the Community Pasture areas. The purpose in life of the PFRA was not to depopulate the Palliser Triangle or turn it back into a vast open range for livestock to replace the buffalo that had roamed it when Palliser passed that way. Its purpose was not only to prevent the land of the Palliser Triangle from becoming a vast desert and to restore its productivity. It was that; but it was also to save and restore the agricultural industry of the Triangle and that could not be done by moving the people out of it. Instead, the whole environment had to be remolded to fit the needs of the inhabitants, and even as they fought the dust, the grasshoppers, the rust and the drouth, they were beginning to get a vision of how that could be done.

Grant Denike's agricultural engineers at Swift Current were becoming entranced with the potential of the rubber-tired equipment that was making its appearance. The self-propelled combines were full of bugs and so were the tractors and cultivators and hammermills and swathers. The local farm machinery dealers knew almost nothing about the equipment they sold, so the farmers had to learn to operate it through trial and error mixed with sweat and tears. Into this knowledge and experience vacuum the Experimental Farms people moved, to tinker and adjust and smooth out the kinks. Nothing escaped their attention, be it V-belts that stretched or frayed, gears that stripped, fan speeds that fluctuated, sieves that clogged, pick-ups that failed to pick up, cutter knives that did not cut. And they experimented and questioned and suggested always with confidence that once the new equipment was perfected, and the farmers learned how to operate it and adjust it and take care of it, some tremendous savings would be made in the cost of cereal production.

At Manyberries, Harry Hargrave had experiments well under way that would drastically improve the economics of livestock production in Western Canada. Most of the farmers in the Palliser Triangle were subscribers to the Ontario school of cattle feeding. They believed that cattle had to be fed heavily in the winter to maintain the flesh they had put on in the summer. When feed shortages developed and the cattle lost weight, the cattle raisers became alarmed for fear they would not survive the winter. At Manyberries they wondered how the buffalo had managed to survive the western winters when the feed was scarce. The conclusion was that they had probably lived off the fat they had stored up in the summer. Could beef cattle not do as well? The Manyberries livestock department decided to find out with a series of long-range tests. When the results were in they had conclusive proof that livestock which was allowed to drop 300 or 400 pounds in the winter could make it back quickly the following summer and be finished and ready for market just as quickly as those which had been kept on heavy winter rations.

"Cattle that are well summered are half wintered," was an old rangeland aphorism for which Manyberries was able to provide conclusive documentary proof. The application of this discovery to the Palliser livestock industry would drastically reduce its winter feed requirements and vastly improve its operating economics.

Similar developments were taking place elsewhere—in the progress of irrigation at Lethbridge, in forage crops at Scott and Indian Head, and in the laboratories of the plant breeders and entomologists. On the farms themselves the endless search for better tillage implements went on continually.

So at a time when a start had barely been made on containing the spreading desert, there was reason for confidence on all sides that agriculture itself could be saved and restored to health. It was for this reason that everything the PFRA did was based upon improving the productive environment for the people who were where they were. It was, of course, no part of anyone's goal to reclaim the abandoned farms so that they could be resettled and rebroken. Rather it was part of everybody's goal to take permanently out of cultivation soil that was unsuitable for cultivation; but to encourage those who were established on good soil to stay on the land, and to take full advantage of the new means that would develop to increase the productivity of their soil.

Any resettlement scheme would tend to defeat these objectives. Thus while the PFRA faced the continuing necessity of moving people off the Community Pastures as this project expanded, resettlement was the least important of any PFRA undertaking.

Dick Painter said:

Things got so bad in some of those years that the cattle seemed to go a little crazy. They'd eat anything in sight and the vets used to find such weird stuff in the stomachs of the cattle that they had to coin a new word to describe it. You won't find it in any of the textbooks, but hundreds of cattle died in those days from what they called "hardware disease." They would eat door knobs or pieces of iron, or hinges that fell off gates, they were that desperate to get something into their stomachs.

CHAPTER Twelve

The Six Who Led the Crusade

*I*n every discussion that is held with the men who played a vital part in the conquest of the desert within the Palliser Triangle, one footnote is always added and surprisingly almost always in the same words:

> Of course we must never forget that we had the most powerful assist from nature at the most critical time, and we must never forget the co-operation we got from the farmers at all times and under all circumstances.

There can be no question of the validity of either point. Certainly for most of the Palliser Triangle, the drouth ended in the late summer of 1937 after the crop had been utterly destroyed. The normal fall rains came back, there was good winter snow and the spring rains came at the right time. The rains ended the speculation as to whether the people of the Palliser Triangle could have survived another year like 1937. Certainly the terrible drouth and heat of that year was morale shattering for the people who had already taken such a buffeting from nature. The unkindest cut of all was that while their crops were withering in the fields, the farmers in Manitoba and Alberta outside the Triangle were reaping very good crops. But the speculation about the people being able to survive was largely irrelevant. Their action in 1938 and 1939 was proof enough of that. When spring came in 1938, they went out again with relief seed and put in another crop. When that crop was eaten by grasshoppers or destroyed by rust they went out again in 1939 and did it all over. There was nothing very heroic in their attitude. They only did what they had to do and perhaps they did it because there was nothing else to do for there was no place else for them to go. The West had run out of free land or any other kind of land on which they would have a chance to settle.

Because they had no other choice, they stayed where they were, living on relief and putting in their crops. The probabilities were that they would have gone on doing that and if the rain had not returned in 1937 or 1938, it would have come back in 1939 or 1940 or 1941. But the rains alone could not have saved the Palliser Triangle. The heavy summer cloudbursts did not stop the soil blowing for very long. Rain alone could not restore the productivity of the soil, contain the encroaching desert or save the agricultural industry within the Palliser Triangle. That could only come with the sequestering of hundreds of thousands of acres into Community Pastures, with the revolutionizing of agricultural techniques, with the long-term development of water resources and the conservation of moisture. In short, it would come only through the plans and the exertions that were under way when the rains just happened to come back. The rains were a big help. They were not the solution.

Similarly, the co-operation which the leaders of the campaign got from the farmers was tremendous. Without it very little would have been possible. Too much land was out of control and getting worse all the time for a handful of Experimental Farms people to have been able to handle the problem alone. It took the combined effort of 50,000 farmers over a period of five years to accomplish that. But without the aid and direction provided by the leaders and their staffs, all the co-operation in the world would have been wasted. It was the equipment, the techniques and their dedication to the cause which made the marshalling of the co-operation of the farmers fruitful.

The retrospective veterans of the campaign have given

nature far too much credit and have taken too little themselves. The explanation may be that to orderly scientific
minds things must have a beginning and an end, and the
return of the rains provided a logical point for terminating
the era. But that would be like ending World War II with the
battle of Stalingrad, which was where the tide turned. The
threat of the desert to the Palliser Triangle was not like a war
with an identifiable beginning and end. It was not even like a
hurricane which, though its origin may be obscure, is over
when the rain stops falling and the clean-up starts. The threat
of the desert never really ended, it only diminished year by
year, until a realization came to the people that it was not
there any more.

It is the lack of both a shattering beginning and a climactic
ending that has kept the story of the conquest of the desert
from recognition as a many-sided triumph. In particular it has
kept a group of dedicated public servants from ever getting
the recognition they deserve from their country. The Western
Canada of the end of Canada's first 100 years is every bit as
much a monument to the men who saved it as it is to those
who opened it up.

Who are these men to whom Canada owes so much?

To single out only five or six of the hundreds who played
vital roles in the struggle may seem grossly unfair. Certainly
there was hardly an employee of any Experimental Farm or
Provincial Government agricultural agency who did not have
a part in the struggle. Many of them had very important parts,
people like Norman Ross of Indian Head, Doug Matthews at
Scott, who worked himself into a nervous breakdown, and
Fred MacIsaac whose premature death was widely attributed
to overwork during the worst of the crisis. There were laboratory scientists turned into extension workers, who organized
Agricultural Improvement Associations, and Experimental
sub-stations; entomologists, plant scientists, agricultural engineers. There were, perhaps as important as any, scores of
municipal secretaries at whose desks the buck-passing
stopped and the bull work started. Finally, there were the

farmers themselves, 50,000 of them and at least 500 self-sacrificing farm leaders who threw themselves into the organization of their neighbors throughout the whole of the dust bowl era. Many of these men could also be singled out for special mention, if anybody is. Yet it would be a worse discrimination to withhold any longer honor that is due because in granting it there is a slight to someone else.

To decide whom to single out as the indispensable men who made the conquest possible a very simple test can be used: Could the agricultural industry within the Palliser Triangle have been saved without the individual contribution which each made? The answer has to be "no" in case of the following:

L.B. Thomson, George Spence, Dr. E.S. Archibald, J. Gordon Taggart, Asael E. Palmer, Rt. Hon. J.G. Gardiner.

The order of precedence does not matter and there will be no attempt made here to assess relative importance. That, indeed, would be impossible for the contribution of each was unique and as such could not be compared with that of any of the others. An objection may be entered that it is unfair to include Gardiner and leave out the Hon. Robert Weir, who was the originator of the PFRA. However it was Weir's bad luck to be bounced out of public office before his brain-child was out of swaddling clothes. Had Weir survived politically he would undoubtedly have done things very much as Gardiner did them. The point is that Weir did not survive and Gardiner came in and took over.

Gardiner made two contributions which were decisive. The first was to focus national attention on the crisis within the Palliser Triangle and to keep it focussed there. The second was to get the Liberal Government of Hon. W.L. Mackenzie King to vote the millions of dollars that were needed to fight the drouth within the Palliser Triangle. In the environment of the depression this was surely no minor miracle. The Liberals had coasted into office without a program on the revulsion of feeling against the sadly discredited regime of Rt. Hon. R.B. Bennett. The Liberals were dedicated to a balanced national budget and an end to tinkering with the economic system. Thus one of their first acts was to fire the Wheat Board of John I. McFarland which had tried without much success to stabilize the price of wheat above the bankruptcy level. McFarland was replaced by James A. Murray who was quickly dubbed "Fire-Sale" Murray by the haste with which he dumped the Canadian wheat carry-over on the world markets. The Liberals had swept everything before them in Quebec and the Maritimes and hence were by no means beholden to the prairie agrarian support.

To have obtained cabinet approval of spending vast sums of money within the Palliser Triangle on concrete projects would have been a difficult task. To obtain the millions Gardiner got for anything as nebulous as was PFRA during its first three years was incredible, but Gardiner managed to bring it off. It should be noticed, in assessing this accomplishment, that antipathy toward pouring eastern money down the prairie rat hole was as prevalent among eastern Liberals as among eastern Conservatives. But whether the money came hard or came easy, Gardiner got it. And it was Gardiner who was able to carry through the livestock rescue program of 1937, at a time when every Conservative politician in the West was trying to set him up in their sights. The history of the cattle business is notorious for sharp practices and low grade schemers. Getting the better of a cattle buyer or a horse trader was regarded as the ultimate test of any farmer's acumen. Thus to have turned scores of cattle buyers, even government buyers, loose with handfuls of government money would have convinced Gardiner's eastern colleagues that he was mad, if they had understood the situation. Yet his agents were able to carry through the entire project without destroying or even splattering the reputation of the Minister of Agriculture.

Gardiner got the money and got the job done. But that was only part of it. During the first years of his administration he was in and out of the dust bowl continually. Not only was he acquainted with the work going on in general terms, he had eaten enough dust to have an intimate and detailed knowledge of almost everything that was happening. Thus he had the explanation for everything on the tip of his tongue and in Parliament and out he was an articulate and convincing spokesman. In later years Gardiner's political opponents tended to ascribe political motives to everything he did, and with some justification. Certainly political consideration can never be far from the top of the mind of anyone so steeped in, and skilled in, the art of politics as Gardiner was. And he could not have been unaware of the possibility of collecting some political dividends from whatever success was made of the PFRA. But to interpret Gardiner's role in the campaign against the desert as only that of a politician on the make would be as palpably false as it would be unfair to the PFRA.

Important as Gardiner's role was as the spokesman for PFRA and money-raiser extraordinary, he made still another contribution. He was impatient to the point of down-right irascibility over delays in getting the PFRA program off the ground. He exerted as much pressure on the Government of Saskatchewan as he did on his own departmental employees in an effort to clear away the legal entanglements that were stifling the efforts to get things done.

The contribution which Gordon Taggart made was less concentrated in time than that made by Gardiner and much wider in scope. It encompassed more than two decades and it embraced every aspect from the fundamentally scientific to politics and public relations. As the first director of the Swift Current Experimental Farm, he set the pattern for the experimental program at the station. If he had done nothing else than set up Sidney Barnes in his wind and soil studies it would have been an important contribution. But everybody at Swift Current got the same sort of freewheeling freedom to pursue their ideas that Barnes had. Shorty Kemp and later Grant Denike were encouraged to launch out in all directions on their machinery experiments, just as he encouraged W.S. Chepil in his wind and soil experiments at Regina. There was room for ideas to develop wide-ranging roots and blossoms profusely at Swift Current and everybody was encouraged to contribute what they could to fields beyond their specialties.

When Taggart quit the Swift Current station and the government service to enter provincial politics in Saskatchewan in 1934 it was, in a way, a one-man protest march against the economy wave that gripped the Experimental Farms service. At a time when an expansion of effort to control wind erosion was needed, vital funds were being denied to the service. There was reasonable comfort and security for Taggart, however, as director of an Experimental Farm, two qualities much sought after in 1934. But Taggart turned his back on both to take on the most difficult task imaginable—Minister of Agriculture for the drouth-ridden and depression-racked province of Saskatchewan.

It was in this post that Taggart made his greatest contribution. He came into office at a time when the flight of the farm families from the dust bowl was reaching its peak. He was faced with the very real prospect that a kind of panicky exodus could develop into a stampede unless somebody did something to restore the confidence of the farmers in the country; and the confidence of the country in the farmers. He undertook the job. Taggart knew, from his knowledge of the work being done at Lethbridge, Indian Head and Scott as well as at Swift Current, that most of the answers were becoming clear to the problems of dry-land farming within the Palliser Triangle. He knew, perhaps better than anyone, how much good wheat land there was within the Palliser Triangle, and what could be accomplished on that land by a change in farming methods and the development of better equipment.

Above all, Taggart was convinced that the Palliser Triangle had a future as a wheat growing area. This confidence was not shared in too many places. Indeed, for 15 years the emphasis had been on moving people out of the dry land. Both Saskatchewan and Alberta had resettlement schemes going before Taggart went into politics. For example, George Headley, the Alberta Minister of Agriculture, announced as late as August 1934 that 405 families were being moved out of 33 crop failure districts within the Palliser Triangle. This of

course was in addition to the thousands of families previously evacuated. Taggart, thus, was faced with a situation
in which the preponderance of opinion was on the side of
evacuating the population. He set himself immediately to
combat the idea. He had two potent arguments. The first was
that the people who left the dust bowl were usually worse off
than those who had stayed. The second was that there was
precious little land around that was capable of absorbing
many resettled farmers.

Taggart's official position in the Saskatchewan Government took him frequently to Ottawa and to Eastern Canada,
usually in a search for additional finances. On these trips he
went to great pains to emphasize that Saskatchewan's problem was not drouth alone, that it might not have been even
drouth primarily. It was the complete collapse of farm prices
that was causing much of the havoc in the West, as well as
unemployment in the East. Money had almost ceased to
circulate in many areas. The publisher of the *Shaunavon
Standard* had switched his circulation rate from $2 a year to
four chickens a year. Many of the small-town merchants
existed on relief orders for without the relief trade they would
have been out of business.

With grain in the good crop districts bringing scarcely
enough to pay for the cost of harvesting and freight, with
cattle and hogs returning little more than trucking charges, it
was ridiculous to blame everything on drouth. In order for the
farmers to be able to take remedial action against wind
erosion, they needed money for new equipment and for
repairs to old equipment. In every crop district within the
Triangle there were farmers who were raising crops, even in
1931 and 1934. But because of low prices they were little better
off than those who raised nothing.

It was Taggart, therefore, who brought a dash of realism
into discussion of agricultural problems on the Prairies. And
it was Taggart who was as responsible as any one man for
getting the Community Pastures into operation. Community
Pastures were not his idea. Co-operative pastures had been

operated on and off for many years in both the United States and Canada. The old Matador Ranch in Saskatchewan had been a Community Pasture for many years. The Saskatchewan Government itself was experimenting with several pastures on a small scale in southern Saskatchewan. But nowhere were any of these undertakings successful enough to start a mad rush to emulate them. In any objective evaluation, there were more signs of costly failure than success.

Yet if Taggart's first principle, that the people had to stay on the land, was to be upheld, something had to be done about livestock. And something had to be done to take the marginal land permanently out of cultivation, particularly land that had been abandoned two or three times. If it could be reclaimed with grass, the farmers on good land in the vicinity could use it to graze their cattle. They could hence expand their wheat acreage to more nearly achieve economically sized units. Two primary steps had to be taken. Ottawa had to be convinced of the feasibility of Community Pastures because it would have to provide the money. The municipalities and then the individual farmers had to be convinced that Community Pastures were in the interests of both. Convincing Ottawa was easy. But to get the municipalities to see the light took all of Taggart's persuasive powers, and they were considerable.

In the early stages, Saskatchewan and Alberta were agreed that Ottawa should provide the money and the provinces would operate the pastures. By being closer to the actual operations the provinces felt they were better able to do the job, and for a lot less money. When Ottawa dug it heels in and insisted that if it put up the money it would have to run the show, and get title to the land into the bargain, it was Taggart who had to get his cabinet colleagues to go along. The fact that Alberta never did come into the Community Pastures project may only indicate that it lacked a Gordon Taggart as Minister of Agriculture.

Gardiner and Taggart functioned in the area of public policy. Archibald, Palmer and Thomson were on the administrative level. The contribution which each made was every bit as vital to ultimate success as that of Taggart or Gardiner. Without the Dominion Experimental Farms, nothing would have been accomplished. It was Archibald who put the Experimental Farms into the very forefront of the struggle. More than that, Archibald more than anyone else was responsible for building the Experimental Farms organization to a point where it was capable of taking over the entire wind erosion problem and putting into practice the measures needed to solve it.

Like Taggart, Archibald was a native of Nova Scotia who came into the Dominion Government service after a stint at teaching. Archibald was professor of agriculture at the Truro Agricultural College in 1912 when J.H. Grisdale, then Director of the Dominion Experimental Farms, picked him as animal husbandman for the Experimental Farms Service. He was then 27, and when Grisdale moved up to become Deputy Minister of Agriculture seven years later Archibald succeeded to the post of Director. In the meantime the number of Experimental Farms in operation jumped from 16 to 28 and under Archibald the number of cattle in experimental projects was increased from 500 to 7,800.

Archibald brought to the Experimental Farms Service an almost total-recall memory and an insatiable curiosity about everything that lived. He seemed able to keep track of everything that was going on at all the farms, of the particular problems of every region being served by the farms, and of the people who staffed the farms. How the Experimental Farms Service was ever able to attract a staff with the salaries and wages paid will probably always remain an unsolved mystery. But a clue is provided in the fact that the service was somehow successful in recruiting the young science students at the universities. It offered them summer employment and immersed them in the atmosphere of the service in the new ground that was being broken everywhere by scientific experimenters. By the time they graduated, the service was in their blood. Under Archibald, the Experimental Farms became havens for young scientists who found nature challenging and new ideas entrancing. They were encouraged to look not into the next month but into the next generation, to think in terms of being a part of a crusade to raise the standard of living and add to the amenities of life on the farms. As most of them had come from farms and ranches in the first place, the milieu of the Experimental Farms became something very difficult to resist, even though salaries were notoriously inadequate.

Grant Denike, for example, spent three years at the Swift Current station as a student laborer. He managed to stay away for a year after graduation, until Taggart tracked him down and brought him back. Until World War II, some of the brightest young minds to come out of the prairie universities were working for the Experimental Farms for less than $100 a month. When P.J. Janzen came back to Swift Current after graduation, he was taken on as a "graduate laborer" at 35 cents an hour. More important than money, however, was the freedom that the young scientists had to spread their wings and pursue their own particular bent. And they had a part in a scientific revolution, in bringing all the latest scientific accomplishments to the farmers on the land. They could play that part in the knowledge that in E.S. Archibald the Experimental Farms had a director that would back them to the hilt and who would share their enthusiasm for anything they were able to accomplish.

Archibald had no part in the drafting of the original plan for the PFRA. But when the law got onto the statute books he quickly assumed responsibility for everything that was done. It was Archibald who picked L.B. Thomson to go out to Swift Current in July 1935 to organize the first meeting of the divisional specialists of the PFRA. It was Archibald who picked the committee which was composed of Sidney Barnes, Dr. S.E. Clarke, A.E. Palmer, J.H. Kemp, Norman M. Ross and W.L. Jacobson, along with Thomson.

It was Archibald who got behind and pushed every constructive suggestion that came out of the Palliser Triangle. He was an enthusiastic supporter of the Agricultural Improvement Associations and the Experimental Farms Sub-stations. From his undergraduate days at the Ontario Agricultural College, his dedication to making the latest scientific knowledge available to the people on the Canadian farms never diminished. He had an awesome, almost reverent respect for the work of the research scientists and he had a genius for taking complex ideas and putting them into language farmers could understand. So the AIAs and the sub-stations were right down the centre of the Archibald alley.

Of all the eastern officialdom, none understood the situation in Western Canada better than Archibald, or was more keenly interested in solving the problems of the drouth. It was the greatest challenge the Experimental Farms had ever met and when the opportunity arrived to face the challenge he seized it with enthusiasm. The sudden flow of riches from the PFRA appropriation gave him a chance to demonstrate to the country what the Experimental Farms could accomplish if only given half a chance. It was not too long before his drive and enthusiasm were building a head of steam under the people on the Farms. As Asael Palmer pointed out, it was a shock to the system to be suddenly released from the iron tight economy wave into an era when there was all the money they needed to finance their activities. Archibald may not have invented the PFRA but he was certainly the one who recognized the bonanza first and married the Experimental Farms skills and energy to the PFRA financial resources.

Archibald had one quality that enabled him to get much more out of his people than might otherwise have been possible. He made the people at each station feel that the work they were doing was as important, in his eyes, as any being done anywhere. When M.J. Tinline at Brandon came up with the idea of building an international peace garden on the Canada–United States border, Archibald gave it his support. When Russell Leslie at Morden developed the concept of fruit trees growing in every prairie farmyard Archibald was for it. He was an enthusiast for the tree-planting program of the Indian Head Forest Nursery Station and that enthusiasm was shared by all the Experimental Farms. Though it was generally accepted that trees used moisture and that field shelterbelts were not reliable in preventing wind erosion, the planting of trees around farmyards was something else. Archibald shared Leslie's belief that a farmer with fruit trees growing in his yard would hesitate long and hard before walking away from his farm. So on the first committee of divisional specialists, Archibald found a place for Norman Ross, the superintendent of the Indian Head forest nursery. And while the others were concentrating on the campaign to beat back the desert, Ross mounted a massive tree planting campaign to improve the amenities of farm living by enclosing the farmstead and gardens in a shelter of greenery that would take the curse of bleakness from homes of prairie farmers.

In addition to his drive and enthusiasm, Archibald was a man who knew his way around the Ottawa bureaucracy. He was a past master of the art of the possible. He knew that in the state of emergency that existed in the West errors of commission would be quickly forgotten while errors of omission would not. The time had come to push ahead boldly and Archibald pushed, and there were times without number when the Archibald push was decisive to the success of the project.

Very often the Archibald push was exerted through the man who was, in a very real sense, Archibald's deputy and field-working alter-ego—L.B. Thomson. There may be differences of opinion about the inclusion of some of the men in this chapter on the men who won the war against the desert. There will be none about L.B. Thomson.

In the interviews I had with Gordon Taggart, Dr. Archibald, Asael Palmer, George Spence and Grant Denike, I asked each to select one man who they thought contributed most to the success in the struggle against the drouth. Without exception, and without hesitation, they chose L.B. Thomson.

Thomson was the kind of person who does not suit first

names. He was known everywhere as "L.B.", and to such an extent that few of the magazine and newspaper articles written about him ever mentioned his given names. They were Leonard Baden and were bestowed on him by his parents in New Zealand in 1900. Thomson enlisted in the New Zealand army in 1918 but the war was over before his unit reached England. He took his discharge, migrated to Canada and got a job shearing sheep on an Alberta ranch. The skill he had acquired as a farm boy in New Zealand paid off handsomely for at 25 cents a head he was able to earn up to $20 a day. For the next year he drifted around Western Canada as an itinerant farm hand, door-to-door salesman and knife sharpener. In 1920 he enrolled at the Olds School of Agriculture and later worked his way through the University of Alberta to a degree in agriculture.

Thomson's first job after graduation in 1925 was to take over direction of boys' and girls' calf clubs in Alberta. Then he conducted a reclamation survey and was hired by the Experimental Farms Service in 1926 as an assistant to Gordon Taggart at Swift Current. When the Government set up the Range Experimental Station at Manyberries, in 1927, Thomson was placed in charge and he remained there until he was moved back to Swift Current to succeed Taggart in 1935.

There was nothing in Thomson's record at Manyberries to indicate the kind of ball of fire he would turn into in 1935. True, he was well on his way to transforming an open chunk of baldheaded rangeland into one of Alberta's beauty spots. He had diked and ditched and irrigated until Manyberries had become a challenge to every rancher in southern Alberta. He had toured the ranch country continually and was on a first-name basis with every cattle raiser within 200 miles of the station. He had set up many of the rangeland pasture management experiments that Harry Hargrave would carry through to successful conclusion. But, after making allowances for the radically different environment of the cattle country compared with the farming country, Thomson seemed to be settling into a comfortable rut at Manyberries. When he was transferred to Swift Current in 1935 and into the struggle to contain the desert, he exploded out of his rut with a force that destroyed all trace of his ever having been in it.

Because the Swift Current station was in the heart of the worst blowing and drifting soil in the Palliser Triangle, it was the logical point for the early headquarters of the PFRA to be established. For the next three years, Thomson ran the Swift Current station with the back of his mind and devoted all the rest of his attention to leading the battle against the drouth. He knew, from the very first, that little would be accomplished without the complete co-operation of the farmers themselves. He set out single-handedly to win that support. He put together several reels of home movies to illustrate how the drifting soil could be controlled. He had slides made of other scenes that did not lend themselves to movies.

He loaded his films and projectors and cords and batteries into a car and set out across the Prairies like a combination missionary and horse-trader. Sometimes he and Taggart and Palmer and George Spence hunted in packs. Sometimes they went alone. But it was Thomson who went farthest and stayed longest. It was Thomson alone who could ignite the dead coals of enthusiasm of his farm audiences and send them out again to their fields with hope and confidence that their livelihood could still be saved.

How he kept up the pace he set for himself no one could explain. He wore out the young "graduate laborers" like Baden Campbell, Herb Purdy and Peter Janzen whom he conscripted as chauffeurs. His days often began with one dawn and did not end until the next. In the first year of the PFRA there were many committee meetings to attend and Thomson tried to attend them all. In between he sandwiched his farm meetings, his on-the-spot investigations and his conferences with his own field workers on what they were accomplishing. All this entailed travelling continually over the worst network of mud and gravel roads extant. Without the dust and grasshoppers Saskatchewan's roads at their best were bone-shaking and car-rattling enough. But with the grasshoppers and dust they were sheer torture at times. The combination of insects and dust clogged the radiators and coated windshields with an opaque gooey mess. Even the government cars, which were newer and better cared for than any others in the Triangle could not stand the gaff. They broke down, sprung leaks, choked up, broke springs and conked out on dust-clogged roads.

Being abroad in the Palliser Triangle during the summers of 1936 and 1937 was not fit activity for man nor beast. Had he chosen to do so, Thomson could have spent his life in peace and comfort at the Swift Current Experimental Farm. This might have been akin to life in a storm cellar, but its inhabitants would have been shielded from continually being reminded of how desperate conditions were.

The physical discomfort which was an integral part of touring around the Triangle was bad enough. But the impact of the disaster upon the mind of the beholder was worse. In the office of the PFRA it was a simple matter to take the reports from the field and draw 50 or 75 circles around the worst blowing areas. Then machines could be assembled and a crew dispatched to do something about the eroding soil. But it was only by actually travelling the area as Thomson did that one was adequately impressed with the awesome magnitude of the disaster, and the awesome magnitude of the task that was going to have to be done; when somebody discovered the best place to start.

Yet neither the physical discomfort nor the mentally depressing atmosphere seemed to phase Thomson in the slightest. Whatever discouragement he may have felt, he felt privately. When he spoke at a farm meeting, or got into private communication with the farmers, he exuded confidence that the worst of everything was over. He was the greatest one-man faith-restorative that ever hit Western Canada. Thomson's confidence, moreover, rubbed off just as much upon his own employees and associates at the other Experimental Farms as it did on the farmers themselves.

In those years, Thomson found his true niche in society,

promoting the welfare and efficiency of the farmers on the land. He caught Archibald's vision of taking the fruits of modern science to the farms and showing the farmers how to use it. When the PFRA was reorganized with a life and a structure of its own, Thomson went back to being superintendent at Swift Current, but only in body. He was still most interested in ferreting out new ideas and putting them to work. When Seamans and Peake perfected the system of trapping sawflies with brome grass, Thomson rushed into a demonstration at Swift Current. Then he tried to get the Province of Saskatchewan to seed down all of its thousands of miles of road allowances to brome grass. When a huge surplus of horses became an embarrassment during the war years, he helped organize and operate a horse-meat canning factory which supplied thousands of tons of tinned meat to Europe. When George Spence left the PFRA for the International Joint Commission in 1948, Thomson was the natural choice as successor.

The PFRA Thomson took over was a far cry from the squalling infant he had helped nurse into life in 1935. Most of the things he had only been able to talk about and hope for had become accomplished facts. The PFRA had now embarked on a new and bigger career than even he had ever envisaged. It was completing the great St. Mary's dam and was at work on the plans for something even bigger, the South Saskatchewan River dam. In the beginning, the SSRD project had not appealed to Thomson, and he had to be convinced that it was sound. Once convinced he became the spearhead of the sub-surface campaign to sell it to the governments. He never lived to see it start for he died in Regina in 1956.

Asael Palmer was probably as unlike L.B. Thomson as a man could be. In contrast with Thomson's ebullient enthusiasm, Palmer was thoughtfully restrained. To his vocation as a technical agricultural scientist specializing in irrigation, Palmer brought respect for the soil that bordered on reverence. As a devout Mormon he had a sense of serving God by his husbandmanship of the earth. He had one quality in common with Thomson, an impatience with the limitations of a 24-hour day. Palmer never regarded himself as being fully employed unless he had several jobs going at once. Thus before he joined the staff of the Lethbridge Experimental Farm in 1921, he operated a farm of his own, was principal of the Knight Academy at Raymond and was irrigation consultant to the Canadian Pacific Railway.

Palmer may not have been in at the very beginning of wind erosion in the Palliser Triangle, but when his interest was aroused at the Board of Trade luncheon in Lethbridge in 1918, he made up for lost time. Thereafter whenever in his travels he encountered blowing soil he stopped to investigate, and although the problem eased very considerably through the 1920s it never quite disappeared from eastern Alberta. It was much more of a problem in the Chinook belt of Alberta in the winter than it was farther east. There was, as a result, more work to be done with the farmers in dealing with suddenly developing emergency situations. As the recognized expert in residence, Palmer was available to the farmers at any hour of the day or night. Anyone's soil drifting problem was his soil drifting problem. In the beginning he had few remedial methods at his disposal. He could recommend that the fields be ridged across the wind, or that strip farming be adopted. What set Palmer apart was his preoccupation with finding a permanent solution for wind erosion that would enable the farmers to go on growing wheat in the arid, high wind areas of the Palliser Triangle. Thus whenever he heard of a farmer doing anything just a little differently he went out to investigate. In that way he saw the possibilities in the plowless fallow developed by J.H. Bohanon at Sibbald, in the sub-surface blade cultivator being perfected by C.S. Noble. Palmer had the knack not only of instantly recognizing a good idea when he saw it but in seeing how it might be improved and adapted. He was quick to pass on anything he found to Gordon Taggart at Swift Current and to get experiments going at Lethbridge. While the search for the perfect solution went on, Palmer never turned his back on an imperfect solution that worked some places part of the time. Strip farming was imperfect, but it worked well in some places. The one-way was imperfect, but it worked under certain conditions. The duckfoot and the rod weeder were in the same category.

Palmer could not only see the possibilities in them all, he had the faculty of being able to encourage farmers all over eastern Alberta to become more deeply interested in the study of their soil. To say that Palmer inspired the farmers of southern Alberta to embark on the wide range of implement and cultural experiments that were so fruitful for prairie agriculture would be an exaggeration. But his encouragement was certainly a contributing factor, and providing encouragement was one of the things he did best. This, of course, would not have been possible without the incisive quality of mind that Palmer brought to his profession. He recognized a good idea when he saw it—instantly. Having recognized it, he became its best salesman, and he sold it with a quiet non-eloquence that engendered trust and confidence with the farmers and thus speeded the revolution in farming methods within the Palliser Triangle.

George Spence, who was the first director of PFRA, did not in fact come into the organization until 1938, when the worst of the drouth was over. Nevertheless he had been part of the leadership of the struggle from the beginning. As Minister of Public Works in Saskatchewan he supplied the engineers and surveyors who laid out the first farm dugouts and stock-watering dams. In his ministerial capacity, he had behind him 30 years of experience as a dry-land farmer in the southwestern border country of Saskatchewan. In those years he had put in his own dugouts and knew from bitter experience the problems inherent in cattle raising when the nearest source of water was 10 miles away. Like all the others, he spoke the farmers' language, though with a tang from the northerly Islands of Scotland that helped give added emphasis to his strongly voiced opinions.

Spence's great contribution, however, was in the realm of

idealism and not on the mundane level of practical reality. It was Spence who raised the sights of PFRA far above anything visualized in the beginning. Not only did he set off the agitation in southern Alberta that led to the construction of the $40,000,000 St. Mary's dam project; he never permitted it to be shunted aside by Ottawa. That alone was no minor achievement in the political climate of the times. It was under his prodding that the PFRA engineers kept up their search for a suitable site on which the South Saskatchewan River dam could be built. When Chief Engineer Gordon MacKenzie found the site, it was Spence who wheedled the money out of Ottawa to get the vital preliminary engineering under way and to keep the work going.

When George Spence took over, the PFRA was little more than the skeleton of an organization. It was no easy task for a non-engineer like Spence to recruit the staff of graduate engineers the organization needed, to say nothing of the lawyers and architects and accountants that were required. It was a task made infinitely more difficult by the scandalous wage levels that prevailed in the government service, even after the war. One former graduate employee of the Experimental Farms Service returned from the war to the offer of a permanent appointment at $125 a month, about half of what he was offered to take alternative non-government employment. Yet recruit a staff Spence did, and in the process he infected it with his vision of the PFRA as a miracle-working organization that would transform the whole of the Palliser Triangle from a disaster-prone distressed area into a Garden of Eden. It was Spence who converted the South Saskatchewan project from an engineering feasibility study into a social crusade of the PFRA. It was his own crusade in turn, which converted a rock-hard, tight-fisted dry-lander into the most eloquent visionary of his time—the vision being the untold benefits of water held captive for use in areas of dire need.

Other observers approaching this period from a different direction and with a different perspective, may conclude, as I have already suggested, that other names should be added to this list. But it would have to be done by way of addition rather than substitution for I have the gravest of doubts that the struggle could have been won at all without the special and completely distinctive contributions made by Thomson, Palmer, Taggart, Spence, Archibald and Gardiner. And that can be said without detracting in the slightest from the important work and the hard work done by so many scores of others who were involved, from the university scientists, Experimental Farms superintendents and research specialists down to the field crews of the grasshopper campaign.

Edna Jaques said:

My brothers farmed near Briercrest, Saskatchewan, and for nine years they never sold a bushel of wheat. One year it came up, not too bad. My nephew was running the binder while his father worked around the place. He saw a black cloud coming up in the west, and started to shiver. Before the boy could get the binder and horses back to the barn, a half-mile away . . . the storm had hit, and not one blade of wheat was left standing . . . my brother cursed the earth . . . the heavens, and all that was there in that day.

My mother loved pansies and she started a few plants in a tin can in March. Then she set them out in a little round flower bed about the end of May. She watered them faithfully every night from a well about ten blocks away. They were in full lovely bloom and we thought sometimes they were the only things that were keeping her sane.

When the grasshoppers struck, she covered the few in the middle with an upturned stovepipe. But by golly . . . they dug under it and by morning there wasn't a shred of pansies left . . . She took one look at them and threw her apron up over her face and cried. She said "I'll never try again." She never did.

CHAPTER THIRTEEN

Machinery That Saved the Day

The most intriguing aspect of the whole saga of the struggle against the desert in the Palliser Triangle must surely be this: At a time when nature was going the worst, and a consensus grew that Palliser had indeed been right, the farmers themselves were engaged individually and collectively in a personal search for farm implements to unlock the secrets of successful dry-land farming.

In Saskatchewan and Alberta, it was not just a question of farming in a way that would prevent soil erosion, it was doing it with the equipment that the farmers had. It would have been futile to recommend they acquire some new type of miracle cultivator or plow that would do a perfect job. There was no such implement, and not one farmer in 100 would have been able to buy new equipment if it had been available. They were faced, therefore, with the necessity of trying to farm properly with improper implements.

It was for this reason that they lost interest in engaging in the plowing matches sponsored by the University of Saskatchewan. What was the sense in vying for the plowing championship when plowing was destroying the topsoil of the Palliser Triangle? Instead, the demand grew for the university to put on farm machinery field days at which the farmers and the experts from the university and the Experimental Farms could get together for a demonstration of what could be done with the machinery they had. In the latter part of the 1920s the agricultural engineering department of the University of

Saskatchewan conducted only seven machinery field days. Ten years later, in 1937, it ran 120 of them or an average of 2 a day during the summer. Had it not been for the growing menace of sawflies, grasshoppers and other insects, strip farming would probably have been the widely adopted practice. But these drawbacks helped to convince the farmers that there had to be a better way. Trash fallowing seemed to be the best answer, and then what was needed was not know-how but equipment to get the job done. It is interesting to note that attention in Alberta turned to the search for some sort of blade that would work in most kinds of ground; in Saskatchewan they concentrated on the disc.

In southern Alberta, the trend toward larger farms was established with the creation of the Special Areas in the 1920s. Because of their larger operations, the Albertans tended to have more machinery, which meant acquiring skills in blacksmithing and machining. Some of the larger spreads had well-equipped shops in which to repair their own equipment. It was perhaps this interest in things mechanical that encouraged them to try to invent new implements. Most of the equipment available to them had been developed elsewhere, and even the best of it had to be modified to work properly under Western Canadian conditions. The standard duckfoot cultivator, for example, worked well on light soil. But it was not made to penetrate the hard, sun-baked fallow. So they tried strengthening the shanks and putting on bigger feet. Then they discovered the heavier equipment could not be pulled by their horses. So they tried something else. At Barons, Alberta, J.B. Turner and Otto Wobick got together and regenerated an old steam-engine breaking plow outfit. They replaced the plows with giant duckfeet they made in their own shops. They christened their new invention "The Paul Bunyan," and it worked better than anything anybody else had yet invented. Unhappily only the steam tractors would pull the cultivators and they were already obsolete. Peter Kooy and Bill Williamson of Monarch made a cultivator equipped with one king-sized duckfoot. Victor Erdman invented a blade with three large duckfeet and eventually built his own implement business in Lethbridge. The most persistent searcher of them all, however, was Charles S. Noble, the most dedicated wheat grower Canada had ever seen.

Born in State Centre, Iowa, in 1873, Noble had moved to North Dakota as a young man and homesteaded there in the early 1890s. In Minnesota and North Dakota at that time were some of the biggest wheat farms on earth—the "bonanza farms" that the crude steam tractors and steam threshing machines had made possible. The biggest was the Cass-Cheney-Dalrymple spread that covered 75,000 acres and, according to Stewart Holbrook, usually had 30,000 acres in crop. The farm employed 1,000 men, 800 horses, 30 steam engines, 100 gangplows and 53 steam powered separators to thresh a 600,000-bushel wheat crop. When Noble came to Alberta in 1902 he brought the "bonanza farm" vision with him and it was with him until his death. He homesteaded at Claresholm, became a part-time land agent for the Canadian Pacific Railway, and by 1908 was selling land at the rate of 1,000 acres a day to American farmers who were being crowded out of North Dakota, Minnesota and Iowa. At the same time he was expanding his own holdings as quickly as he could get the land broken. In 1913 the 2,800 acres he had in oats averaged 102 bushels per acre.

By 1916 Noble was operating six different farms and in 1917 acquired the Cameron farm, a spread of over 30,000 acres, 36 miles east of Nobleford. In 1918 it was broken by 11 steam tractor crews to whom Noble offered a prize of $1,000 to the outfit which broke the most acreage. But the crop of 1919, instead of launching Noble into financial orbit, was the forerunner of a series of disasters. Crop failure followed crop failure and by 1922 his creditors foreclosed and Noble, at the age of 49, was flat broke and back where he started without even a half-section homestead. But not for long. He leased his old home place, the four-section Grandview farm, and after renting it for two years was able to buy it back again. By 1930,

C.S. Noble was once again one of Alberta's biggest and best grain farmers. He was also a firm believer in stubble mulching and, as previously mentioned, was the prime mover in the conference of the local farmers on the dust problem in 1932. In 1934 he and his sons Gerald and Shirley developed a huge rod weeder that they thought would take the weeds out by the roots and leave the stubble on the surface. It was made of an inch-and-a-quarter steel bar but when they got it into the soil it was much too heavy to pull.

In the winter of 1934-35 Noble went on a vacation to California and visited a former farm hand who was running several fruit orchards. Here Noble encountered a beet lifter that gave him the idea for the Noble Blade. It was a plow-like gadget attached to a tractor. A vertical blade was pulled down the edge of a row of beets. At right angles to the bottom of the upright was a six-inch by twelve-inch flat blade which ran under the beets, cutting off the roots and lifting them to the surface without disturbing the surrounding soil. For the rest of his holiday Noble worked in a local machine shop putting together a 48-inch blade that would do the same job on the weeds of his Alberta wheat farm.

When he returned to Nobleford in the spring he had Asael Palmer come out from Lethbridge to see it work. It worked well enough to convince Palmer that the invention was very much worthwhile. He became its public relations godfather and more than anyone else was responsible for getting widespread acceptance for it. Before that, however, the bugs had to be worked out and that took time. The showers that fell soon after the first tests quickly revealed some basic flaws in the design. The weeds that had been undercut by the blade sprang back into life. The blade had not shaken the roots free enough from the soil. Everybody went to work on that problem—Noble, Palmer, L.B. Thomson and Grant Denike. It was quickly solved by tilting the blade at a 35-degree angle so that the back end pushed the weeds up and free of the soil. Then it was discovered that the blade was too hard to keep in the ground. That was fixed by piling weight on the frame and later by curving the blade and sharpening the leading edge to give it adequate suction.

Noble's blade cultivator quickly attracted the attention of the neighborhood and the Noble farm machine shop was transformed into a factory to make blades for the farmers of the district. Within a year the Noble Cultivator Company was incorporated and the Noble family was in the farm implement manufacturing business. In 1938 the United States Soil Conservation Service bought a dozen of the blades and the use spread steadily until it covered the continent.

For C.S. Noble and his family, it seemed as if the invention of the blade was the poorest idea he had ever had. A decade and a half passed before the implement company started to make a profit and for many years the income from the farms had to be plowed back to keep the implement company going. When he died in 1957, Noble's implement company and farming operations were all well into the black. He died, however, before his invention was to receive its crowning accolade. After the Russian Government under Nikita Khrushchev launched its program to develop the arid areas of Siberia for wheat production, it sent to Nobleford for a shipment of Noble blades.

Charles Noble was a man who believed fervently in the productive potential of the Palliser Triangle but he was two generations ahead of his time in his conviction that the best way of achieving it was with large-scale mechanization. Even in the late 1930s he could still hitch and drive a 20-horse team and cut a 36-foot swath. He was convinced too that answers could be found to most problems if a person never stopped looking. Ken Liddell recalled interviewing Noble before his death in his office at Nobleford. Noble interrupted the conversation to reach into a drawer of his desk and pour himself a drink from a small bottle. It was carrot juice, he explained, and he had heard that it had been effective in the treatment of leukemia. He said, with shattering casualness, that he had leukemia.

In Saskatchewan the farming population was almost exclusively preoccupied with the disc—the disc plow, the disc harrow and the one-way disc. None was completely, or even moderately satisfactory. The disc plow cultivated too deeply and the disc harrows did not go deeply enough and left the ground ridged. The one-way was an attempt to solve both problems. It first made its appearance in Saskatchewan in 1925 and was soon being distributed by all the machine companies.

H.A. Lewis, who was lecturer in agricultural engineering at the University of Saskatchewan under Dr. Evan Hardy, said that the word for the one-way was "cantankerous." It had a considerable and very bothersome side draft, it had to be weighed down to get adequate penetration on hard ground and most of all it presented hitching problems that seemed insurmountable to many farmers.

The beginning of the dust bowl years intensified the interest of the Saskatchewan farmers in farm machinery field days. The hitching and the draft problems, the need to avoid deep tillage combined with the necessity of keeping the stubble on the surface of the soil, all combined to thicken the air of bafflement that surrounded grain growing. Both the Experimental Farms and the university tried to help out by expanding the number of farm machinery field days held each year. In the intervals between these demonstrations the farmers kept looking around for their own solutions. It seemed to scores, perhaps to hundreds of them, that some sort of combination of a one-way and a disc harrow was needed. They began to trek to Saskatoon and Swift Current with their ideas, their half-ideas, and their vague hunches. As Lewis has said, the experts often learned more from the farmers than they were able to provide in the way of helpful advice.

The great variety of land within the Palliser Triangle was at last being recognized and reflected in the wide range of both ideas and problems. What would work on the light soils didn't work on the heavy soils. One-way discs that worked on level land were impractical on rough land or stony land. More and more farmers concluded that what was needed were short lengths of discs attached to a frame so that they would follow the contours of the soil and maintain a uniform depth of cultivation. It took the better part of 15 years and the brainstorming of hundreds of individual farmers before the first practical discer was developed in Saskatchewan.

After he retired in 1962, Lewis compiled a short history of the development of the discer. It is considered by many to be the best account of the machinery-inventing binge that developed in Saskatchewan as the dust bowl era came to an end. By this time the farmers had become obsessed with the need to find profitable ways of cultivating their land without bringing back another dust bowl. What follows here is an edited version of the Lewis paper:

> The first operating machine that our department saw working was inspected by Prof. Hardy in 1930. It had been built by L. Weckman at Rouleau. His machine was not of the same general type as our present day discers, but was flexible rather than using a solid gang like the one-way. It did a similar class of work to the present day discers with the side thrust absorbed by wheels and the tractor hitch. It had to be transported from field to field on a long stoneboat as there was no provision to lift the discs out of the soil.
>
> About 1938 we viewed a machine made up by using the right hand disc gangs from disc harrows attached to a six-by-six-inch timber by drag chains. No supporting wheels were used and all of the side thrust was absorbed by a triangular arrangement of logging chains from the timber to the drawbar of a heavy steel-wheeled tractor. The angle of cut was varied by changing the length of the chains. For transporting, the angle was changed till the timber was at right angles behind the tractor and the discs simply rolled out on the surface. M.T. Allen of Neville made the machine and for several years he sold plans for the construction of this machine for one dollar apiece to western farmers through an advertisement in *The Western Producer*.

By 1940 several people had visions of machines similar in general principle to our present machines but in most cases lacked the money, initiative or facilities to actually build a working model. Russel Fyke at Sceptre had even gone as far as drawing scale plans of a machine which used a three-wheel suspension and independently mounted disc gangs, which he was not able to build until some time later.

At about the same time, Mr. Fielding at Eastend, developed a machine which used two very small, flat faced wheels in front to support the weight of the front frame and act as a hitch cart. It had two vertical wheels from the front end of a Fordson tractor on the back end of a tubular frame to take the side thrust. His gangs were all linked together by universal joints, and were pulled by short chains from each gang to the tubular frame. He was not able to build his own machine so he obtained assistance from a Mr. Jensen of the same district. Their machine met with some approval and they later arranged with Norman Hall of Shaunavon to build some machines for them in his machine shop.

The machine had serious side problems and tended to drag the rear end of the tractor sideways as well as interfering with the steering. For this reason it worked better behind steel wheeled tractors than the recently introduced rubber tire tractors. Under severe operating conditions the disc gang would hump in the middle leaving some of the land entirely unworked. I just saw one of these machines in operation at a field day south of Weyburn on the farm of Ernest Kyle in the spring of 1942. While it had many good features I was not particularly impressed with its overall performance.

All of the ideas and machines up to 1942 were quite varied in their design and in the way in which the weight was carried as well as the methods of absorbing the side thrust. In fact about the only thing that they all had in common was the use of old disc harrow gangs for the main tillage medium. In most cases the absorbing or offsetting of the side thrust was their biggest stumbling block.

During 1942 and 1943, R.A. Johnson of Beadle visited us several times to discuss his ideas of a machine that would use conventional disc harrow gangs in a flexible type of mounting to a frame somewhat similar to the conventional one-way. He visualized a constant angle to the direction of travel with the main frame and minor gang angle varied through lever control.

He also visualized a second lever to apply spring pressure to the rear of each gang as required to maintain a level depth of cut. A third lever of a latch of some sort would lift each gang to a transport position for moving.

We had several conferences on probable loads, strength of materials required, probable draft and consequent size of machine that his I.H.C. WD9 tractor could pull and the ranges of desirable angles of cut. On one occasion we spent several hours with chalk, drawing up full scale designs on the smooth cement floor of the tractor laboratory to get the information that Johnson wanted. Finally he was able to make up a machine in the winter of 1944 and the early spring of 1945 with the assistance of Dave Johnston, the blacksmith at Kindersley. They used parts from an old tractor frame and a discarded Bissill disc harrow as their materials, keeping down expenses as much as they could until they found whether it would work or not.

Professor Hardy and I visited the Johnson farm on May 1st, 1945, to see the machine on its trial run. So intense was the interest that quite a crowd gathered to see the machine in operation. With some changes that we were able to make to the hitch and the positioning of the rear wheel plus extra weight on the rear wheel to assist in holding against the side thrust, the machine worked as Johnson put it, "much better than it ever had even as a new disc harrow." Johnson's machine was the first operating machine in the province, as far as we know, to use the now conventional three wheel support and two point flexible mounting of the disc gang to the set angle main frame.

Les Wyman, the Massey Harris dealer at Kindersley had been following R.A. Johnson's work with considerable interest and had started to assemble parts from his repair stock to build a machine of his own. The blacksmith had also started to develop a machine of his own. After the successful trials on May 1st, 1945, they and a number of local farmers requested that a field day be held later in the spring to try out the proposed three or more models that they expected to have ready. Both Wyman and Dave Johnston promised to have machines of their own ready to go by the middle of June. Professor Hardy and I attended the field day on June 11th, 1945, with two assistants. We planned to test, as we thought, some three machines, but on arrival at Kindersley we discovered that five machines were in the field. They were R.A. Johnson's original machine, one built by D. Johnston the blacksmith and sold to M.G. Cressman and three Wyman built machines, one built on rubber tired wheels and two on steel wheels. He had sold one of the steel wheeled machines to S.L. Watley who pulled it with a D 2 caterpillar. This was the first time we had ever seen side thrust controlled so adequately that a track type tractor could be used.

During the late seeding operation Cressman mounted a seeding box from an old drill on his machine. The drive was taken from the land wheel. The box was only long enough to serve the front four gangs with seed and the machine was operated with the two rear gangs raised. This machine was very likely the first discer to operate with a seeding attachment.

A crowd of over 500 interested people, some of whom had driven over 200 miles to be present, were on hand. With minor adjustments all of the machines worked well and I think over half of the people present went home resolved to build a machine of their own. I still look upon June 11th, 1945, as the day that the big swing toward discers started in Saskatchewan. During the balance of that summer and the spring of 1946 I saw and tested more than a hundred machines while several other members of our staff must have come in contact with at least that many more.

Almost every well equipped machine shop or blacksmith's shop and many farmers with good shops started building discers to supply the local community demand. The limiting factors in production became time and availability of parts. Junk yards were scoured for heavy steel pipe, old plows, one ways and other machines were dismantled for wheels, shafting, discs, bearings etc. A distinct change was rapidly taking place in Saskatchewan tillage.

The war itself intensified the search for the perfect cultivator probably more than the drouth. The economic position of the farmers improved and they would have been able to buy better equipment if it had been available in any quantity. Instead they had to pretty well make do with what they had. When one farmer made a break-through, as Johnson had done, it got blacksmiths and machinists all over the province rushing into the act. Norman Hall at Shaunavon built several machines, the Wymans at Kindersley got into the agricultural implement manufacturing business. Fred Schneider and Mike Poppowill of Eston and scores of others were turning out discers. How one idea led to another, and different people came up with the same idea simultaneously, is illustrated by the case of Allan McKinnon of Regina.

He had been a student in agricultural engineering under Dr. Hardy and was farming at Regina. In the winter of 1945, Dr. Hardy gave him a picture of the Johnson discer but McKinnon was not too much impressed. He came to the conclusion, however, that it might be quite useful with a seed box attached to it so that it would be possible to seed directly into the stubble. He spent the winter making an 18-foot machine of his own and fitting it with a seed box and attachments. When spring came he used it to plant his crop and it worked fine.

His operation also attracted widespread attention. The International Harvester Company sent out a couple of photographers on a half-ton truck to follow his operation. The Cockshutt agent came out and both measured it and photographed it from all angles. Dr. Hardy came down from Saskatoon and held a field day on the McKinnon farm. Within a year the discers were coming off the assembly lines of all the farm implement companies.

How much of the machinery development activities on the farms of the Triangle could be attributed to the intensive propaganda drive to which the farmers had been subjected and how much of it was spontaneously generated will remain an unanswered question. Nevertheless, within the Palliser Triangle during little more than a decade, an amazing transformation had occurred in the thinking of the masses of the grain growers. From an overwhelming majority belief in the efficacy of maintaining a black summerfallow, the pendulum had swung to the opposite extreme. Now the main objective was to discover the best way to grow wheat while leaving the trash on the surface of the soil. Certainly this change of mind had to be attributed in very large measure to the effectiveness of the gospel preached in season and out by the Experimental Farms experts like Chester, Sherriff, Foster, Purdy, Janzen and MacIsaac to the AIAs and the Experimental Sub-station field days.

And there was much more to this revolutionary change of thinking than merely stopping the soil from blowing. Unless the productivity of the soil could be substantially increased there would be no long-term gain from the mere tying down of the topsoil. The concentration of attention on stubble mulch moved the whole of the Palliser wheat economy in through the backdoor of one of the basic theories that Sidney Barnes had proven at Swift Current. That was: Evaporation of the moisture could be substantially reduced by insulating the surface of the soil from the turbulence of the hot winds.

In the words of Grant Denike, the whole of the northern Great Plains was little more than a gigantic evaporation basin left over from the ice age. On its surface, the sun and air would evaporate twice the amount of free water the land received from the rain and snow that fell. It was therefore necessary to use the moisture of two years to grow one crop of grain—but by keeping the stubble standing upright on the surface of the soil through which the hot winds could not reach down to suck out the moisture.

This discovery meant that large crops could be grown on moisture supplies that would previously have been inadequate. In a real sense, the discoveries made at Swift Current had the same effect as if the rainfall within the Triangle had been increased by an inch or two. But it was a result which could only be fully achieved by finding the best equipment to destroy the weeds and leave the stubble on the surface. The stubble had to be left on the surface to prevent wind erosion; so the search for implements to prevent wind erosion became, in a real sense, the unknowing search for implements that would provide the crops with the equivalent of another couple of inches of rainfall.

The science of meteorology is no place for outsiders to go wandering, and it is a field in which general conclusions can seldom be drawn with much confidence. Average precipitation figures can be distorted by single thunderstorms and temperature and wind velocity can affect the value of the measured rainfall. Drouths vary in intensity over comparatively small areas. In the three summer months of 1937, the disaster year, there was 13 inches of rain at Waskada, Manitoba, rainfall was normal at Beechy, Saskatchewan, and two inches above normal at Lethbridge, Alberta. Nevertheless there are generally dry years and generally wet years and 1961 was a severe drouth year almost everywhere. In many areas of

Saskatchewan there was less rain that year than in the year 1937, though the drouth was less severe on the western edge of the Palliser Triangle in the vicinity of Swift Current and Medicine Hat. With all due allowance for the dangers of drawing conclusions from weather statistics, Saskatchewan in 1961 produced 186,000,000 bushels of wheat compared with only 37,000,000 in 1937 and 110,000,000 in 1936. Over the whole of the Prairies, the 1961 crop was 260,000,000 bushels compared with only 159,000,000 in 1937, when Manitoba and Alberta had good crops.

To attribute the gain exclusively to improved equipment and the application of improved cultural practices and farming techniques might be difficult to justify. But regardless of precipitation statistics, if the farmers of 1937 had had the blades, discers and big chisel cultivators far less land would have blown and a great deal more moisture would have been conserved. That would have been true, even with horses. Had the tractor revolution taken place in the 1920s instead of the 1940s, it would have enabled the farmers to get onto their land quickly and repair the damage being done by the wind and blowing soil. When it came, the tractor enabled the farmers all over the Triangle to reach out for more land with which to put optimum-sized farms together.

The existence of Community Pastures enabled them to stay in beef production. The land that was put back into grass in the 1930s was infinitely more productive, thanks to the discoveries of the plant scientists and soils experts, than it had ever been before it was broken. Where the old short-grass range could carry only a single steer on 100 acres, it became possible to put 10 of them on 100 acres of the new grasses and legumes.

The perfection of the combine carried large-scale wheat production and mechanization even further. And the further it was carried the greater the production and the lower the cost. With the combine, there was an added dividend. With it the straw and chaff went back on the land, to be worked in to maintain soil fertility instead of lighting the sky in post-harvest bonfires. For this the farmers also could thank the Swift Current station for the work that was done over the years on farm equipment. When Swift Current ordered its first combine, the manufacturer thought so little of the future market for combines in Western Canada that the station had to freight it out at its own expense. It was fortunate for Canadian farmers that it did. At Swift Current the machine was thoroughly tested and literally dozens of faults were found in its operation. By the time the farmers of the West were in shape financially, many of the flaws had been removed and improvements made.

The development of the rubber-tired tractor was also an important contribution of Swift Current. It was not alone, of course, for the American tractor companies were also beginning to produce tractors with rubber tires in the early 1930s. Swift Current, however, was in the very forefront in the solution of the problem of getting traction on the farms of the Triangle with low pressure tires. With the development of rubber tires, the usefulness of the tractor was at least doubled on most farms. What was true of the testing of the combines and tractors was true as well of hay balers, swathers and most other items of equipment used on prairie farms.

One fact should never be forgotten, in the development of the equipment with which agriculture was to be saved in Western Canada, the farmers and their scientific advisers did it on their own. Not the least surprising fact was the complete lack of interest on the part of the farm machinery industry in the problems of the Palliser Triangle. It was only after Swift Current, Lethbridge and the University of Saskatchewan had collaborated with the Nobles and Johnsons and their scores of compatriots in solving the problems that the manufacturers came around to take possession of the ideas. Perhaps that is explicable on the grounds that most of the implement agents within the Triangle had gone broke long since, or lived from hand to mouth, deeply in debt to their suppliers. When the PFRA was established and an emergency appeal went out for excavating contractors, graders, scrapers and tractors with which to tackle the dust bowl, the reply was an awesome silence. Nobody had much of anything in working order, least of all the implement dealers.

Though they contributed little or nothing to solving the problem of dry-land farming, no one can ever accuse the implement companies of being reluctant to take hold of an idea once the people of the Palliser Triangle had proven its worth. The Canadian Co-operative Implement Company rushed out and copyrighted the word "disker" and got a clear jump on the other companies in marketing the Johnson invention. Within a matter of months, however, all the major machinery makers were pushing the sales of their own modifications of the original design. Nor was the use of the discers confined to the Palliser Triangle. The implement became one of the most popular all over the Great Plains area. Similarly, the use of the Noble blade spread widely and rapidly across the United States, particularly in the light soil area where the farmers were fortunate enough to have big power tractors.

It was not machinery development alone where Canada made an important contribution to the productivity of the dry lands of the continent and eventually of the world. The idea of maintaining a trash cover on the surface of the soil was one that had occurred to many farmers before Bohanon tried it successfully. But it was the development of practical trash-cover know-how in Canada that made it possible for farmers everywhere to grow wheat on the erosion-prone lands of the Great Plains, and grow it successfully. Yet even if these machinery developments and farming techniques had not spread across the world, even if they had been confined exclusively to the Palliser Triangle, the impact would have been beyond exaggeration. Time and again the grain grown on these prairies has been used to prevent famine or allay hunger in Russia, China and India.

Canada, of course, cannot claim exclusive credit for any of these developments. The inspiration for the Johnson and Noble inventions came from discs and blades that had been previously developed in the United States for different purposes. Similarly, Canadians owed the credit for the first crested wheat grass tests to American experimenters. The Americans imported the seeds from Russia and got some excellent results with them. But these results might have been unnoticed for years if Dr. Lawrence Kirk had not stumbled over them and used them as a basis for his own work. Once Kirk had recalled the worth of the grass to their attention, the Americans were quick to grasp its potential worth and to make the most of it.

And so it was that after the wounds of the Palliser Triangle were bound up and healed, its productivity was marvellously restored by the blades and discer seeders developed by Noble and Johnson with the help they got from the Palmers, Chesters, Thomsons, Denikes, Matthews, Hardys and Lewises and all the rest. And it was these, with such other exclusively Canadian developments as summerfallowing, strip farming, trash fallowing, trap stripping and grasshopper poisoning, that helped transform the agriculture of the earth and to make unproductive lands productive, and brought the hope of an adequate food supply to millions of the ever-hungry people of the world.

$\mathcal{I}$NDEX